More Language of Letting Go

Hazelden Meditation Series

More Language of Letting Go

366 New Daily Meditations by Melody Beattie

Melody Beattie

Hazelden
Publishing

Hazelden
Center City, Minnesota 55012-0176
hazelden.org/bookstore

ISBN: 978-1-56838-558-7

2020   13 14

Cover design by Lightbourne
Typesetting by Universal Press

This book is based on actual experiences.
In some cases, the names and details have been
changed to protect the privacy of the people involved.

This book is dedicated to God, my readers, and
Brady Michaels and his family—Mom, Dad, and Brother.
Like you taught us Brady, Live Big.
We miss you and love you.

CONTENTS

ACKNOWLEDGMENTS AND CREDITS

I gratefully acknowledge and thank:

Lawrence Hans for his masterful creative content and ideas, Rebecca Post for her superb editorial work and detaching in love, and all the staff at Hazelden for the many dutiful, unseen tasks that allow bits and particles of electricity to turn into a book that ends up in someone's hand.

Honorable Mentions

For being part of my life, lessons, and this book, I acknowledge and thank Kyle, Nichole, Julian, Andy, Pat, Old Dude, Peg, Martin, Frank, Rob the flight instructor, Alex, Betsy, Lob, John, and of course, Karl, the coolest pilot in the world.

INTRODUCTION

This is a book of essays, meditations, and activities—one for each day of the year. You can use it to begin your year on January 1. Or you can begin your year on your birthday, the day some people believe begins their personal new year. It's a companion book to the original *Language of Letting Go* (not a replacement or updated edition) and can be used by itself or in conjunction with that book. You can roll along with your life and use the book to address issues that arise. Or you can use this book as a workbook—or "playbook"—to address specific areas and issues you'd like to focus on in the upcoming year, such as releasing an outdated relationship or behavior, achieving cherished goals, or moving to the next level in work, in love, or in life.

The essay that falls on the first day of each month explores the theme for the month. Each monthly topic is a major component in the process of letting go. You will also notice that skydiving, my new passion, has turned out to be a beautiful metaphor for the art of letting go and letting God do for us what we can't do for ourselves.

I use God as the predominant word for references to God, Higher Power, Jehovah, or Allah. I may use He or She as the pronoun for God, depending on my mood. I mean no harm, nor is it my intention to discriminate or offend. Substitute whatever word pleases you to describe your idea of God.

The prayers and ideas are meant as suggestions.

May God bless you, your family, friends, and loved ones in this year to come. And may you guide yourself joyfully through the journey you choose, or have been called, to take.

January

Trust That Good Will Come

It was a slow, boring January day at the Blue Sky Lodge. We had just moved in. The house was a mess. Construction hadn't begun yet. All we had was a plan, and a dream. It was too cold and rainy to skydive or even be outdoors. There wasn't any furniture yet. We were lying around on the floor.

I don't know who got the idea first, him or me. But we both picked up Magic Markers about the same time. Then we started drawing on the wall.

"What do you want to happen in your life?" I asked. He drew pictures of seaplanes, and mountains, and boats leaving the shore. One picture was a video-camera man, jumping out of a plane. "I want adventure," he said.

I drew pictures of a woman tromping around the world. She went to war-torn countries, then sat on a fence and watched. She visited the mountains and the oceans and many exciting places. Then I drew a heart around the entire picture, and she sat there in the middle of all the experiences on a big stack of books.

"I want stories," I said, "ones with a lot of heart."

Across the entire picture, in big letters, he wrote the word "Woohoo."

As an afterthought, I drew a woman sky diver who had just jumped out of the plane. She was frightened and grimacing. Next to her I wrote the words "Just relax."

On the bottom of the wall I wrote, "The future is only limited by what we can see now." He grabbed a marker, crossed out "only," and changed it to "never."

"There," he said, "it's done."

Eventually, the house got cleaned up and the construction finished. Furniture arrived. And yellow paint covered the pictures on the wall. We didn't think much about that wall until months later. Sometimes slowly, sometimes quickly, and sometimes in ways we'd least expect, each of the pictures we'd drawn on that wall began to materialize and manifest.

"It's a magic wall," I said.

Even if you can't imagine what's coming next, relax. The good pictures are still there. The wall will soon become covered with the story of your life. Thank God, the future is never limited by what we can see right now.

The wall isn't magic.

The magic is in us and what we believe.

Before we start speaking the language of letting go, we need to understand what a powerful behavior letting go and letting God really is.

God, help me do my part. Then help me let go, and let you do yours.

Activity: Meditate for a moment on the year ahead. Make a list of things you'd like to see happen, attributes you'd like to gain, things you'd like to get and do, changes you'd like to occur. You don't have to limit the list to this year. What do you want to happen in your life? Make a list of places you'd like to visit and things you'd like to see. Leave room for the unexpected, the unintended. But make room for the possibility of what you'd like, too—your intentions, wishes, dreams, hopes, and goals. Also, list what you're ready to let go of, too —things, people, attitudes, and behaviors you'd like to release. If anything were possible, anything at all, what are the possibilities you'd like to experience and see?

The surest way to become Tense, Awkward, and Confused is to develop a mind that tries too hard—one that thinks too much.
— Benjamin Hoff, The Tao of Pooh

The universe will help us, but we need to do our part as well. Here's an acronym, *My Part*, to help you remember what it means to do that.

Manifest
Your

Power
Accept
Relax
Trust

Too often, we tell ourselves the only way to get from point A to point B—or Z—is to tense up, obsess a little (or a lot), and live in fear and anxiety until what we want takes place.

That isn't the path to success. It's the path to fear and anxiety.

Accept. Relax. Breathe. Let go. Trust yourself, God, and the universe to manifest the best possible destiny when the time is right for you.

God, help me make the journey from fear and control to letting go and stepping into my true power.

There is a Zen story about two monks walking down a street after a heavy rain. Arriving at a corner, they came upon a beautiful girl in fine clothing unable to cross the muddy street without getting filthy.

"Here, I'll help you," said one monk. Lifting her in his arms, he carried her to the other side. The two monks walked in silence for a long time.

"We've sworn a vow of celibacy and are not supposed to go near women. It's dangerous," the second monk said to the first. "Why did you do that?"

"I left the girl back at the corner," the first monk said. "Are you still carrying her?"

Sometimes, we may find ourselves in a situation where our ideals conflict. Being kind and loving to another person may conflict with our value of being committed and loving toward ourselves.

When one ideal imposes on another, then use your judgment. Do the right thing by others. Do the right thing by yourself, too. Then let the incident pass and move on.

For the monks in our story, right action usually meant not having contact with women. However, when encountering a stranded person on the road, right action became helping others. Ideals remain. Right thought, right action, right speech—but the path to those ideals may twist and turn throughout life. Be sensitive and aware that you are following an ideal and not a rigid belief.

God, help me learn when it's time to let go.

Activity: In an earlier activity, we explored our goals and dreams list. Now, let's determine the ethics and ideals we want to live by, the code of conduct we want to follow. What's of foremost importance to you, whether or not your dreams come true and you achieve your goals? Examples of ideals may be staying clean and sober, honoring your commitments to others, and honoring your commitment to yourself. Many people choose additional spiritual values, such as compassion, honesty, tolerance. Some people choose to live by an ideal they call "Christ Consciousness," some "Buddha consciousness," some the "Twelve Steps," and some the Ten Commandments. List your ideals, and put that list with your goals. Let these ideals be a light that guides your path and allows you to live in harmony with others and yourself.

January 4   Know when to compromise

Sometimes compromise is important. Sometimes it's better to give in to someone else's wishes in order to have fun as a group or as a couple, or for the benefits of the team. Sometimes compromise is dangerous. We need to guard against compromising our standards to gain the approval or love of someone else.

Decide when you can, and when you cannot, compromise. If it's not harmful and you are ambivalent about a decision, then compromise. If it could lead to breaking your values, compromise isn't a good idea.

Is it okay to have lunch with an attractive colleague if you're married? Possibly, but not if lunch will lead to dinner, which then leads to more time spent together, culminating in an affair. Is it okay to go to the bar with friends after work? Maybe, but not if it leads to one rationalized decision after another until you have broken your commitment to stay sober.

Remember that what may be an acceptable compromise for

one person might not be acceptable for you. Know your limits, know your values, and be aware of the dangers that can come from compromising them.

God, help me be aware of my limits. Give me the strength not to compromise the values that I need to help me on my path.

January 5   **Move when it's time**

We were touring the ruins at Hovenweep National Monument in the southwestern United States. A sign along the interpretive trail told about the Anasazi who had lived along the small, narrow canyon so long ago. The archaeologists have done their best to determine what these ancient Indians did and how they lived their lives. The signs told about the strategic positioning of the buildings perched precariously on the edge of a cliff, and questioned what had caused this ancient group to suddenly disappear long ago.

"Maybe they just got tired of living there and moved," my friend said.

We laughed as we pictured a group of wise ancients sitting around the campfire one night. "You know," says one of them, "I'm tired of this desert. Let's move to the beach." And in our story they did. No mystery. No aliens taking them away. They just moved on, much like we do today.

It's easy to romanticize what we don't know. It's easy to assume that someone else must have a greater vision, a nobler purpose than just going to work, having a family, and living a life. People are people, and have been throughout time. Our problems aren't new or unique. The secret to happiness is the same as it has always been. If you are unhappy with where you are, don't be there. Yes, you may be here now, you may be learning hard lessons today, but there is no reason to stay there. If it hurts to touch the stove, don't touch it. If you want to be someplace else, move. If you want to chase a dream, then do it. Learn your lessons where you are, but don't close off your ability to move and to learn new lessons someplace else.

Are you happy with the path that you're on? If not, maybe it's time to choose a new one. There need not be a great mysterious reason. Sometimes it's just hot and dry, and the beach is calling your name.

Be where you want to be.

God, give me the courage to find a path with heart. Help me move on when it's time.

January 6　　　　　Take responsibility for your life

Before you can jump out of the airplane, before you can fly solo in an airplane, before you can go on the whitewater rafting trip, before you can make a bungee jump, you have to sign a waiver.

The waiver is a document that says that you realize the dangers in what you're about to do, that you and you alone have made the decision to participate in the activity, and that you and you alone are responsible for the outcome.

You sign away your right to sue, whine, complain—to do anything except risk your life for a new experience.

You sign the waiver to protect others from being liable in case of an accident. I think waivers are a good reminder that ultimately no one is responsible for my life but me. There is no one to blame, no one to sue, no one to ask for a refund. I make my own decisions and I live with the results of those choices each day.

So do you.

It's your life. Sign a waiver saying that you take responsibility for it. Set yourself and others free.

God, help me understand the inherent powers I have. Help me take responsibility for my choices, and guide me about what decisions are best for me.

Activity: Read the following waiver carefully. Fill in the blanks, and be aware of what you're signing. It is your life, after all. Take responsibility for what you do.

WAIVER

I understand that during the course of my life I will be required to make many decisions, such as where I want to live, whom I want to live with, where I work, how much fun I have, and how I spend my money and time, including how much time I spend waiting for things to get better and people to change, and whom I choose to love.

I understand that many events that occur will be out of my hands and that there are inherent dangers and risks in all decisions I make. Life and people have no obligation whatsoever to live up to my expectations; I have no obligation to live up to the expectations of anybody else. Life is a high-risk sport, and I may become injured along the way.

I agree that all the decisions I make are mine and mine alone, including how I choose to handle the events that are beyond my control. I hereby forfeit my right to recourse as a victim, including my rights to blame, complain, and whine or hold someone else responsible for the path I choose to take. I am responsible for my participation—or lack of it—in life. And I take complete responsibility for the outcomes and consequences of all decisions I make, understanding that ultimately it is my choice whether I become happy, joyous, and free or stay miserable and trapped.

Although people may voluntarily nurture and love me, I and I alone am responsible for taking care of and loving myself.

Signed:_____

Dated:_____

January 7   Save your life in a journal

Are you saving your life by writing about it in a journal?

Sometimes I use a file in my computer for my journal. If I'm rambling, ranting, or raving—writing something that could embarrass me if seen—I lock the file with a code. My words in my journal, whether it's in a computer or a green Italian notebook, are meant only for me.

There are many ways to write in a journal. We can go on and on about whatever comes to us. That's helpful, especially if we're stuck. We can use our journal as a record, writing down what we did that day. It's a good place to write our goals and to explore our fantasies and dreams. We can write poems or short stories. We can write letters to God or our Guardian Angel, asking for advice. Or we can just say what happened each day, and then write how it feels.

People may think there's a right and wrong way to write in a journal, but I don't agree. There aren't any rules about journals. It's just a way to record and save our lives.

Do you think your life is worth saving? I do. If you've been neglecting to do that, ask yourself "why?"

God, help me be aware of and respect the details of my life.

Activity: Transfer your goal list to a journal, and begin writing your responses to the meditations and the activities as part of your journal entry for each day. Use your journal as a logbook, to record what you're doing and whom you're doing it with as you pursue your dreams. Or use it as a way of exploring how you feel, who you are, and what you want to do. Save your life in whatever way makes sense to you.

January 8   **Letting go to save our lives**

I crouched in the doorway of the airplane, next to my skydiving coach. I held on to the doorway with my right hand for balance. With my left hand, I firmly grasped my coach's gripper, a padded piece of cloth on his jumpsuit.

It was up to me to give the count. "Ready," I hollered. "Set . . ."

I backed up and took another breath. "Ready, set . . ."

I heard a snicker. "Get out of the plane," someone hollered. "Go."

I released my grip on the door, closed my eyes, and dived headfirst into the air—with my left hand firmly attached to my jump master's gripper. We wobbled around for a moment. The plan was, we would turn to face each other in the air, I would grab his other shoulder grip, get my balance, then I'd release him.

He turned to face me. I grabbed his other grip. Now I was falling stable and holding on with both hands. He nodded, giving me my cue to let go.

I shook my head, carefully, so as not to lose my balance.

He looked confused, then nodded again.

I shook my head again, clinging more tightly.

I looked at my altimeter. Six thousand feet. Thank God. It was almost time to pull. I released my grips. I just let go. Obviously, I couldn't safely pull my rip cord while I was hanging on to him.

It was time to save my own life.

My coach backed away.

I signaled, then pulled my rip cord. My parachute made that sweet whooshing sound, the one I had come to identify as the sound it makes when it opens correctly and fills with air, slowing my fall into a float.

Wow! I thought. *This is really fun!*

Sometimes we're so scared, all we can think to do is hang on. Hanging on in this case was a silly illusion. We were both falling through the air. Holding on to a relationship that's not working, a negative self-image, a job that isn't working, moments and times that have passed, or emotions such as fear and hurt can be a silly illusion, too.

To save our own lives, sometimes we have to let go first.

God, show me what I need to let go of, and when it's time to do that.

January 9   Detach in love

In the original *Language of Letting Go*, I told the gerbil story. It's one of my favorite stories about letting go. Here it is again.

Many years ago, when I lived in Stillwater, Minnesota, my children wanted a pet. They wanted a puppy, but I said no. We had tried a bird, but its feathers fell off. I suggested a goldfish, but we settled on a gerbil instead.

One day, the gerbil got loose. It got out of its cage and scurried across the floor. It ran so fast that none of us could catch it. We watched as it disappeared under a crack in the wall. We stood around, wondering what to do, but there wasn't much that could be done.

In the months that followed, the gerbil made timely appearances. It would scurry out from behind the walls, run across the room, then dart back into the walls. We'd chase it, lunging after it and screaming as we ran.

"There he is. Catch him!"

I worried about the gerbil, even when we didn't see it. "This isn't right," I'd think. "I can't have a gerbil running loose in the house. We've got to catch it. We've got to do something."

A small animal the size of a mouse had the entire household in a tizzy.

One day, while sitting in the living room, I watched the animal scurry across the hallway. I started to lunge at it, as I usually did, then I stopped myself.

"No," I said. "I'm all done. If that animal wants to live in the nooks and crannies of this house, I'm going to let it. I'm done worrying about it. I'm done chasing it."

I let the gerbil run past without reacting. I felt slightly uncomfortable with my new reaction—not reacting—but I stuck to it anyway. Before long, I became downright peaceful with the situation. I had stopped fighting the gerbil. One afternoon, only weeks after I started practicing my new attitude, the gerbil ran by me, as it had so many times, and I barely glanced at it. The animal stopped in its tracks, turned around, and looked at me. I started to lunge at it. It started to run away. I relaxed.

"Fine," I said. "Do what you want." And I meant it.

About an hour later, the gerbil came and stood by me, and waited. I gently picked it up and placed it in its cage, where it happily reestablished its home. Don't lunge at the gerbil. He's already frightened, and chasing him just scares him more and makes us crazy, too.

Is there someone you'd like to get close to? Is there an irregular circumstance in your life that you can't change? Detachment, particularly detaching in love, helps.

13

God, show me the power of using detachment as a tool in all my relationships.

January 10   **Push a different button**

If you keep pushing the same button, you will get the same results. If you don't like the same results, maybe you could try pushing a different button.

"I try and I try and I try. Nothing seems to change. I don't know why he can't try to please me a little more; I've done so much for him." "The people at work just don't appreciate my efforts after all that I've done."

If you find yourself reacting to the same situations with the same responses over and over again, waiting for a change, stop! If you've been pushing the same button again and again, maybe the only result you're going to get is the one that's been taking place.

Look at your relationships. Is there a situation that has been moving steadily downhill despite your best efforts to push the right button? Do you find yourself responding to the same situations in the same way over and over, never satisfied with the results? Are you trying the same thing over and over, waiting for something outside of yourself to change instead of doing something differently yourself? Maybe it's time to stop pushing the button, walk away, and do something else.

God, give me the clarity to see the situations in my life honestly and to act with wisdom and responsibility in the associations that I have.

"I think of letting go as being like throwing a baseball," a friend said to me. "The problem is, I just don't want to let go of the ball." Hanging on to the ball is a temptation. We've got it in our hands. Why not keep it there? At least if we're dwelling on the problem, it feels like we're doing something. But we're not. We're just holding on to the ball, and chances are we're holding up the game.

There's nothing wrong with trying to solve the problem or offering requested advice. But if we've done everything we could, and there's nothing left to do but obsess, the person we need to stop is ourselves.

Here are some rules:

- If you've tried to solve a problem three times, and obsessing doesn't count as a problem-solving skill, then stop yourself. Let go. Throw the ball. At least for today.
- If others ask for advice, give them the advice once. Then throw the ball to them. Say no more.
- If a person hasn't asked for advice, or if you've offered advice and were told no thanks, there's nothing to throw. The ball isn't in your hands.

Remember the times you've willingly let go. Think about how things worked out for you then. Now remember those times you resisted letting go. Whether you wanted to or not, did you throw the ball in the end?

God, please show me the benefits of letting go.

Letting go can be like a tug-of-war with God.

Have you ever played tug-of-war with a puppy and an old

sock or a toy? You pull. He pulls. You pull it out of his mouth. He grabs hold again and shakes and shakes and says *grrrrrr*. The harder you tug, the harder the puppy tugs. Finally, you just let go. Then he comes right back again, for more.

I have never successfully treated or solved one problem in my life by obsessing or controlling. I've yet to accomplish anything by worrying. And manipulation has not wrought one successful outcome. But I forget that from time to time.

The best possible outcomes happen when I let go. That doesn't mean I always get my way. But things work out and, ultimately, the lesson becomes clear. If we want to play tug-of-war, we can, but it's not an efficient problem-solving skill.

God, help me surrender to your will.

January 13   **Take care of yourself**

For once a person begins on this path of knowledge they will only look inward, learning how to fix themselves, instead of trying to fix other people.

— *Rav Brandwein*

Letting go doesn't mean we don't care. Letting go doesn't mean we shut down.

Letting go means we stop trying to force outcomes and make people behave. It means we give up resistance to the way things are, for the moment. It means we stop trying to do the impossible—controlling that which we cannot—and instead, focus on what is possible—which usually means taking care of ourselves. And we do this in gentleness, kindness, and love, as much as possible.

Have you tricked yourself into believing there's someone you can control? If you have, tell yourself the truth. Stop trying to have power where you truly have none. Instead, exercise your will in a way that will bring results. The one power you always have is the ability to let go and take care of yourself.

God, help me make letting go and taking care of myself a way of life.

January 14   **Say *yes* to yourself**

Are you balanced? Do you share your time, your energy, your life, as much with yourself as you do with those around you? We all know how simple it is to say "yes, yes, yes" each time someone makes a request. After all, it makes us feel good, makes us feel needed, makes us feel loved. And the more we say *yes*, the more they ask of us. And we tell ourselves this is an example of even more love.

But soon we say *yes* to too many things. We get bitter about our relationships. *Can't they do anything for themselves? Nothing would get done around here if it weren't for me. Isn't there anyone else who can help?* After a while, things don't get done, promises go unfulfilled, relationships break down. And so do we.

It doesn't have to be that way. Know your limits. You are one of the most important people you need to look after and love. Balance your time, your energy, your life with those around you. You will be able to give more freely and joyfully as a result, and you'll be more open to the gifts of the universe.

It's not wrong to give to others. But it's okay to say *yes* to ourselves, too.

God, help me live a balanced life. Help me learn when it's time to say yes to myself.

*It may sound odd, but the way to give up being over controlled
is to become more disciplined about letting go.*
                    — *Stella Resnick*, The Pleasure Zone

I was sitting at home worrying one day when a friend
called. He asked how I was. I told him I was worrying.
Actually, I was crossing the line into obsessing about something that was going on in my life then. "There's nothing you
can do about it," he said. "Just relax. It's out of your control."

What my friend was really talking about was practicing the
discipline of letting go. After I hung up the phone, I deliberately put my worries and obsessions aside. I surrendered to
the way things were. I simply relaxed. It was like a miracle. I
was able to move forward with my life.

When we begin letting go, it may seem almost impossible
just to relax and let go. As with anything else, with practice
and repetition, we will become more skilled. That doesn't
mean we won't need to remember to do it. It just means letting go will become easier, in time.

If you've become highly skilled at worrying, obsessing, or
trying to control, deliberately practice relaxing and letting go
until you're good at that, too.

*God, help me make the discipline of relaxing and letting go a daily
part of my life. Teach me to let go with poise, dignity, and ease.*

How do you let go? *I just can't let go? It's impossible to let go
of this.* These are thoughts that may run through our minds
when we worry, dwell, and obsess.

Pick up something around you. Pick up this book. Hold it tightly. Then just drop it. Release it. Let it fall right out of your hands.

That's what you do with whatever you're obsessing and dwelling about. If you pick it up again, drop it one more time. See! Letting go is a skill that anyone can acquire.

Passion and focus can lead us along our path and help us find our way. But obsession can mean we've crossed that line, again. We can be compassionate but firm with ourselves and others as we learn to release our tight grip and just let things go.

God, help me know that if I'm obsessing about a problem, it's not because I have to. Dropping it is always a choice available to me.

January 17   Relax. You'll figure it out

Let the answers come naturally.

Have you ever gone into a room to get something and by the time you got there, you forgot what you went to get? Often the harder we try to remember, the worse our recollection.

But when we relax and do something else for a minute—just let go—what we're trying so hard to remember pops naturally into our minds.

When I suggest that we let go, that's all I'm suggesting that we do. I'm not saying the problem doesn't matter, or that we have to entirely extinguish all thoughts of the subject from our minds, or that the person we care about isn't important anymore. All I'm saying is that if we could do anything about it, we probably would have by now. And seeing as we can't, letting go usually helps.

God, help me relax and let my answers about what to do next come naturally from you.

January 18   **Let go of the past**

I was sitting outside on the patio one morning. A foggy mist gently covered the peaks of the Ortega Mountain Range. The birds were singing. My mind wandered back to ten years ago and my life in Minnesota with my children, Shane and Nichole.

Shane was still alive then. Nichole was still living at home. Our love, our family bond, was so strong. "We'll always get together for birthdays," we had vowed. "Our bond, our love, will live on." It had been the best year, the happiest year, of my life. I wanted that time back again. *If I could just see him again, for one minute. If the three of us could just be together again, for one day,* I yearned, *life would be so good.*

Later that morning I picked up an Osho Zen meditation card—not to tell the future, but to get insights into now.

My card talked about "clinging to the past."

It said, "It's time to face up to the fact that the past is gone, and any effort to repeat it is a sure way to stay stuck in old blueprints that you would have already outgrown if you hadn't been so busy clinging to what you have already been through."

"Silly me," I thought, coming back to the patio and to the Ortega Mountain Range. "Even though life is different and I miss the children, life is pretty good now."

Let yourself have all your emotions and feelings about losing people and moments you loved and cherished. Feel as sad as you need to. Grieve. Then let the feelings and the past go. Don't let your memories stop you from seeing how beautiful and precious each moment in your life is now.

God, help me let go of yesterday so I can open my heart to the gifts of today.

January 19   You're connected to life and the universe

"My friend died, and I was upset," a man told me one day. "I took off on a trip, wandering around the Southwest, hiking through Bryce Canyon. I saw the snow in the caverns, the rich red carved peaks sticking up. I saw the vastness of the universe, and the beauty in all of it. I had set off on my trip to prove how unique and isolated I was in my grief. By the time the trip ended, I realized just how connected to this world I am."

Part of letting go is recognizing that you are a part of this universe and not separate from it.

Perhaps a situation has come up in your life recently that signals an ending—the passing of a relative, the end of a relationship, the loss of a job. The people we love and the things we do contribute to our sense of who we are. When the people and things we love are threatened, taken away, we can rebel. We want to hold on to the known and don't want to see what's on the other side.

Let go of the uncontrollable in your life. You're not a solitary being in this great universe, set to struggle against all of the forces; you're part of the whole. And the changes that come—whether they're joyous or sad, easy or difficult—are just a part of the growing process that each of us goes through.

Feel the pain when you have a loss. Feel the joy when you triumph. Then let go and continue to grow.

See how connected you are.

God, help me recognize that I am a part of your creation and don't need to fight it. Help me live in peace and celebration of life.

There is no such thing as complete acceptance. When you can remember a loss with a little distance and much less pain, you have accepted the loss and mourned it fully. You accept that life is different now and move on.

— *David Viscott*, Emotionally Free

There are certain events that we may never accept fully. What can be accepted, though, is that we are required to live with these losses and find a way to go on.

Some people were horribly abused in childhood, beyond what anyone can be expected to endure. Some of us have experienced unthinkable losses later on in life. A spouse may have betrayed us. We may have lost our family through divorce. We may have lost our physical health through an accident or illness. A loved one may have died.

It's okay to stop waiting for and expecting total acceptance of the unthinkable in your life. Instead, gently do one thing each day to demonstrate that you're willing to move forward with your life.

God, grant me compassion for myself and others. Help me learn to be gentle with broken hearts, including my own.

Activity: Make a list of all the questions you have for God, the "why's." For instance, why did so-and-so have to die, why did I have to lose my family, why did this have to happen to me? Then, as much as possible, do not dwell on those questions. Trust you'll get your answers possibly later, possibly when you can talk to your Higher Power face-to-face. For now, let those questions be the unsolved mysteries of life.

When we hoard what we have been given, we block the door to receiving more. If you are feeling stagnant in your life, share some of what has been given to you.

Let go of some of the sorrow that you have experienced by sharing your experience and the compassion that you have learned from it with another. Share your success by teaching someone else your methods. Share in the abundance given to you; donate to a favorite charity or church. Give of your time, your money, your abilities. When you give, you open the door to receive more.

Sharing our experience, strength, and hope is key in a Twelve Step program. It's a key to all of life, whether we're recovering from addictions or not.

Find some way to share of yourself. Maybe it will be as simple as picking up the tab at lunch. Volunteer to help with a local project. Just find one small way to give. Give without any thought of compensation. Don't look for a thank you; give without expectation. Be aware of how you feel in the act of sharing; be aware of the glow that you feel in the deepest part of your soul. Then, do it again. Keep sharing small pieces of your gifts—your experience, strength, and hope— until sharing becomes a natural part of you.

Open your heart to all you've been given by sharing your gifts with someone else. That small glow you first felt in the bottom of your soul will soon overflow in your life. Maybe we gave compulsively and without joy at some time in our lives. The answer isn't to permanently stop giving. It's to learn to give with joy.

God, help me give abundantly of what's been given to me. Teach me how to give, so that both my giving and my receiving are healthy and free from attachments.

January 22   Let go of your plans

Letting go can feel so unnatural. We work hard for a promotion, a relationship, a new car, a vacation. Then the universe has the gall to come along and mess up our plans. How dare it! And so, rather than opening ourselves to the experiences that await us, we hold on to the plans that we made for ourselves. Or we hold on to bitterness about our plans going awry.

Sometimes losing our dreams and plans for our future can hurt as much as losing a tangible thing. Sometimes accepting and releasing our broken dreams is part of accepting a loss.

Let go of your expectations. The universe will do what it will. Sometimes your dreams will come true. Sometimes they won't. Sometimes when you let go of a broken dream, another one gently takes its place.

Be aware of what is, not what you would like to be, taking place.

God, please help me let go of my expectations and accept the gifts that you give me each day, knowing that there is beauty and wonder in each act of life.

January 23   Remember to let go

A friend called me into the next room. I didn't want to move. I was head-deep in obsession, fretting about something I couldn't change, at least not at that moment. I reluctantly walked to the window where he stood, walking in that stiff, unnatural way we jerk about when we're obsessing.

"Look at the moonlight reflecting off the waves," he said.

I stared at the white shimmering ripples in the ocean, like diamonds in the night.

We talked for a moment, about whether it was phosphorescence—that delightful and rare phenomenon that causes the sea to glow in the dark—or whether it was simply moonlight bouncing off the waves. We decided it was light.

I walked away, a little more relaxed. Letting go isn't something we do to manipulate the universe into giving us what we want. It's a way of opening our hearts to receive the gifts it and God have for us.

God, help me remember that I don't have to let go today, but I'll be happier if I do.

January 24   Learn to let

Someone said, "Let go and let God," and this is a wonderful recipe for overcoming fear or getting out of a tight place. In any case, the rule for creation is always to let.

— *Emmet Fox*

Darren, a friend of mine, keeps Light Show in his computer. It's a program of his own making. In this file, he records all incidences of Divine Guidance, Divine Intervention, answered prayers, and serendipitous events in his life. Whenever he begins to doubt the presence of a Benevolent Force, whenever he stops trusting life, whenever he feels abandoned or wonders exactly how wise it is to trust God, he turns to his own light show to remind himself how powerful and wise it really is to let go.

People can tell others how miraculous it is to let go, how beneficial it is to practice a hands-off policy when it comes to manipulating or controlling the affairs of others, how stunning it is to let go of goals and let nature take its course. I could tell you how beneficial letting go is in creating healthy relationships.

But that's my light show. Why not create your own?

Don't try, don't force, don't make it happen. *Let.* Let it happen.

Let go and let God.

God, show me how letting go can benefit my life.

Activity: Start a file in your computer or dedicate part of your journal to a light show. Document how you try to control a problem, or a person, or the outcome of a particular situation. Enter that incident into your light show. Then, practice letting go. Make notes about what helped you, any tools you used such as meditation or prayer. When the problem gets solved, or the goal gets accomplished, or you simply get the peace and grace to live effortlessly with an unsolved problem, enter that into your logbook. Whenever you need reassurance, refer to your light show.

January 25   What do you want?

Imagine walking up to the counter at the local fast-food restaurant and asking if they had your order ready. "What order?" the counterperson would ask. "Did you phone one in?" "No, but I thought you might have something for me behind the counter anyway."

It's absurd, you might say. *How could I expect them to have food ready for me when I hadn't yet placed my order?*

Exactly. And how can you expect the magic of the universe to start bringing you the things and experiences that you want for your life if you haven't named them yet?

Have you placed an order yet? Maybe you thought about it at the beginning of the year, but put it off until you had more time to think about it. And every day, you wake up and stand at the counter of life asking, "What do you have for me?"

If you haven't asked for anything, you may have to settle for whatever life hands your way. Why not take the time to ask? You don't have to be too specific; just ask for what you want. Want adventure? Put it on the list. Want love? Write it down. There is no guarantee that you'll get everything you request. Life may have other plans for you. But you'll never know whether you can get what you want unless you know what that is, and ask for it first.

God, help me have the courage to bring the desires of my heart to my conscious mind, and to you.

January 26   Be a thermostat

There's a thermometer on my back porch. It tells me when it's hot enough to go for a swim.

Inside the house, there's a thermostat. The thermostat not only tells us how hot or cold it is, but will actually do something about it as well. If the temperature gets too warm, the thermostat tells the air conditioner to cool off the house. If it gets too cool, the thermostat tells the heater to warm things up a bit.

Which are you? Are you a thermometer—only reflecting the attitudes of those around you? Or are you a thermostat—determining your own course of action and following through with it? Thermometer people often know where they are; they just don't do anything about it. *I'm stuck in this relationship. I'm really angry, resentful, and upset.* Thermostat people are aware of where they are, too. They just choose to do something about it, as well. *I'm in this relationship, and I will do everything that I can to improve it. But if necessary, I will walk away from it.*

Being a thermostat means we take appropriate action to take care of ourselves.

God, help me learn to respond to whatever environment I'm in by taking the appropriate actions to take care of myself.

January 27   Find the adventure in your life

He had quit his job eight weeks earlier, a prodigal son off to find his story in the world. He arrived back in town dirty, unshaven, tired, and smiling. He had $4.38 in his pocket, he said. Enough for a burger and fries, if someone would give him a ride—there wasn't enough gas in his car to get him to the restaurant and back. We were just getting ready to go to dinner and one of the others asked if he wanted to come along. "My treat," a friend said, "as long as you tell us some stories."

He did.

And oh, what stories he told from his trip through the west—high mountains, deep canyons, altitude sickness, frigid nights. Story after story poured out as we listened over plates of tacos.

"But what will you do now?" I asked later. "You only have four dollars to your name."

"It's okay," came the reply. "I'll just go back to work for a while."

"And then?"

"Take another trip. Next year I'm going to Europe to see what's over there."

Take a chance. We don't have to settle in and live in the first safe, comfortable box that we find. We can live in the moment, pull all that we can from it, then stretch our wings and fly someplace else. I'm not saying to quit your job and go off on a backpacking adventure, unless that's what you want to do. I'm just saying you might want to follow your heart. Learn to cook, learn to paint, share what you know by teaching a class. Find the adventure in your life, calculate the risk, then take it.

God, put the adventure back in my life. If I've gotten too safe in my little world, help me take a risk. Help me learn to live big.

January 28   There's magic in our beliefs

There's a church in the town of Chimayo, New Mexico. Rumor has it that the soil surrounding the church has special healing properties. Long before the church existed, there was a spring gushing up from the ground nearby. The Tewa Indians of the area believed that this spring held special magical properties and thought that by drinking the water, their infirmities could be healed. The waters eventually stopped bubbling up, leaving only a muddy pool, and still the pilgrims came seeking healing. Finally, even the mud dried and turned to dust, and still the Tewa came. They ate the dust or mixed it with water and drank it. And many times it healed them.

Then the Spanish built a church in the area. When the stories of the magical healing dust persisted, the church decided to blend with the local beliefs instead of trying to eradicate superstition.

Today, people still come to the Santuario de Chimayo to be blessed or to take a little dirt from El Pocito, the little well in a back room. They still believe that the dust will heal them. And many times it does.

Is the dust magical? I don't know. But there's magic in what we believe.

Our beliefs tell our future better than any crystal ball or

psychic can. As a man thinketh in his heart, so is he, one holy book says. Be mindful of your thoughts and beliefs. What you think and believe today, whether it's *I can't* or *I can*, is what you will manifest tomorrow.

Do you have any beliefs right now that are holding you down or back? What are your *I can's* and what are your *I cant's*? Take a moment. Look into your heart. Examine what you believe to be true. Is there an area of your life that could be benefited by thinking and believing something else?

If you're going to use the power of your mind, use it to form a positive belief. Sometimes, the littlest bit of magic is all we need to change our lives.

God, help me come to believe what is right and true about myself, life, and others. Show me, and help me understand, the power and magic of what I believe.

January 29   Protect yourself from negative influences

After a long rainstorm in the desert, I watched little drops of runoff splashing off of a rock face into little indentations in the rock. Each drop fell in exactly the same place as the drop before, and over the years, the procession had dug a tiny hole into the stone. I looked around at the other rocks in the area and saw that they, too, were pockmarked by the slow but steady effects of erosion over the years.

Poor relationships can be like that rain. We start out on a course of learning and self-improvement with the best of intentions, but little by little our efforts are undermined by the associations that we choose. We do have an advantage over those rocks though.

We can move.

Maybe you have allowed your efforts to be sabotaged by

wrong friends, wrong thoughts, or negative input of some sort and kind. You have a choice. You can choose to stand in the rain of negativity and slowly be worn down by it, or you can find shelter, a support group of like-minded people, a good book or program, a minister or mentor, a helpful and positive friend.

Be aware of the negative rain in your life. If even a stone can be worn down over time by constant falling rain, how much more must we be aware of the influences in our lives. Seek out that which is edifying, and find shelter from that which can erode your resolve.

God, protect me from negative influences, which erode my beliefs. Help me protect myself. Surround me with that which is positive, edifying, and uplifting.

January 30   See the good in yourself, too

"Let me see your hands," she said, gently holding my right hand up close to hers. "Look," she said. "We have the same hands."

My daughter was thrilled by the discovery that our fingers were the same size, curved the same way; even our wrists were the same shape. I was at her house visiting her, her child, and her husband that afternoon. We had snuck away for a few quiet moments together. Later that evening, when I returned home, she called me on the phone.

"You seem so excited and interested in our hands," I said.

"I've always thought your hands were so beautiful. Then I started looking at my hands, and I thought maybe they looked just like yours, but I wasn't sure until we looked at them today. It's just so cool," she said, "that my hands look just like yours."

It's so easy to see and notice what we like in other people. Sometimes, it's not as easy to see the attributes and beauty in ourselves. It's good to see the beauty in others. But sometimes, take a moment and get excited when you notice what's beautiful in yourself, too.

We hear so much about people mirroring our negative qualities back to us. You know—what you don't like in others is probably what you don't like in yourself. And often that's true. But people can also mirror our desires, our hopes, our attributes, and our strengths back to us. Chances are that what you see and admire in others is probably a mirror shining your good qualities back to you.

God, help me see the beauty and the good in life. Help me be aware of what I like in others, so that I can better define what I aspire to become.

Activity: Choose five people in your life whom you like and respect. Make a list of the qualities they have that you admire. Now, see how many of these qualities might correctly be used to describe yourself, as well. If you don't believe you already possess these qualities, could you be selling yourself short? Or do these qualities describe who you aspire to be? If you define some new aspirations, transfer them to your goal list. See how easy it is to begin defining and clarifying our dreams?

January 31   **Speak the language of letting go**

Sometimes in our lives, we can let go in an instant. We recognize that we're dwelling on or obsessing about a particular situation, and we just let go. We drop it. Or we run into someone who has a problem, and we instinctively adapt a hands-off posture, knowing that it's not our responsibility to take care of other people. We say what we need to say, and we almost automatically let go and focus on taking care of ourselves.

Other times, it's not as easy. We may be entangled in a situation that feels utterly impossible to let go of. We get enmeshed with a problem, or a person, that seems to compel us to hang on more tightly when letting go is the key.

We know we *shouldn't* be obsessing, but we can't seem to stop.

One day, many years ago, back in Stillwater, Minnesota, my son was hugging me tightly. He didn't want to let go. I started tipping over. I lost my balance.

"Shane," Nichole scolded, "there comes a time to let go."

Sometimes letting go happens in stages. Sometimes it means becoming more aware. Sometimes it involves going deeply into the feelings hidden underneath our behavior. Learning to let go may involve gaining more confidence and self-esteem. Sometimes it means simply practicing gratitude for the way things are.

Be gentle with yourself and others as you learn to practice the language of letting go.

Sometimes, no matter how much we know, letting go takes time.

God, help me remember that letting go is a powerful behavior, one that can change my life and impact the lives of others. Help me be patient with others and myself as letting go becomes a way of life.

February
Say Woohoo

I put on my skydiving gear and headed for the airplane. Here I was again, ready to go. My hands were already sweating; I could feel the quiver in my lip. Why did I keep doing this to myself?

Once I boarded the airplane, I started what had become a routine for me. *I don't have to do this,* I told myself. *I'm volunteering to skydive. It's not mandatory.* Not wanting to overly embarrass myself in front of the other, more experienced sky divers, I coped with my anxiety by fidgeting. I fidgeted with the altimeter on my hand. I fidgeted with the strap on my helmet.

I wanted to tell my jump master I couldn't jump because I was having a heart attack, but I knew he wouldn't believe me. It was just anxiety, fear building up to an unmanageable, uncontrollable level.

A friend was sitting across from me, watching. "How are you doing, Mel?" he asked.

"Scared," I said.

"Do you say *woohoo*?" he asked.

"What do you mean?" I said.

"When you get to the door and jump, say *woohoo*," he said. "You can't have a bad time if you do."

I walked to the door of the plane, hoisted myself out, and waited for the nod from my jump master, signaling that he was ready for the count.

"Ready, " I said. "Set." Then with all my might, I yelled, "WOOHOO," so loud the sky divers in the back of the plane heard me.

My jump master followed me out of the plane and then positioned himself in front of me. I looked at him and grinned. Then I grinned some more. *So this is why I'm doing this*, I thought. *Because it's so much fun.*

It was the best jump I'd had yet.

We're jumping into the unknown, when we have a baby or a new job.

Sometimes, however, we don't choose our experience. I can recall sitting on the edge of the bed in the hospital room after Shane's death, knowing that the journey I was about to embark upon would not be an exhilarating one. *God, I don't want to go through this*, I thought. *It's not going to be over in three months or a year. This one I'll live with the rest of my life.* I can remember standing in the parking lot outside the courthouse after my divorce from the children's father. I took one deep breath, feeling exhilarated and free. The next one was filled with terror and dread. My God, I was now a dirt-poor single parent with two children to raise.

Sometimes we jump out that door voluntarily. Sometimes we're pushed.

Feel your fear, then let it go. Dread is just a prejudice against the future. After having examined all the probabilities and possibilities, we decide ahead of time that we're going to have the worst experience possible. So let go of dread, too.

Fidget if you must. Ask yourself what you're doing here. Then walk to the door and give the count. See how much fun it can be when you jump into the unknown and feel the rush of being fully alive.

God, help me take a deep breath and holler woohoo.

February 2   Let go of unreasonable fears

We had planned on this day for a month. Now it had finally arrived. My friend and I were going kayaking in the ocean—it was going to be a first for us both.

We had the kayak and the life preservers. He showed up at the house, ready to go. The sun was shining, and the surf was pounding gently enough to be safe. He had gotten himself all ready for his event. He was wearing a hat, a Hawaiian shirt, and big floppy sandals on his feet.

We put on our life jackets. The man showed up at the door to train us in the proper way to kayak. First it was my turn. I was scared, but not too scared. I knew if we turned over, I'd just float.

I jumped in. The instructor pushed us out before the big wave came. He jumped in. We paddled like heck. When the big wave came, I yelled "ahh" and raised my oar high over my head, like the man said, to be safe. We went through three more of these waves. They looked big. I was scared each time. But soon we passed the surf, and we came to a quiet, clear place. We paddled around for a while. Then it was time to go back to shore and train my friend. I was excited. A little more training, and my friend and I would be ready to go out on the boat together.

I got out of the kayak. My instructor held the boat. My friend began to climb in, so they could push out. Just then a wave came. My friend got nervous and shaky. He screamed. The boat tipped over. He fell out.

He lay there in the surf. The boat slipped over close to his head. He started screaming some more.

"It's just a piece of plastic," I said quietly. "All you have to do is move it away."

"I'm drowning," he said, gasping mouthfuls of water.

"No, you're not," I said. "You're still on the shore. You've got water in your mouth from screaming. All you really need to do is sit up."

My friend sat up. The instructor politely said the waves were getting a little high, and he didn't think he'd be able to train my friend that day, and then he left. My friend and I quietly put the kayak away.

Sometimes, saying *woohoo* means working through our fears. Fear can be a good thing. It can signal danger and protect us. Sometimes our fears are bigger than life and bigger than they need to be.

Many of us have panic and anxiety attacks. It's nothing to be embarrassed about. But sometimes we can calm ourselves down by reinforcing a little reality. Maybe we're not really drowning, after all. Maybe all we have to do to save our lives is just sit up.

Explain to yourself that your fears are unrealistic and you don't need to be that afraid. Instead of screaming for help and upsetting yourself, learn to calm yourself down.

God, help me let go of my unreasonable fears, the ones that are preventing me from living my life.

February 3   Deal with panic and anxiety

I can still remember the day. It was shortly after my divorce. I was a single parent with no money and two young children. It came upon me suddenly, out of the blue. I couldn't breathe. My chest hurt. My heart hurt. I couldn't stop it. I panicked. The more I panicked, the worse it got.

I called 911. The ambulance came. They gave me some oxygen, then politely told me not to worry; it was just a panic attack. I had experienced another one of those attacks, a long time ago. Right after I first married the children's father, I had shut myself down from anxiety. I couldn't breathe, couldn't speak from the fear I felt.

Many people experience panic and anxiety attacks. Maybe it's happened to you. Maybe you've had only one or two incidents of it; maybe panic and anxiety make regular appearances in your life. Most people I've met have experienced fear.

These are a few little clues I've learned that have helped me to deal with my own attacks.

- Breathe. Whenever we panic, our breath comes in shallow, awkward spurts. By deliberately breathing slowly and calmly, we can slow our panic down. We feed it by breathing fast. We put our bodies on hyperalert. If we breathe as though we're relaxed, our bodies will start slowing down.

- Don't respond to your panic with more fear. Sometimes we double what we're going through by having an emotional reaction to our initial reaction. We're afraid, because we're feeling fear. Let yourself go through the original feeling without reacting to yourself.

- Instead of focusing on your fear, let yourself be aware that you're feeling it, but deliberately do something that calms you down. You won't want to do this. Your panic will want you to do something else, something that feeds panic and makes it grow. Do something calming and quiet, even though that activity doesn't feel right to you. It could be reading a meditation, listening to some quiet music, taking a shower, or saying a prayer. We all have things that help calm us down. Find something that works for you.

If panic and anxiety are a continual problem, seek professional help. But if they are only isolated incidents in your life, you may be able to help yourself. One tool that has never let me down when it comes to anxiety and fear is working Step One of the Twelve Step program. I admit that I'm powerless over my panic and fear, and my life has become unmanageable. Then I ask God what I need to do next.

Don't let your fears run your life. Make it a goal to get through them. Ask them what they're trying to tell you. You may be on a path that's new, and your body is just reacting to that. There may be a hidden emotion underneath all this fear, something you'd rather not see. Or maybe you and your life are just changing so fast that everything in your world is brand new. Be gentle and loving with yourself and others.

God, help me welcome all the new experiences in my life. Give me the courage to calmly walk my path today, knowing I'm right where I need to be.

February 4   Don't let fear throw you off balance

Lay a two-by-four on the ground and walk its length without falling off. Easy, isn't it? Now place a couple of bricks under the two-by-four, raising it off the ground by a few inches. Walk it again. A little harder this time? Now imagine that same two-by-four suspended at the height of your house with no safety net under it. Would you care to try again?

The higher the stakes, the harder it is to maintain our balance. That's what fear does in our lives.

When we're faced with simple situations in life, it's easy to do the right thing. But as the stakes get higher and higher, it becomes increasingly difficult to focus on the task. We imagine "what ifs" and what might happen if we fail.

Look at the two-by-fours that you have to cross every day in your life. Are you allowing fear of a worst-case scenario to upset your balance? Put the situation back on the ground. Rarely will failure result in permanent damage. Remove the fear that your mind has created around the possibility of failure and just walk along the plank.

God, help me do the tasks that I have to without the balance-upsetting confusion brought by fear. Help me do what is right simply and easily each day.

February 5   Stare in the face of your fears

Examine your fears.

Sometimes we're afraid of specific things. Sometimes we fear the unknown. And sometimes we're just afraid, because that's the way we usually feel.

Are you nervous, anxious, upset? What's scaring you right now?

Have a little talk with yourself. Take a look at what you fear. Are you starting a new relationship or job? What are the risks? What's the worst that could possibly happen? Sometimes it helps to go through our fears, one by one. We don't need to dwell on the negative, but we need to be certain that we're willing to take responsibility for the risks involved.

Then look in the other direction, and see the entire positive potential there. What can you gain by taking that risk? Does the thrill of victory outweigh the potential loss?

We may emerge from the list saying, *No, I choose not to risk that.* Or, we may look at the risks and say, *Yes, I've been through worse. I can handle this, too.*

Someone once told me many years ago that fear was a good thing. "If you're not feeling afraid, it means you're not doing anything differently. You're just repeating the same old thing." If fear is haunting you, stare it in the face. See what's making you feel afraid. Then either back off, or stare that fear down.

God, help me sort through my fears, one by one. Then guide me in deciding which risks I want to take. Help me not be foolhardy. But help me let go of timidity, too.

February 6   Revel in the void

In the original *Language of Letting Go,* I talked about the in-between places in our lives. Those are the uncomfortable places along the journey where you're not where you were but you're not where you're going yet, either. I talked about accepting that place, no matter how difficult it might be.

Let's look at this place again. Only now, we'll call it the void. Take another look at that moment when one door has closed behind you and you're standing in that dark hallway, but no door opens up. Or you let go of whatever you've been grasping so tightly and stand there with an empty hand. Don't say *woohoo* just when you begin something new. Feel the *woohoo* of this moment, too! Embrace the void. This wonderful in-between place holds the keys to all creation. In the biblical story of creation, God began with a clean slate like the one you may face now. It was the magic and mystery of the void that allowed all of this wonderful creation to be.

If you're at an in-between place, don't just accept it. Revel in it, embrace it, rejoice at your opportunity to sit in the birthplace of all that will come along your path. Relax into the void and allow creation to flow.

God, help me embrace the void and allow it to bring forth what it will, rather than trying to force something that really doesn't fit.

February 7   Replace dread by saying *woohoo*

Let go of dread.
Treat it like a feeling. Identify it. Accept and acknowledge

it. Then release it. Do whatever you have to, to get it out of your system. Because dread is more than just a feeling—it's really a curse.

We throw this dark gray blanket of dread over our lives for hours, sometimes days, months, and sometimes years. We convince ourselves that certain situations will be terrible. Then what we've predicted comes true.

Dread is not living in the present moment. It's living the future before we get there, and living it without any joy. There's a lot of good about the future that you don't know. There's your power to flow. There's the creative power that exists in the void. There's your ability to intuitively handle what comes up. And there's a lesson, a pulsing potential in the experience that you can't see yet. There may be a delightful consequence or outcome from this experience on which you haven't planned. Or it may simply be something you need to get through to experience growth.

If you're feeling cursed because you're living in dread, take the curse off yourself.

God, help me open my heart to the full potential of every moment in my life.

February 8   Watch out for that *woohoo*

That's not flying. . . . It's falling, with style.
— *Woody,* Toy Story

There is a term in skydiving called *relative work.* That means you're controlling your fall rate to match those of the other jumpers in the air—falling in formation with them.

"We *are* flying," said a sky diver, flush with adrenaline after a jump, "relative to each other."

"Sure you are," I said. "But relative to the earth, you're falling, and that's all that counts."

It's easy to get caught up in the *woohoo* of the moment. But don't forget about humility and reality, too. We can make the right moves, assert ourselves, realize our dreams—but our plans need to be brought down to earth.

Find a path with heart, and walk it. Do things. Enjoy your activities. But also be aware that while you may feel like you are flying, there is a big green planet rushing toward you at 120 miles per hour that begs to differ.

Say *woohoo*. Have confidence. Then remember that there's always a power greater than you.

God, help me remember to be grounded and humble in all that I do.

February 9   Get to know yourself

I opened the curtains in the King David Hotel overlooking the walled city in Jerusalem. This entire trip had been an adventure, but not the exciting kind. Nothing had gone as I planned. Usually on my excursions, I met people, connected with them, learned lessons, broke bread, and had fun. This trip had been different. I had barely spoken to anyone.

One night in the hotel restaurant, a woman had motioned for me to join her for dinner. She spoke Hebrew. I spoke English. We sat and ate in silence. I had been to Egypt, the Sinai Peninsula. Now here. And that's the closest I came to human contact on the entire trip.

The past week, I had traveled through Safad, a town in the Holy Land. It was the home of the kabbalah, the mystical sect of Judaism, and one of the places where the purest, most intense form of meditation had been born. Although I had just wandered lightly through that land, something peculiar

45

had happened to me, ever since I'd been there. I could hear my every thought. I was acutely aware of each emotion I felt.

It was as though my life had become a walking meditation.

But I was feeling lonely, and feeling bored.

"What's wrong?" I asked. "Why haven't I connected with anyone on this trip?"

"Yes, you have," was the gentle answer I heard. "You've connected with yourself."

Rays of light were streaming in through the window, in those first few colorful moments when the sun fills the sky. Music from a flute floated up from the courtyard below. Maybe even when we're bored and lonely, all is well in the world.

Take some time on a regular basis to write in a journal, to meditate, or to do both. You'll meet an interesting, exciting person. You'll get to know yourself.

God, help me welcome those quiet spaces in my life as opportunities to connect with myself.

February 10   **Say *woohoo* even if you don't like where you are**

"Once you get into the desert there's no going back," said the camel driver. "And when you can't go back, you have to worry only about the best way of moving forward."
— *Paulo Coelho*, The Alchemist

Sometimes we get into situations and we can easily get out. We date someone, it's not right for us, and we stop seeing that person. We experiment with drinking or drugs, decide that this isn't for us, and we stop experimenting. We accept a job, it's not what we wanted or hoped it would be, so we leave and find another. We may even marry someone who's not right for us, and we get out. No children. No excessive property or financial entanglements. It's a mistake. We're sorry. There may be a few emotions involved, but correction is relatively painless and easy.

There are other times when it's not so easy. We don't just date the person. We get married, have one or more children, and then realize we've made a mistake. We begin using alcohol or drugs, and wake up one day to find that our life is out of control. What we need to do is stop drinking, and it's the very thing we can't do, at least not without help. Or we accept the job or sign a contract, one with serious legal entanglements and consequences.

These are the situations that bring us to our knees. It is in these situations that we work out our destiny. If we've hit a point of no return with some situation in our lives, the only way out is through.

Surrender to the experience. You may not have bargained for this, may not have consciously desired it. Learn to say *woohoo* anyway. You're meeting your destiny head-on. A spiritual adventure has just begun.

God, help me be gentle with others and myself as we each work out our destinies, karma, and fate. Give me the courage, help, insight, resilience, and grace to learn all the lessons I came here to face.

Activity: Write your memoirs. This is an extensive activity. If you take the time to do it, you will learn much about yourself. Break down your life into stories. Don't worry about writing a literary masterpiece. Just break your life down into sections and write about what you learned. Write about what you went through—how you thought it would be, what it actually turned into, how you struggled against this, and

47

how you finally saw the light and learned the lesson at hand. We all have ways of keeping a timeline of our lives; for instance, graduation, marriage, divorce, getting that big job, our sobriety date. This is a journal you may want to keep and add to for the rest of your life. It is your book of life. An interesting twist on this activity is to give your memoirs to your children, or ask your parents to do this activity as a gift. Reading our parents' memoirs can be an enlightening and healing event.

February 11   Grief

No one ever told me that grief felt so like fear. I am not afraid, but the sensation is like being afraid. The same fluttering in the stomach, the same restlessness, the yawning. I keep on swallowing. . . . Not that I am (I think) in much danger of ceasing to believe in God. The real danger is of coming to believe such dreadful things about Him. The conclusion I dread is not "So there's no God after all," but "So this is what God's really like. Deceive yourself no longer."

— *C. S. Lewis,* A Grief Observed

There's no way to prepare for deep grief, for the pain that shatters a heart and a life when a beloved leaves.

No one can coach us on it. Those who could, who knew exactly how it felt, who could describe it in detail, wouldn't do it, would not presume to encroach on this most intimate part of our relationship with a loved one. Those who casually say, "Aren't you over that yet?" don't understand.

This much I will tell you about grief: If there was ever a second, or a moment, when you suspected or knew you had been betrayed at the deepest level by someone you adored, and a splintering pain began to shred your heart, turn your world grimly unbearable to the point where you would consciously choose denial and ignorance about the betrayal rather than feel this way, that is one one-millionth of what it feels like to grieve.

Grief is not an abnormal condition, nor is it something to be treated with words. It is a universe, a world, unto itself. If you are called to enter this world, there is no turning back. We are not allowed to refuse that call. Grief is like nothing else, with the possible exception of the pounding waves of the ocean. To the untrained, casual eye, each wave looks the same. It is not. No two are the same. And each one washes away the old, and washes in the new.

Gradually, almost imperceptibly, whether we believe it or not, we are being transformed.

God, take care of me those moments and hours when I cannot find the will or power to take care of myself. Transform me, if not in the twinkling of an eye, then over the slow movement of the years, into who I will become.

February 12   Starting over

How many times do we have to start over?

Many changes in our lives signal a major ending or beginning: death, birth, graduation, marriage, divorce, moving to a new home, getting sober, losing a job, or beginning a new career. We look around and think, *Here we go. I'm starting over again.*

Sometimes we don't catch on at first. Sometimes it just feels like day after day of the same old thing as the old fades away and the new begins. Sometimes it feels like our lives have just stopped. Whether we believe it or not, when one cycle ends, a new one begins.

If life as you have known it is disappearing, it may be time to let go. Even if you can't see it now—and you probably can't—a new life will begin fading in to take its place. You and your life are being transformed.

How many times do we have to start over? As many times as life as we know it ends.

Say *woohoo*. You're being born again.

God, help me trust that a new life awaits me if life as I've known it is fading away. Give me the patience and trust to sink joyfully into the void.

February 13   You're not alone

I felt a searing pain in my heart. It was physical—I swear it was—when that nurse asked me if I had someone I could call. Over the next few days at the hospital, I was surrounded by people, but at no previous time in my life had I ever felt this isolated and alone. I knew that the path I was about to walk, I had to walk alone.

Later, another nurse walked over to me. She looked straight into my eyes. "It's going to be difficult, harder than you can imagine," she said. "And it'll take about eight years. But you can do it. You'll come through. I know. I lost a child, too. My daughter was nine when she died."

There are places in our lives that we're called to go alone. People can surround us, call us, and offer support. But the journey we're about to take is solely and uniquely ours. People can watch us, reach out to us, and even say they know how it feels. But the world we're entering is ours, and ours alone.

Slowly, as we walk this path that life has thrust us on, we begin to see the outline of a few faces—way out in the distance, waving to us, cheering us on. As we continue along the path, the faces and forms fill in. Before long, we see that we're in the midst of a large, large group. *Where did all these people come from?* we wonder. *I thought I was alone.*

No matter what path you're on, others have walked it before you, and some will follow you there. Each step you take is uniquely yours, but you are never, never alone.

While many experiences are isolated and uniquely ours, we're simultaneously part of a collective force. What we go through and what we do matters—sometimes much more than we know.

God, help me know how much you care. No matter what I'm going through, help me see the other faces along the way.

February 14   Say *woohoo* because there's hope

The doorbell rang one day. I was slumping about in the big house I had just purchased in Minnesota. It was going to be the dream home for the children and me. The problem was, Shane had been killed the day after I closed the deal. Now Nichole and I were rambling around wondering what to do.

I answered the door. The FedEx man asked me to sign for a delivery. I did. And he handed me a large cardboard box. I brought it into the living room and put it down without opening it up. I didn't get excited about much of anything back then. I was sad and angry. People, my readers, said they liked my writing because it gave them hope. The problem was, I didn't have any of that hope for myself. I couldn't see how life could or would ever make any kind of sense again. The one thing I wanted—my son alive and well, and my family intact—would not ever come to pass.

One day I got around to opening that big cardboard box. I

took a knife, sliced it down the center, and looked at what was inside. It was filled with stuffed animals. A big green parrot with a fuzzy beak was sitting on top. There were monkeys, bears, and assorted things. They didn't look brand new, but they were happy, cheerful little things. I took out the card and read the note inside. This is what it said:

"I make my living out of taking all the stuffed animals that people throw away. Then I take them home and clean them up. I guess I like doing it just to prove a point," the woman wrote. "Sometimes, we start thinking something's no good anymore, so we throw it in the trash. Sometimes we throw things away too quickly, but all they really need is a little tender, loving care to bring them back to life. I heard about your son's death. I thought maybe getting a box of my reborn animals might help."

Many years have passed since then. I've gotten rid of a lot of my possessions, especially when I moved from Minnesota to California in 1994. But one of the things I've held on to—in fact he's still sitting in this room with me next to my desk—is the happy green parrot with the big fuzzy beak.

He's a gentle reminder that even something as broken and scraggly as I was can be brought back to life again. Some things in life are true, whether we believe them or not.

Hope is one of those things.

Even if you have to say it in disbelief, say *woohoo.*

God, help me believe in me as much as you do. Thanks for getting me through those tough spots when I lose my faith.

February 15   Let a friend be there for you

I was at a carnival somewhere, sitting on a bench, eating blue cotton candy and experiencing the noise and color and the big carousel. Garishly colored horses bounced up and down, round and round; lights flashed; people whirred past. The little girl was on the verge of tears as her mother brought her up to the gate. She stalled, trying desperately to convince her mom, that no, she really didn't want to go on the merry-go-round after all. Mom was reassuring but firm, and finally a deal was reached. Daughter would go on the big ride if Mom would go, too.

They gave the man their tickets and walked around, the little one in awe of the multihued beasts that surrounded her. Finally, she settled on a white one with a gold mane and tail, and directed her mom to sit on the blue one next to her. Mom smiled, a little embarrassed, but complied with her daughter's request.

Then the music started. And suddenly, they were both five years old, shrieking and laughing as their horses bounded away. I laughed, too, watching from my bench. They raced around an imaginary track through valleys, over rivers, across plains. The music screamed, the lights flashed, and for a few minutes, they could fly.

They were still laughing when the ride ended. "Again Mommy. Let's go again!" laughed the girl excitedly. So they turned and got back in line. In letting go of her fear, that little girl was able to feel the wonder and excitement of a new experience, and in helping her daughter to overcome fear, the mother was able to recapture some of that thrill, as well. In our everyday lives, there are times when we are frightened, times when we need a friend to give us courage, and times when we can be a friend giving courage to someone else. Be grateful for those who have helped you find strength. Be grateful for the times when you have helped your friends find courage of their own.

Both sides of the coin are winners, and sometimes, experience is sweetest when shared.

God, help me reach out my hand in friendship and strength to those I meet along the way. And when I'm scared, help me give up my pride and ask a friend to stand by my side.

February 16   Joy is your destiny

Adam fell that man might be, and men are that they might have joy.

— *Book of Mormon*

In the garden, original man was perfect, unchanging, never knowing sickness or the sorrow of separation. It was only after the fall that we could learn the contrast between joy and sorrow and truly learn what joy is. More than the absence of sorrow, it is the embrace of life in all its turmoil. To live joyously means living with full awareness of how impermanent each life on earth is—how precious each moment, each conversation, each sunrise is.

Each day is the beginning of another new adventure, another opportunity to take a chance and live life to its fullest.

Look around you. Find the joy in your world.

After all, that's why you're here.

God, help me find and create true joy and peace in my world.

February 17   Lighten up

"Mom, can I sleep over at Johnny's house again tonight? Please?" Shane begged.

"Why?" I asked.

"For fun," he said.

"You just slept over last night," I said.

"Who said you can't have fun two days in a row?" he asked.

While ideas such as discipline and focus are undeniably important, so is the idea of having fun.

With a small amount of effort, we can extract all the fun and joy out of most parts of our lives—our relationships, our work, even our leisure time. We can put so many restrictions and should's on everything we do that our very lives become dull, overly ponderous, and routine. Before long, we find ourselves living up to a set of rules—and we're not certain where the rules came from or whose they are.

I relented, and let Shane have the sleepover he asked for. He had fun. He had a lot of fun that entire year. So did I.

Let yourself go. Have a little fun with life. Or, have a lot of fun with life. If you've spent years being extremely disciplined, reliable, and somber, maybe part of achieving balance is having a decade of fun.

Dig out your goal list, the one you placed at the back of this book. Add another value to your list: have as much fun and joy as possible in the days, months, and years to come.

It's time to lighten up.

God, please show me how to put ideas like fun and joy back into my life. Show me how to have more fun in work, in love, and in play.

February 18   Remember how to play

We don't stop playing because we get old, we get old because we stop playing.

— *Herbert Spencer*

I was sitting on my back porch watching a group of children playing in the surf. As the waves came surging in, they would turn to face the shore on their body boards and paddle like heck to try to catch the wave. I watched the surf crash down on top of them, one by one. There would be nothing for a few moments but the torrent of water, and then a little while later a green foam board would pop up and a little while later, a laughing head and body. They'd shriek and laugh, then one by one turn around, go back out, and do it again.

Later toward sunset, I saw two gray-haired men in ocean kayaks paddling near the shore. They would wait for the perfect wave and then paddle as hard as they could, trying to catch it and ride it into shore. Again I watched as the waves reared up and crashed down on the little boats. A kayak would get pushed up on the beach, followed a few moments later by a laughing gray-haired man, who would then paddle back out and do it again.

I have a friend in his thirties who is determined to make it. He doesn't know where he's going; he just knows that he is going somewhere. And no, he doesn't have time to go to a basketball game or Magic Mountain. He's busy and doesn't have time to play.

I have a friend in his fifties. He's in excellent health. He sits in his house, feeds the dog, and complains about the pain and the shortness of life. He doesn't play because his poor body just isn't what it used to be.

We can play or we can *not* play. It doesn't make any difference one way or another, except that at the end, you will have had a much more enjoyable time if you did.

God, help me start having some fun.

My house renovation project was way behind schedule. Spring was right around the corner. Stress was a pounding ache in the back of my head.

Then we went to the toy store. "Oh, these will be great," he said, grabbing two Nerf dart guns off the shelf. "And how about a bow-and-arrow set, too?"

When we got home, we took some markers and drew a big target on the wall in the living room. We started shooting at it, but soon grew tired of that game and started shooting at each other instead.

A friend walked in the front door.

We shot him. Two to the belly and one to the forehead.

He threw me into the hot tub.

And I forgot that the ceiling wasn't done, and that the walls weren't painted, and that the carpet would have to be delayed. That night we had a barbeque, and our friends took out the markers and drew pictures of themselves, their experiences, and their hopes on the unpainted walls of the house that was behind schedule. And we laughed, and no one cared that the house was unlivable.

We can't always control the timing of our plans, but we can have fun along the way. Friends don't care if the project is finished; they just want to be a part of the magic of life.

Look at things from a new perspective. Laugh. Be grateful you're where you are at this moment. Don't worry about trying to hurry the future along. Look for the joy in life now.

Maybe a visit to the toy store would help you, too.

God, if I can't see the joy in life, help me look again.

Activity: Go to the toy store today. Buy something that appeals to you, or buy something ridiculous—a twirl-o-paint, an Erector set, a game of Operation, a bead-o-matic. Break out of your mold; look at life from a new perspective. Learn how to play, again.

February 20   **Take a side road**

Adventures don't begin until you get into the forest. That first step in an act of faith.

— Micky Hart

We were driving along highway 166 in central California on another road trip. The trip had been a long one, started on the spur of the moment, as they usually are, and now we were anxious to get back home. Then we—Andy, Chip, and I —all saw it: a small road leading up into the mountains behind an open gate. It wasn't on the atlas. The road turned to dirt. Cows lounged on the path and we had to wait for them to move out of the way. The GPS (Global Positioning System) got lost. The path degraded. We hit a patch of black mud and the truck struggled for a moment. Chipster gunned the motor and we leapt ahead.

"Think we should turn around?" he asked

"No, this road must go somewhere," said Andy

"Aaaah," I said

We came to a small lake in the middle of the path.

"You can make it," said Andy, rolling up his window.

"Aaaah," I said.

Chip switched into four-wheel drive and gunned the motor. Muddy water poured in through the open sunroof.

Much later—after we moved rocks out of the way, splashed through more puddles, saw stunning views from a high ridgeline, and drove far too close to the edge of the cliff—we came across an old man pushing a bicycle up the road. We asked, "How much farther is it to get out of here?"

"Well," he replied, "how far in have you come?"

"We didn't come in this way."

A puzzled look crossed his face. "How did you get here then?"

"We drove over the ridge."

He shook his head in disbelief and walked on.

Ten miles later we came to another gate. The cell phone started to work again.

The GPS decided that we were still on the planet after all.

Sometimes, we find the biggest adventures when we deviate from the map and drive through the gate into new territory just to see where it goes.

God, help me remember that I don't have to follow the map all the time. Give me the spirit of adventure. Bring a little woohoo *into my life.*

February 21   **Say *woohoo* wherever you are**

I walked into the beach house after a day of work to find my friendly tormentors, Chip and Andy, standing by the window that drops down to the beach. Actually, Chip was standing next to the window; Andy was outside, hanging by a climbing harness. The rope led into the house and was tied off around one of the main support beams.

I didn't ask what they were doing. I just grabbed the climbing harness that was lying on the floor at Chip's feet and asked if I could try, too.

Rappelling from the house down to the beach is not my ordinary daily activity. But sometimes, even the smallest, most ridiculous thing can be a chance for a *mini-woohoo*. That night, I learned to rappel in the moonlight on the beach from the living room of my house.

Be open to new experience in your life. If it isn't life-threatening, maybe it's okay, even if it is a little odd. Don't be afraid to be ridiculous, look a little uncool, and even let out an *aaaah* now and then.

Have you had a *woohoo* lately? Have you got one on your list? Or maybe in your garage? Put on some Rollerblades, buy a surfboard, get out your sled. Order something new off the menu. Take a different road. Find the *woohoo;* then carry it with you into your ordinary world and let it lighten your spirit.

Woohoos are the moments we'll remember all our lives.

God, help me lighten my spirit by putting a little woohoo *into my daily life.*

February 22   Stop throwing that blame around

"There are two kinds of people in the world," a friend explained to me one day. "There are the ones who blame other people for everything that happens. And there are the ones who blame themselves."

Have you ever watched a movie where one of the actors used a flamethrower? In a movie I watched one day, they called this instead a "blame thrower." It's a lit torch of fiery rage that we throw at either others or ourselves when situations don't work out the way we planned.

Blaming can be a healthy stage of grieving or letting go. But staying too long in this stage can be unproductive. It can keep us from taking constructive action. Blaming ourselves too long can turn into self-contempt; blaming others can keep us heavy and dark with resentments, and fuel the victim within.

If you're going through a loss, or if life has twisted on you, pick up your blame thrower—in the privacy of your own journal. Give yourself ten or twenty minutes to blame without censorship. Get it out. Write out everything you want to say, whether you're throwing blame at someone else or at yourself.

It may take longer if the loss is larger, but the point is to give yourself a limited amount of time for a blame-throwing session, then cease fire. Stop. Move on to the next stage in living, which is letting go, accepting, and taking responsibility for yourself.

God, help me search myself to see if I'm holding on to blame for myself or someone else. If I am, help me get it out in the open, then help me let it go.

February 23   Learn to fly

Take your life in your own hands and what happens? A terrible thing: no one to blame.

— Erica Jong

There is always someone else to take the fall if our plans don't work out: "I would have been more successful, but the economy was slow this year." "Well, that sounds nice, but my therapist says that I should avoid too much stress." "I wanted to do that, but my husband didn't like the idea."

What a frightening prospect it is to take your life into your own hands, to decide whether or not you will accept full responsibility for all of your actions and choices.

What an amazing—and sometimes terrifying—freedom

complete responsibility for your actions brings! Sometimes we make mistakes. Sometimes we stumble and fall. But oh, the feeling when you finally get it right, when you decide to take that step and it works! That's when you discover that those fragile butterfly wings on your back are not there just for ornamentation. You can fly!

Take charge of your life. Take responsibility for your actions. Ultimately no one chooses what you will do but you, anyway. Enjoy the freedom. You've had it all along.

God, help me take complete responsibility for my own actions. Give me the guidance, and power, to steer my own course according to the dictates of my heart and my conscience.

February 24   Seek the adventure in your life

. . . adventure is not made up of distant lands and mountaintops, rather it lies in one's readiness to exchange the domestic hearth for an uncertain resting place.
> — *Reinhold Messner,* Free Spirit

It isn't necessary for us to travel the world in search of the next high mountain or wild, desolate place to find an adventure. Adventure lies in our perspective and in our attitude. It is our approach to life, rather than the actual circumstances of it, that determines how much adventure we have. Adventure for one person may mean seeking out a dream that has been long neglected. Perhaps adventure for another means losing weight, changing an outgrown image, getting sober, learning to be in a love relationship, or simply experiencing joy.

It's good to make ourselves comfortable, but don't get so comfortable in front of that hearth that you never want to grow or change. Water that never moves become stagnant and poisoned; so it is with the human spirit. We are given life to live.

Look at your life and see if there is some area where you, too, can seek out an uncertain resting place. Maybe work, love, or an area of spiritual growth? Some new or long-forgotten lesson is waiting to be discovered or rediscovered by you.

Say *woohoo*. Be uncomfortable for a while. It's never too late to learn and experience something new.

God, instill in me a spirit of adventure as I pursue my life.

February 25   Let God and your intuition lead the way

I define synchronicity as an external event which triggers an internal knowing. It has to do with events that are significant coincidences, such as when you are trying to solve a problem and someone "just happens" to call. During the conversation the caller "just happens" to give a clue or answer to the difficulty.

— *Nancy Rosanoff,* Intuition Workout

I was talking to my friend Kyle one day. I was in the final stages of writing *Playing It by Heart*, but I didn't know what the ending was. The book was an in-depth life review. I was astounded by the number of experiences I've had.

"I've been a pauper, a drug addict, a codependent, a midwestern housewife, a married woman, a single parent on welfare, a secretary, a journalist, a chemical dependency counselor, a book author, a bereaved parent, and a Californian. I've traveled to the Middle East, across the United States, ran a bookstore, and now, although I've taken the long hard road to get there, I live at the beach," I said. "There's nothing left for me to do."

"I know one thing you want to do that you haven't done yet," Kyle said.

"What?" I asked. There was a long silence. I thought maybe he hung up.

"Just a minute," he said. "I'm thinking."

"I know," he said. "You've never jumped out of a plane."

I forgot about the conversation. Within a few days, the phone rang. A man who had worked on my house about nine months before was on the line. He reintroduced himself. Then he explained why he called. He said he was a sky diver, and he asked if I'd like to go to the drop zone with him sometime, and maybe make a tandem jump.

A few months later, I went with him to Skydive Elsinore. I learned that day that jumping out of airplanes was something I very much wanted to do. And the skydiving experience was exactly the ending I needed for my book.

Trust your inner guidance. Our Higher Power works in mysterious ways. Listen to people, and watch for signs that trigger your inner knowing.

God, help me be open to all the ways you speak to me to help guide me along my path.

February 26   Open the door to fun experiences

You will do foolish things, but do them with enthusiasm!
— *Colette*

It was nighttime. A light breeze ruffled through my hair as I sat on the bench looking out over the lights of Las Vegas. *How did I get here again?* I thought. Then I remembered. It had been another one of Chip's wrong turns that had led us from southern California into the unknown.

The man wrapped a thick cloth around my ankles and then attached the cord to it. Another backup cord ran to the harness around my waist.

I was on a tower 150 feet above the ground getting ready to bungee jump. By my feet. At night. In Vegas. Again.

Sometimes the first step is the hardest. Sometimes it's the second step that gets you. The thing about a new experience is that you have no expectations; there is no frame of reference. But the second time. . . . I remembered the feeling of looking down off the platform to the ground below, the unnatural, terrifying step into nothingness, then my stomach jumping up into my chest, the long second when time seemed to freeze, the plunge toward the ground, and the tug of the cord slowing me. I remembered the rebound, the hanging there, waiting to be pulled back up. I remembered it all, and it grew in my mind. And besides, this time it was night, and I was going to be hanging by my feet.

I walked to the edge of the platform. I wasn't holding on. But I was shaking.

"5-4-3-2-1-go!" came the count. I closed my eyes and let myself fall.

And I laughed and I screamed, and I laughed at myself for screaming. It was fun.

Later, as we headed farther down the road, farther away from home on another intuitive road trip, I was still smiling.

Growth is self-perpetuating. Each new experience opens the door for further experiences. Today, remember something that you may have done only once, something you liked; then do it again. Allow your mind to fill you with uncertainty as you remember all of the experiences of the first time. It doesn't have to be work-related. Maybe you went to a play instead of watching TV. Camped in the woods. Or wrote a poem. Find something that was fun, and do it again. Then, bring that feeling back to your ordinary world. Bring the *woohoo* of the second time into the third, forth, and fifth times that you do a thing.

Keep the life in your life.

God, please remind me of some fun, interesting things that I like to do. Then help me get out of my chair and do them.

February 27   Live your life

A painting of a rice cake does not satisfy hunger.
                                                    — *Ancient saying*

An old man was telling his grandson about how poor he was when he was younger. "Why when I was a kid, we couldn't even afford cheese for the mousetraps," he said. "We had to cut out pictures of cheese and use that."

"Wow, did you catch anything gramps?"

"Yes. We caught pictures of mice."

I have a picture in my house of a Buddhist ceremony in Tibet. The picture was taken by a photographer who lives close to the Blue Sky Lodge. She told me all about the picture when I bought it from her—told me about the smells in the air, the temperature, the crush of the people around her, the tastes, smells, and sights of that place. When I close my eyes and remember her words, I can almost go there. Almost, but not quite. I hope to travel there sometime, to see those things and to feel my soul filled with the spirituality of a monastery high on a hill. The picture is like a menu. It sits on the counter, tempting me with all that is offered in it. But it doesn't satisfy my hunger.

We can share our experience, strength, and hope with each other. But I can't learn your lessons and you can't learn mine.

I'm planning my trip to Tibet, as I write this book. Will it all work out like the trip in the picture? I don't know. I do know that I won't get the experience—the sights, sounds, tastes, smells, and the impact on my soul—from looking at the picture on my wall.

Have you been trying to gain sustenance from looking at a picture of an experience—reading books, taking classes, going to seminars, listening to mentors—instead of going out and living life for yourself? Take another look at your menu, the list you wrote at the beginning of the year. Order something from it.

Stop looking at the picture and go live for yourself.

God, help me start living my life.

February 28   Experience life for yourself

We learn to do something by doing it. There is no other way.
— John Holt

"I'm an armchair adventurer," I've heard more than one person say. This means that they never actually go out and do anything. They let others take all the risk. Through books, they've climbed Mount Everest, sailed around the world, hiked the Pacific Crest Trail, and snowshoed to the South Pole. *They* were even able to tell me all about how to fly a plane before my first lesson.

It's one thing to spend our time reading books or listening to lectures about how to do this or that—how to have a successful relationship, how to build a business, how to live life more fully, whatever comes after *how to*. The trick is to finally put the books down, walk away from the lecture, and do it. Getting information, support, and encouragement is helpful. Necessary, too. But life was meant to be lived, not studied. The only way that you'll have a successful career, relationship, or hobby is to go out and get one for yourself.

God, help me take the risk of actually doing something I want to learn to do.

February 29   Let go of timidity

Live big!

— *Brady Michaels*

Sometimes, that's the best advice we can hear. Win or lose, succeed or fail, go for it, and go all the way. As my flight instructor told me on the first day of flying lessons, "Keep one hand on the throttle and one hand on the yoke." "Aahhhhh!" I would say during my early lessons as the plane lifted into the air, but I kept the throttle pushed all the way in.

There are times when it's wise to be cautious. And there are times when the best thing we can do—the only thing we can do—is go for it by living big. Ask her out. Request the raise. Say no—and mean it. Learn to drive a race car or climb a tall hill. Learn to snorkel or surf. Dreams remain dreams until you act upon them. Then they become real life.

Will you throw a few coins into the beggar's cup, or will you bring him a hamburger and fries from the local fast-food place? Will you do an average job at work, or will you look for ways to go big—really give it your best—in the everyday areas of your job? Will you put your all—your heart and emotions—into the relationship with the people you love? Will you wait for another, more convenient time to pray, or will you start genuinely trusting God?

You don't have to get a life. You've already got one. Live it, and live big.

God, help me let go of my fear and timidity, and learn to live big.

March

Learn to Say Whatever

"Do you have issues with drama addiction?" I asked my daughter one day, in a serious, interviewer kind of voice.

"Of course I do," she said. "I'm the original drama queen."

"Can I interview you about it?" I asked.

There was a long pause on the phone. "I've got a better suggestion," she said. "Why don't you interview yourself?"

I've been addicted to many things this lifetime—alcohol, heroin, morphine, Dilaudid, cocaine, barbiturates, Valium, and any other substance that physically or psychologically promised to change the way I feel. I've been addicted to caffeine, tobacco and nicotine—cigarettes and Cuban cigars—and opium and hashish, too. I've been caught up in other people's addictions to these substances as well. Some people might say I have an addictive personality. I don't know if I agree with the concept that we can become addicted to people, but if the folks that say you can are right, I've probably been addicted to certain of those, too.

But of all the addictions possible on this planet, I've found my addiction to drama absolutely the hardest to recognize, accept, deal with, and overcome. The rush of emotional energy I feel from drama at the theater, on television (small or big screen), in a book, and most preferably acted out in real life (mine) is the last legal, legitimate jones that society allows.

It's not politically correct to smoke, act out sexually, be a nonrecovering alcoholic, or shoot drugs. But despite all the evolution in consciousness that's unfolded and gotten us to this point, drama addiction is more than politically correct.

Drama addiction is in. Right now, for many people, it's one of the only things giving meaning to life.

Potential guests line up, volunteering to have their relationship and court battles—things which once were guarded secrets—broadcast on international cable and satellite TV. Our society can't wait to peek and snoop into their lives. Broadcasting real-life soap operas guarantees the ratings will soar.

In 1999, I wrote the above words in a chapter on drama addiction in my book called *Playing It by Heart*. But the concept of drama addiction, and transcending it, has been around for a long, long time.

In 1937, author Emmet Fox wrote an essay in *Find and Use Your Inner Power*. The essay's title was "Don't Be a Tragedy Queen."

"Self pity, by making us feel sorry for ourselves, seems to provide an escape from responsibility, but it is a fatal drug nevertheless," he wrote. "It confuses the feelings, blinds the reason, and puts us at the mercy of outer conditions. . . . Don't be a tragedy queen—whether you are a man or a woman, for it is not a question of gender but of mental outlook. Absolutely repudiate a crown of martyrdom. If you cannot laugh at yourself (which is the best medicine of all), at least try to handle the difficulty in an objective way, as though it concerned somebody else."

Maybe the antithesis to being a drama king or queen has been around even longer than that.

Three tiny Buddha statues sit before me on my writing desk. One is Serene. One is Smiling. One is Sorrowful, doubled over in compassion for the world. All you can see is the top of his head.

"The Kingdom of Heaven is within you," Jesus said.

"Nirvana is a state of consciousness," wrote Anne Bancroft, in an introduction to the Dhammapada, a book containing the teachings of Buddha.

Enlightenment and paradise aren't places we visit. They're within our hearts and heads.

Say, "It's a nightmare," if you must. Even say, "Oh my God, I can't believe this is happening, much less happening to me." But whether you say the words with calmness and serenity, bursting with laughter or a mere giggle, or doubled over with compassion for the pain of the world, learning to speak the language of letting go in the days, months, and years of the millennium ahead means learning to say *whatever*, too.

God, help me let go of my need to create drama to have a life.

March 2   Don't stir the emotional pot

"My bill collector called today," a friend said to me one day. "I love it when she calls. Every time she does, we have a good fight. She tells me that I owe her company money. Then I say I know. She tells me that my balance is due. I tell her I know that, too. Then she asks why I haven't sent a payment. I tell her that the reason I didn't send a payment is because I told her last month I could send only twenty dollars a month and she said not to send it, because that wasn't enough. That's when the screaming starts. Then she yells at me to get a job. I scream back that I'm trying and she ought to get a better job herself. Then we both slam down the phone and don't talk to each other until she calls again next month."

Some of us intentionally stir up drama to release emotions, get the pot brewing, and add a little energy to our lives. Sometimes we can cause trouble in areas where we'd be better off without it. Turning our home into a battleground doesn't leave us a good place to live.

Sometimes when we're stressed, we just like to get those emotions out. And what better way to get them out than by engaging in a good, old-fashioned fight. Just make sure you're not making an enemy out of someone whom you'd rather have as a friend. And check to see that you're not taking your stress out on an innocent bystander, a lover, family member, or friend.

God, help me let go of my need for dysfunctional drama in my life. Help me make sure I'm not taking my stress out on the people I love. If I am, show me another way to release my emotions.

March 3   Don't take storms personally

Somewhere out in the Pacific, a storm brewed and swirled and thrashed and died without ever touching the land. Three days later, under a clear blue sky, the storm surge reached the California coast near Los Angeles. The sea threw rocks at my house, and the waves stacked up and crashed down against the pilings of the foundation. Farther up the street, the ocean ate the back porch of two houses. All night the shoreline trembled and shook from the power of the sea.

The next morning the tide pulled back, the swells calmed, and the sky stayed blue. I walked down the beach, impressed at the way the ocean had littered it with huge chunks of driftwood and rocks. Then I walked back upstairs and drank my morning coffee.

Sometimes, storms aren't about us.

Sometimes, friends or loved ones will attack us for no apparent reason. They'll fuss, fume, and snap at us. When we ask them why, they'll say, "Oh, I'm sorry. I had a bad day at work."

But we still feel hurt and upset.

Hold people accountable for their behavior. Don't let people treat you badly. But don't take the storms in their lives personally. These storms may have nothing to do with you.

Seek shelter if necessary. Get away from curt friends until they have time to calm down; then approach when it's safe. If the storm isn't about you, there's nothing you need to do. Would you try to stop the ocean waves by standing in the surf with your arms outstretched?

Say *whatever.* Let the storms blow through.

God, help me not to take the storms in the lives of my friends and loved ones too personally.

March 4   Allow for differences

He's rational. He wants examples of the problem and wants to focus on and find a solution.

She wants to talk about how she feels.

He wants to sit in front of the television and click the remote control.

She wants to cuddle on the couch and look into his eyes.

He deals with his stress by playing basketball with his friends, tinkering with the car, or going for a hike.

She wants to go to a movie, preferably one that makes her cry.

I spent much of my life thinking that men and women—and generally all people—should just be the same. It took me a long time to realize that while we have much in common with other people, we're each unique.

It took me even longer to realize that the practical application of this meant I had to learn to allow for differences between the people I loved and myself.

Just because we have something in common with someone, and might even think we're in love, doesn't mean that each person is going to respond and be the same.

So often in our relationships, we try to get the other person to behave the way we want. This forcing of our will on them will ultimately become a great strain. It can also block love. When we're trying to change someone else, we overlook his or her gifts. We don't value the parts of the person that are different from us, because we're too busy trying to change the person into someone else.

Allow for differences, but don't just allow. Appreciate the differences. Value what each person has to offer and the gifts each person can bring.

Learn to say *whatever*, with a spark of amusement and curiosity, when someone isn't the same as you. Try getting a kick out of the unique way each person approaches life.

God, help me understand the rich gifts that letting go of control will bring to my life.

Activity: This activity is designed to help you allow for and appreciate the differences between you and someone important in your life. That important someone might be a child, a spouse, a best friend, a colleague, or a parent. The purpose of this activity is to promote awareness. Make a list in your journal. Put your name on top of it. Next to your name, put the other person's name. Now, list what's different and what's the same about you and the other person. Maybe some of the things that are different are attributes you'd like to attain for yourself. Maybe not—maybe the differences are simply that—different ways of coping with and responding to life. Maybe your ideals and behaviors are truly incompatible and being around this person just isn't acceptable for you. At the least, this list should give you some ideas for areas where you could practice letting go.

Cheryl's husband was a tyrant. His anger controlled most of her moves. He didn't get angry often, but when he did, he exploded in a rage. He broke things; he carried on. His rage terrified her.

"I've never done well with anger," Cheryl said, "either my own, or someone else's. I spent my childhood walking on eggshells, trying not to annoy my dad. Then I married a man whom I allowed to completely control me by the mere threat of his rage."

Whether we call them rageaholics, tyrants, or bullies, a lot of people in our world get their way by being mean. We may find ourselves instinctively walking on eggshells around these people, praying to God we don't set them off.

Anger is a powerful emotion. But we don't have to let anybody else's rage take control of our lives. If somebody you know or love is a bully or a tyrant, don't take it on yourself. Stop walking on eggshells and letting their rage control your every step. Instead of taking on their problem, try something different. Give their problem with being a bully back to them.

How do you deal with anger? Does somebody in your life use anger as a way of controlling you? It may be time to let go of your fear of setting off people.

If you are in a dangerous situation, then by all means, get out. If you are just allowing yourself to be controlled by the fear of an emotional outburst, then learn to say *whatever* when someone spouts off.

God, please don't let anyone's anger, including my own, be the master of my life.

Unless you want a fight or an argument, don't give people anything to push against.

Here is a key to harmonizing with people who are upset or have a point of view different from your own. Stay so relaxed when you talk to them that you allow yourself to empathize with how they think and feel. That doesn't mean that you give in to people's every whim. It means, instead, that you are so clear and focused that you can genuinely let other people be who they are, too.

It's both naïve and egotistical to think that everyone thinks and feels the same as us. It's ridiculous to believe that everyone will agree with our point of view. One of the true signs of a person who is growing in consciousness is that he or she recognizes that each person has individual motives, desires, and feelings.

"Instead of meeting a verbal attack with a verbal counterattack you respond first by coming around to your attacker's point of view, seeing the situation from his or her viewpoint," wrote George Leonard in the *Way of Aikido*.

He was talking about using a concept called "blending" to deal with verbal confrontations in our daily lives. "The response, whether physical or verbal, is quite disarming, leaving the attacker with no target to focus on. It's a means by which you can multiply your options in responding to any kind of attack."

If the person espousing his or her point of view is just trying to get us to react or has no desire for reconciliation, we can still neutralize the conflict by staying relaxed, letting the other person be, and responding by saying, "hmmmm." It's a polite way of saying *whatever*, when expressing your disagreement would only lead to a senseless fight. At the least, you'll become a great conversationalist, a respectable art to be acquired. At best, you'll bring about world peace, at least in your corner of the world.

God, help me be so clear on who I am that I can generously afford to let other people be who they are, too. Help me to set aside my defensive behavior, and teach me to blend with other people and see their point of view while not relinquishing my own.

March 7   **Recognize manipulations**

Herein lies an irony: the person who is trying to manipulate you views you as having greater strength or power than he or she does.

— George H. Green and Carolyn Cotter,
Stop Being Manipulated

George Green and Carolyn Cotter describe manipulation as an encounter in which someone else attempts to control how you feel, behave, or think—without your permission—and it causes you discomfort as a result.

Most of us use manipulation, from time to time, to get what we want. Sometimes our manipulations are harmless, even cute. Both people know a low-grade manipulation is at hand. Both people basically want what the manipulator is working so hard to get—dinner out, a movie, a walk through the park. It's not a big deal.

Other times, the stakes are higher and the people involved don't agree. That's when manipulations can be harmful. When we don't know what we want, when we're not clear with others and ourselves about how we feel, a manipulation is in the air.

Sometimes manipulations are conscious and deliberate.

Other times, they're unconscious, foggy attempts to get what we want.

"Let's simplify our definition of manipulation," suggest Green and Cotter. "If an encounter leaves you feeling crummy, it probably involves manipulation of some sort."

Isn't it ironic that sometimes the very feeling we're trying to deny is exactly what we need to be feeling to take care of ourselves?

Next time you're faced with a situation that leaves you feeling crummy, take a moment to see if a manipulation was involved. Remember that whenever others try to manipulate you, they perceive you as having something they want and as being more powerful than they are. If you're powerful enough to be a target for a manipulation, you're powerful enough to take care of yourself.

God, help me let go of my belief that I need to manipulate other people to get what I want. Help me stop letting others manipulate me.

March 8   Learn to deal with manipulations

Even if you understand and follow all of the rules for more effectively engaging manipulators, life with them is not likely to be easy.

— *George K. Simon Jr.*

Sometimes they want something. Sometimes they want someone. Sometimes they want someone to give them something or to feel a particular way. They want power, in some way, shape, or form. Manipulators prey on our weak spots.

Obsession and guilt are weapons.

Manipulators get us to use these weapons on ourselves.

Sometimes we can disengage from manipulators—walk

away, set a clear limit, be done with them. Other times, it's not that easy. We may be at least temporarily stuck with a boss or authority figure who indulges in heavy manipulation. One of our children may be going through a relentlessly manipulative period. We may have a parent whom we care about deeply who has adapted manipulation as a way of life.

Learn how to effectively deal with manipulators. Not everyone means what they say. People fling words about to hit our guilty, vain, or frightened spots. Recognize that tinge of guilt or coercion you feel when other people are trying to force you to do it their way. Learn to recognize when others are telling you what they believe you want to hear. Learn to not react, stay clear, practice nonresistance, and stay true to yourself.

Be gentle with yourself, if you have a manipulator in your life. You're not responsible for the other person's attempts at manipulation. You're responsible for staying clear.

God, help me let go of the weak spots in myself that allow me to fall prey to manipulations. Help me stay clear of guilt and obsession so I can decide what's best for me.

March 9   Know your limits

While it's good to be compassionate, we can become overly compassionate, too. Don't work so hard at not judging other people that you forget to pay attention to what you don't like.

"I know what it feels like to be abandoned and left. I don't like the feeling, so I'm not going to leave my boyfriend," Clara says. She's living with a man who abuses her, emotionally and physically.

"I'm not going to judge her," Ralph says about his new

wife. She's using cocaine and stealing money from him to get high. "She's had a hard life, and I haven't walked in her shoes."

"I need to be compassionate and nonjudgmental with my son," Robert says about a child who's driving him to distraction with his manipulations and lies. "He's had a hard life. His mother died when he was three. And I'm the only person he's got left."

You can set boundaries with someone, without judging that person. You can decide that behaviors are inappropriate and hurt you, without condemning that person.

Don't forget, you have a right to say "ouch."

We can say *whatever* with compassion and still take care of ourselves.

God, help me set appropriate limits with the people in my life.

March 10   Let it be

Life is a series of letting go's—an "infinite" series of letting go's. All things in life are given us on loan. Stand face-to-face with life, learn to let go, and whatever comes our way—success or failure, joy or sorrow, support or betrayal, light or darkness—it all blesses us. Once we have learned to let go, we are prepared for whatever life gives us. And death itself is nothing to be feared.

— *Matthew Fox*

For many years, I resisted the concept of letting go. I resisted mostly because I didn't understand what people were talking about. I'd be loudly obsessing about something. "Just let go," they'd say. "Okay," I'd say. Then I'd walk away and wonder what they meant, and mostly how to do it. Soon, I caught on.

If I didn't want people harping at me about letting go, I needed to obsess silently. Privately. Or at least in the presence of someone who wouldn't lecture me about letting go.

As the years wore on, I was forced into letting go. Eventually I even wrote a book called *The Language of Letting Go*. I thought it was the end of my need to practice letting go.

When my son died, I learned that writing the book was only a prelude, an introductory course, in letting go. Over the years that followed, I gradually began to learn a new respect for this behavior called *letting go*.

Letting go is a behavior we can practice each day, whatever the circumstances in our lives. It's a behavior that benefits relationships we want to work. It's a helpful behavior in insane relationships, too. It's a useful tool to use when we really want to bring something or someone into our lives, and in accomplishing our goals. It's a helpful tool to use on outdated behaviors such as low self-esteem and manipulation.

Letting go takes the emotional charge, the drama, out of things and restores us to a sense of balance, peace, and spiritual power.

Letting go works well on the past and the future. It brings us into today.

Paraphrasing the mystic writer Matthew Fox, everything that comes, comes to pass. Demystify letting go. It's not as complicated as it sounds. Learning the art of letting go really means learning to calmly let things be.

God, help me learn to let go.

A healthy friend dies participating in a sport she loves. A husband works hard on his marriage only to come home one day and find his wife in bed with another man.

A knock at the door, and a starving family opens it to find bags of groceries piled anonymously on the porch. A large order comes in just as a company is getting ready to close its doors, and the owner's dream is given new life.

Sometimes life twists. Sometimes it goes the other way, too. Things happen. Sometimes we label these events *good*, sometimes *bad*. We cannot always see the reason or purpose in them, but most of us choose to believe there's a Divine plan.

I don't know *why* I've received some of the blessings I've been given; I don't know *why* some of the sorrow has come my way. All I can do is trust that whatever comes my way, there's a lesson at hand.

Are you focusing on the circumstances of your life instead of the lessons? The circumstances are the tools. Be involved in them. Feel the pain of loss and the elation of victory. Let compassion works its way into your soul. Learn caring and kindness for others and yourself, too.

Instead of asking *why*, learn to ask *what* the lesson is. The moment you become ready to accept it, the lesson will become clear.

God, help me accept all the twists and turns along my path. Help me learn to say whatever to the good and the unfortunate incidents that come my way.

March 12   Don't cut yourself on your gifts

Mishaps are like knives, that either serve us or cut us, as we grasp them by the blade or by the handle.

— *James Russell Lowell*

Success rains down for no apparent reason. Tragedy strikes like a freight train. We're left to deal with the results. We can allow our egos to swell over our sudden good fortune, or we can humbly accept the fruit of our labor and continue to better ourselves. We can lie down and give up after a tragedy, or we can grieve, get up, and begin taking steps to move on with our lives.

Look at the situations in your life. Have you been given success? Are you learning the lessons of loss? Perhaps yours is the gift of the ordinary. Don't walk too boastfully through your successes, nor remain too long in your grief. And don't sleep through an ordinary life. You'll lose your sense of wonder and awe, and when it ends, you won't know where you've been.

We cannot always control what will happen to us. We need to let go of any false thoughts that we can. We can choose how we'll handle the situation just like we choose how we'll pick up a knife—by grabbing the handle or the blade.

Watch out for the cutting edge.

What you do with what you have been given is important.

God, thank you for what I've been given.

March 13   Say *whatever* when it's out of your hands

We cannot control everything that happens to us. But we can control our response to those things. We cannot control the feelings of others—their fear, their power trips, their issues. All that we can choose is how we want to respond.

Maybe you have been wronged. Maybe you have had a dream taken from you due to the actions of another. What are you going to do about it? You can give up and give in, or you can make the best of the situation, move on if you can, or make a life where you are.

Say *whatever.*

Learn to live and let live.

You can start over, again and again, if necessary.

God, give me strength to stand up when the actions or thoughts of others drag me down. Help me practice right thought and right action. Help me walk the path that is set before me, no matter what it may bring.

March 14 **Learn something new about yourself**

Wildfires scorch large chunks of the western United States every summer. It's part of the natural cycle of things. After a while, nature decides that it's time to start over and a patch of the woods goes up in smoke.

This year, one fire burned near Mesa Verde National Park in southwestern Colorado. I read the news wires with interest, hoping that the archeological sites there wouldn't be destroyed. The crews worked on the fires, and though there was damage in the area, the main ruins were left unharmed. While the fires had burned thousands of acres around the park, they had also done something else—they had burned away the undergrowth that had sprung up around twelve previously undiscovered sites.

Sometimes life sends fires raging through our lives, too. Those fires are also part of the natural cycle of things. Life, nature, or our Higher Power says it's time to start over, again.

Use misfortune as an opportunity. Who knows? That fire rampaging through your life just might clear away the brush of the past. Keep your heart open and stay aware. You might learn something new and previously undiscovered about yourself.

God, help me stay alert to the lessons of today.

March 15   Let go of the controls

"You have the controls," my flight instructor says. "No, you have the controls," I say back. "No I don't," he says. "You do."

My banter with my flight instructor can be amusing at times. It's not so funny when we fight about issues of power and control in our lives. And usually it goes the other way. We don't want to give the controls to someone else; we want those reins ourselves.

We want to get our way. And we get upset when things don't work out. Sometimes, after we've been working on ourselves and our control issues for a while, we begin to get complacent. Because we've been so effectively using and directing our power, we rarely get in battles we can't win. Things work out smoothly. We mostly get our way, because we're not trying to control what we can't. That's when it's easy to think we're more powerful than we are.

Are you engaged in a power struggle with someone or something you can't change? Spend a moment thinking about it. Is that really the way you want to use your energy and power, trying to do the impossible, creating rifts, and fighting battles you can't win? When we try to control someone else or events beyond the scope of our power, we lose.

When we learn to discern the difference between what we can change and what we can't, we usually have an easier time expressing our power in our lives. Because we're not wasting all our energy using our power to change things we can't, we have a lot of energy left over to live our lives.

Learn to say *whatever* when you don't get what you want. Learn to let things be the way they are.

God, help me to let go of my need to control and to be open to the flow of the universe.

March 16   Don't be a backseat driver

I was walking through a toy store one day when I saw a little toy steering wheel attached to the tray of a stroller. The child could play with the wheel and pretend that he or she was controlling the direction of the cart. The steering wheel wasn't attached to anything; someone else was behind the stroller, pushing it here or there. The child could steer all he or she wanted to, but if Mom was going to the hardware department, then the child was going there, too.

What a good lesson to teach children at such an early age: no matter where you steer, something bigger than you is going to push you wherever it wants.

We soon outgrow the stroller and then burst into adulthood. First we learn to drive—finally a wheel that does something! Now we've got real freedom! But the car needs gas, we have a curfew, and there are speed limits and driving laws. Or we graduate from school and move into the real world. Finally no more parents controlling our every move. But then there is rent, and the boss, and the roommates, or a spouse and children to consider.

No matter how much we grow, where we go, or how old

we get, there is someone else above, someone bigger, pushing us in this direction or that. Sorry, no new car this year; you've got a different lesson to learn.

We can want things, pray for things, and hope that things will come to pass. But ultimately, we're not in control. Instead of spending our time and energy trying to get someplace else, we can learn the lesson and enjoy the beauty of the life we've been given.

God, help me realize that while I am not in control of everything that happens in my life, I can choose how I'll respond.

March 17   Don't avoid the void

I was sitting at dinner with a group of friends in a restaurant one evening. Everyone but one person was done eating. Feet were shuffling under the table. We were ready to go. One member of the group, an older woman, was picking at her meal. She had ordered dessert, but hadn't eaten it yet. Instead, she slowly sipped her coffee.

"I don't eat my dessert until I've finished coffee," she said, when the waiter asked if he could take her plate.

All eyes at the table watched as she took a tiny sip, placed the cup down, and chattered, telling stories and jokes, making meaningless conversation. We watched eagerly as she started to pick her fork up to take a bite of dessert, then sighed quietly as she changed her mind, set the fork down, and began to tell another story.

She was alone, widowed, and her children lived in another state. It was obvious that she was trying to stretch dinner out with her friends as long as she could. She was trying to fill up that empty, silent place we call the void.

There's a lot of talk in life and in this book about doing,

achieving, and going for what we want. There's much spurring on to activity that shouts, "Yes, I'm alive. And I'm fully and richly living my life the best I can."

In all this busyness and living, there needs to be mindfulness and careful attention paid to another part of life, too. That part is the repetitive and natural cycle that some people call "the void."

It's an empty space in our lives.

The void can be a small space in our lives—lasting a few days or weeks. Or it can go on longer. That relationship has ended. We're alone. We don't know what to do next. Or that cycle in our lives has ended—maybe we've graduated from school or college, and we don't know where to go next. Maybe our time as a parent has ended. Maybe someone we loved, a roommate or best friend, who was an important part of our lives has moved away.

Don't be afraid of the void. Postpone it for a while, if you must. Linger at dinner with friends, refusing to finish your dessert. As dark, cold, and empty as it feels, the void is a friendly place. Its rhythms are slower and often more confusing than other cycles in our lives, but the rhythms of this cycle are still there.

Remember those quiet times in your life, the ones you've gone through before, when one cycle has ended and another has not yet begun. Remind yourself when that void comes along that you don't have to be frightened of it. It's not the end. It's only a creative and necessary pause, a cycle of its own, in the cycles and rhythms of life.

God, give me the courage to step into the void in my life with dignity, faith, and a sense of humor. Help me cherish the unknown as much as I enjoy activity and clarity.

"Sometimes I talk myself out of praying," Sheila said. "I convince myself that it's just more work, because even if I pray about something, I have to do all the work, too."

I sit down to write. The energy's not there, but the deadline is. *God, please help.* I remember a joke I heard from someone, somewhere: "I love deadlines. Especially the whooshing sound they make as they go flying by." I write anyway, putting one word in front of another. Then, from out of nowhere, comes a string of words I didn't plan on, a new idea, a fresh perspective, a story, complete with ending. *Wow! Where'd that come from?*

An issue comes up in a relationship with a friend. He's hurt and angry. His hurt and anger evoke more hurt and anger in me. I try to reason things out, listen to him, get him to see things my way. He feels justified. So do I. Day after day, we work on the relationship. The strain continues. I don't know what to do next. "God, please help me with this situation. Show me what to do next." I keep talking to my friend. He keeps talking to me. Then one day, I feel less defensive and guilty. A new feeling surrounds the relationship. "I'm sorry," I say one day. "So am I," he says, too. *Wow,* I think. *Where did that come from?*

I stand on the scale, glaring at the numbers. I want to lose ten pounds. I start eating less, exercising more. A few days later, I get on the scale again. *Dang. Gained a pound.* I continue to eat less; the numbers don't move. *God, please help me drop this weight. Why am I holding on to it?* I continue to watch my caloric intake and pay attention to exercise. One morning, I get on the scale. *Wow! I've lost five pounds. How did that happen?*

Pray. Let go. Then act as if you need to do all the work.

Don't plan on magic and miracles. But leave room for them, too.

God, help me remember that when I run out of myself, I run right into you.

March 19   Lighten up

The matter at hand is serious. It's grave. We need to get serious about the relationship. We need to get serious about the task.

Maybe what we really need to do is learn to lighten up.

Nations rise and fall, heroes are born and die, the sun rises and sets, and you want me to take seriously the notion that arriving to church wearing the right clothes is going to make any difference at all?

What matters is what's in our hearts.

"The reason angels can fly is that they take themselves so lightly," G. K. Chesterton once wrote. Once you stop taking yourself so seriously and let go of the gravity of all that you do, you can learn to fly, too.

God, help me lighten up.

March 20   Let go of what others think

We had gone for a walk in the snow down into the bowl of Bryce Canyon in Utah earlier that day. After a quick shower in the hotel room, we headed down to the restaurant for dinner. Our boots were soaked from the snow, so we wore our flip-flops to the restaurant.

The hostess was the first to notice. "Hey, you've got the wrong shoes on!" she admonished. "There's snow outside!"

"Yeah, I know. We're from California," Chip replied.

"Humph," the hostess sniffed, as she showed us our table.

When our server approached our table, the hostess was right there again, quick to point out our inappropriate footwear to him. We tried to explain that we had been hiking and our boots were wet, but it only set her off more.

"I certainly hope you didn't wear those," she said. "There's snow on the trails." Then she trotted back to her station.

Our server didn't care. He listened to the story about our hike, told us one of his own, and kept our glasses full.

Later during the meal, the hostess guided another couple past our table and pointed at our feet. "Look at these people," she said. "They're from California and they're wearing the wrong shoes!"

We giggled all through dinner that night, all because our hiking boots got soaked.

Sometimes what's appropriate for a situation just doesn't work for you and you're forced to improvise. Wear the wrong shoes if you must, but don't miss the party because of what someone else might think.

God, help me remember that the important thing is how I live, not how I look.

March 21   Letting go of finances

Letting go doesn't mean we don't care. It's about having faith that things will work out. Let's take a look at how letting go applies to the issue of money.

John had been an alcoholic for years. Over time, the disease destroyed his life, including his financial health. He hit bottom and finally began recovery. After a while, he was able to start making progress in life. But his finances were in terrible shape. For a while, he hid all the bills in a drawer. Then one day, he took out the bills and started to make a plan. Instead of feeling hopeless and overwhelmed, he applied the Twelve Steps to this area of his life. He called his creditors. He gave himself a budget. He did the best that he could and he let go of the rest.

Slowly, over the years, he began to rebuild his credit. He paid off his debts, a little at a time. He applied for a credit card, the kind you have to pay in advance. Then after a year, his limit was raised. He doesn't use the card for credit; he uses it for a credit rating. He's now got a checking and a savings account. He pays his taxes and manages to save a little every week.

Sometimes things happen. Cars break down. People get sick. The rent gets raised. That unexpected expense comes up, out of the blue, just when you thought you were ahead.

There were many years I couldn't do my budget on paper. No matter how I arranged it, more had to go out than I could see coming in. I did my best, took responsibility for myself, then let go.

Worry never helped.

An attitude of taking responsibility for myself did.

What we cannot do for ourselves, God will do for us. And God knows we need money to live here on earth. What was that the Bible said? Seek money first, and then you'll have peace? Nope, I got that backwards. "Seek ye first the Kingdom of God and all else shall be added unto you."

Manifest what you need from a place of responsibility, trust, and peace.

God, teach me to let go of worrying about money.

Many years ago, in ancient times, Moses led a group of slaves out of Egypt and back to their homeland. Along the way, they had to wander for many years through the Sinai Peninsula, a barren, rocky, lifeless stretch of land.

During their extended stay in the wilderness, God provided them with manna, a food that appeared out of nowhere and sustained the people with the nourishment they needed each day. The trick to this rhythm of trusting God, and receiving what they needed, was that any manna they received had to be used that day.

Manna couldn't be hoarded. It could not be stored or saved up for a rainy day. If the people hoarded their manna, it would spoil and rot away. Or it would mysteriously disappear as magically and certainly as it had appeared.

Most of us know what it means to receive our daily bread. It's the love, the guidance, the grace, and the material things we need each day on our journey.

Sometimes, we can sit down and anticipate the times to come. We can look at our money, our strength, our abilities, our stamina, and say wearily, "There just won't be enough." That's because we're looking too far ahead.

Look around at what you have available, this moment or this hour. Use the resources and gifts you've been given. Tomorrow's manna will come at its appointed hour.

God, help me enjoy the road to freedom, even when that journey takes me through the wilderness. Help me remember the rules about manna: living one day at a time.

We call it keeping up with the Joneses. They buy a boat and we buy a bigger one. They get a new TV and we get a big screen. They start a business and we start planning our articles of incorporation and the first stock release. And while we're so busy keeping up, we ignore our soul, the inner voice, that's telling us that it really wants to teach children to read.

While it helps to identify with each other, we're not the same. So why compare ourselves on the basis of material things?

Follow your own talent and heart. It may be that you are a talented public speaker, able to sway hundreds of people with your words. Or maybe you have the talent of friendship, and you've been sent to quietly, one-on-one, help those close to you walk their own path.

If you must compare yourself to something, compare your daily life to your ideals and dreams. Do they match? If those ideals and dreams bring great material wealth, that's great. If they mean a life of quiet, anonymous service, that's great, too. Yes, material goods can be fun. But they can also be a trap.

Are you walking a path with heart in your own life, regardless of what others have?

God, help me let go of the trappings. Teach me to walk my own path.

March 24   **Cultivate inner peace**

According to my experience, the principal characteristic of genuine happiness is peace, inner peace.
                                        — *His Holiness the Dalai Lama*

Cultivate a sense of peace, an abiding inner peace that doesn't depend on outward circumstance.

So much chaos, so much drama, so many emotions surge through us. It is so easy, so tempting to believe that once we get through this circumstance, once we achieve this goal, once we solve this problem, then we will be peaceful.

That's an illusion.

"I'm happy when I get what I want," said Kent. "For a few minutes."

Getting what we want may cause us to feel happy for a moment, but it will bring a limited, transient happiness. The next problem or emotion will present itself. Or we will begin resenting that person or job, because he, she, or it did not bring the happiness we believed it would. Like a carrot on a stick, happiness will always be the next problem, acquisition, or emotion away.

Be peaceful now.

Be happy now.

Take the limits off your joy.

God, help me remember to be peaceful first, no matter what situation I face.

March 25   Let go of resentments

Resentments are sneaky, tricky little things. They can convince us they're justified. They can dry up our hearts. They can sabotage our happiness. They can sabotage love.

Most of us have been at the receiving end of an injustice at some time in our lives. Most of us know someone who's complained of an injustice we've done to him or her. Life can be a breeding ground for resentments, if we let it.

"Yes, but this time I really was wronged," we complain.

Maybe you were. But harboring a resentment isn't the solution. If it was, our resentment list would resemble the Los Angeles telephone directory. Deal with your feelings. Learn whatever lesson is at hand. Then let the feelings go.

Resentments are a coping behavior, a tool of someone settling for survival in life. They're a form of revenge. The problem is, no matter who we're resenting, the anger is ultimately directed against ourselves.

Take a moment. Search your heart. Have you tricked yourself into harboring a resentment? If you have, take another moment and let that resentment go.

God, grant me the serenity that acceptance brings.

March 26   Say *whatever* with as much love as you can

There's an old story about compassion, detachment, and Mohammed, the prophet of Islam.

Mohammed had a neighbor who had a garbage problem. This neighbor was a cranky old man who let his garbage pile up and spill out all around his yard. The mess was unsightly, but Mohammed practiced tolerance and compassion. He didn't say anything to the annoying neighbor, for years.

One day, the unsightly mess from the garbage disappeared.

Mohammed went over to his neighbor's house and knocked on the door. The neighbor answered the knock.

"I got worried when I didn't see your garbage," Mohammed said. "I was just checking to make sure you were all right."

We need to set boundaries, be clear, and stand up for ourselves. We need to check regularly to make sure we're taking care of ourselves. But once in a while, we also need to check to see if we're allowing ourselves to become irritated and upset by nonessentials and forgetting the essential of love.

Learn to say *whatever,* but learn to say it with as much compassion and love as you can.

God, help me learn to take care of myself and live with passion, compassion, and an open heart.

March 27   Set yourself free

I'll let go tomorrow; I'm having too much fun torturing myself today. No, that's not really it. I'll let go tomorrow; the things I'm holding on to need me to hold them today. Yes, that's closer to what it is. I'm not enjoying myself at all today, but I have to keep holding on to my desires, my guilt, my limitations, and my worries. I am defined by them. And you want me to let go of them today? Sorry, maybe tomorrow. And so we hold on. And the ulcer grows. And the pain in our hearts from unfulfilled expectations keeps gnawing away at us. What we're really putting off is the freedom we get from letting go.

Yes, I know that what you're holding on to is important. Everything that I have ever had to let go of was important to me, too. If it wasn't important, letting go wouldn't be a struggle. We'd just put it down and walk away.

You've been given today. Will you use it or will you miss out on today's wonder because you're too preoccupied with holding on to things that are beyond your control?

God, help me let go, today.

Some of us get attached to outcomes. We think a project or a relationship has to go a certain way.

Sometimes we get so attached to the outcome of a thing, we don't pay attention to how that thing feels. We may be so focused on marrying that person we're dating, we forget to pay attention to whether we like him or her. We may be so interested in that book of photographs getting published and achieving fame that we can't recollect if we have any passion for what we're taking pictures of. We may be so focused on everyone congratulating us for a wonderful party that we forget to relax and have fun.

We're putting in the effort. But we're trying to control both the flow and the way the thing turns out.

"God is in the details," a writing teacher once said.

What he was talking about was paying attention to each little detail in our writing: the color of the sky, the texture of the couch, the nuances of the feelings of the main character, the twinkle in her eye.

There's another way to interpret this saying, though. And that's to trust that God is present and interested in the details of our lives. Know what your dreams are and pay attention to what you want. But focus on the details of your life—how you feel each moment, the details of what you do. Don't be so attached to outcomes that you forget how much fun it is to live.

Remember that God is in the details, especially in how things work out.

God, help me be clear with you and myself about what I want in life. Help me learn to be present for the details of each moment of each day, doing what I do with passion.

You can clear the land, plow the field, spread the fertilizer, and plant the corn. But you cannot make it rain. You cannot prevent an early frost. You cannot determine exactly what will happen in your life. The rain may or may not fall, but one thing is certain: you will get a harvest only if you planted something in the field.

It's important to do everything in our power to ensure our success, but we also need to let the universe take its course. Getting mad won't help. Dwelling on a situation only takes energy away from us, while yielding few positive results.

The Serenity Prayer comes to mind. It begins: "Grant me the serenity to accept the things I cannot change."

Clear the land, plow the field, plant the crop, and then let go. Things will work out, sometimes the way we want them to, sometimes not. But they will work out.

Sometimes all you can do is shrug your shoulders, smile, and say *whatever*.

Thy will, not mine, be done.

God, help me take guided action, then surrender to your will. Help me remember that true power comes from aligning my will, intentions, and desires with you.

I was standing in my kitchen, many years ago, cooking Thanksgiving dinner. The children were racing around the house. I was expecting company. Dinner wasn't coming out the way I'd planned. And then I noticed, to my dismay, that one of my acrylic nails was missing. I looked around frantically, then realized it was most likely where I feared: inside the turkey, in the stuffing.

I called my best friend and explained things to her.

"Just relax," she said, in the cheery voice I liked so much—sometimes. "Go with the flow."

"How?" I said, quietly.

I don't remember the details of how that day worked out, but it did—I think Nichole found the nail. And so did the next. And so did the next. In time the lesson became clear—learn to relax, and go with the flow. From that relaxed place, you will learn to naturally manifest your power.

Some people call it ki, some chi, some the Holy Spirit, some the Way, the Tao, God's will, or the force. Whatever we choose to call it, there's an energy flow, a path, that will lead us through any situation we encounter in life.

I spent many years resisting this flow, this universal life force. I expended a great deal of energy creating dramas around each incident that took place. I spent as much time resisting a feeling or an event as I spent dealing with it. I lived in a state of fear.

The answer will appear. A solution will come to you. You'll be led to the next place, person, or event. You'll get the opening you need, along with the inspiration, courage, and wisdom. Feelings will come and go.

The lesson isn't that things will be okay. It's that things are okay, right now.

God, teach me how to give up resistance and go with the flow.

March 31   **Change what you can**

There are times when it's best to say *whatever* and times when it's best to say *enough*. Be aware of the differences in these times, and be ready to say both.

103

Are you being abused or merely annoyed? Is your anger based on a legitimate hurt, or has someone just not lived up to your expectations? Be aware that there's a difference. Then learn to apply the strategies, as needed, for that particular situation.

Are there any rules for knowing? No, there aren't. You need to decide and choose what's best for you at any given time. Trust yourself and your Higher Power. You're wiser than you think.

Seek balance in your life. Learn when it's time to let go, and learn when it's time to act.

God, help me let go of situations that are out of my control and help me take action, when it's time.

April

Learn to Say What

It was one of those luxurious mornings. The surf was pounding—just loud enough to be heard. We stood on the balcony, watching the rising tide.

"Its rhythms vary so much," I said. "Sometimes you can't walk on the beach in the morning. Other times it's way up in the late afternoon." Then I pointed out to a spot about a hundred feet away. "And sometimes it's way out there."

"We really need to get a tide chart to help us understand what's going on. A lot of businesses hand them out free."

Then, that thought and those words were gone.

"Let's go get some breakfast," he said.

"I have an idea," I said. "Let's go to the seafood place."

The traffic was gentle and easy that morning. We didn't need reservations. We immediately got a place to sit. Twenty minutes later, we were picking away at a huge plate of crab legs and Key lime pie. It wasn't on the breakfast menu, but it was what we wanted, we said.

Next we drove down to the cove, a hidden inlet down the coast. We had to walk and walk to get there. And once we did, we still had to walk down a hundred stairs. So we slid and clambered down the hill, instead. We wandered around the tiny bay, getting our feet wet and dirty in the sand. We climbed on rocks and stared at each of the beautiful things we saw, things that God made.

"What's this?" I said, barely touching a round ball of prickly things.

"A sea anemone," he said.

I didn't want to touch it completely, so I picked up a piece of a shell and touched the anemone with that.

The prickly, fuzzy ball of stuff just opened up and sucked that crab shell in. *Crunch. Crunch. Crunch.* I giggled. I wanted to see it do it again.

We strolled around the bay. Starfish, rocks, and pretty shells lined the way. "No Nude Bathing," a weathered sign commanded. A patrol helicopter flew by, just to make certain we complied. We climbed back up to the street. We didn't use the stairs this time either.

When we got back in the car, we drove to town again. The surf shop was open, so we ambled on in. We looked at sunglasses, wet suits, kayaks, and shorts. We didn't want to buy anything, so we said thanks and headed out the door. As we were leaving the store, a man suddenly burst out after us, shouting and waving something in his hand.

"Don't forget your tide chart," he said, giving the little booklet to us.

We looked at each other, then laughed at loud. Even though we had forgotten what we said we wanted, the universe remembered and insisted on giving it to us.

There's a lot of things we have to let go of. Probably everything, in fact. But it's important to say what we want first— before we let go—because sometimes when we let go, what we want comes back to us.

An important part of speaking the language of letting go means learning to identify and say what we want.

April 2   Learn to say *yes*

Learn to say *yes*, and mean it.

How long has it been since you've said *yes* to someone in your life? *Yes, I'd like to do that. Yes, that sounds good to me. Yes, I'll take a chance.*

How long has it been since you've said *yes* to yourself? *Yes, I recognize what you're feeling. Yes, I heard what you want. Yes, I realize you're tired. Yes, we'll rest for a while.*

When opportunities come our way—whether for personal, spiritual, or business growth—don't always be so cautious and shy. So what if saying *yes* means you're not living up to someone's expectations? Sometimes we learn to say *no* so well that saying *no* becomes a habit. We don't even consider what we're turning down.

A well-timed *yes* is as important in manifesting our power as learning to say *no*. It's a sign of an open heart.

Next time someone asks you out, suggests an opportunity, or your body tries to talk to you, stop. Instead of immediately saying *no*, like a parent on automatic pilot, listen to the offer. Could it be an important one? Something that might help guide you along your path? Maybe you're scared. Maybe you're worried that you aren't up to the occasion. Maybe you like the safety of saying *no* all the time.

Learn to say *yes* to life.

Honesty, openness, and willingness to try. Hmmmm. Sounds a lot like *yes* to me.

God, help me learn to say yes *and mean it, when that's the appropriate response.*

April 3   Pray and manifest your power

The Sufis have a saying: Praise Allah, and tie your camel to a post. *This brings together both parts of practice: pray, yes, but also make sure that you do what is necessary in the world.*
— Jack Kornfield, Seeking the Heart of Wisdom

It's easy to play the martyr. We spend our lives in struggle and turmoil longing for the sweet by-and-by when everything will be fine.

Today is the sweet by-and-by. Yes, right now. It's here. If

we're to have good in our lives, it's up to us to seek it out.

Here are two things the Bible teaches about faith: One, it says that faith is like a mustard seed. The tiniest bit of it can grow tall and in its own time will sprout. The other thing the Bible says is that faith without works is dead. If you're not doing something, then you're not keeping your faith alive.

Pray. Turn it over to God. But do something, too.

Stop waiting for someone to come along and rescue you.

Learn to rescue yourself.

God, help me take guided actions today to make my life a better place.

April 4   Ask for guidance

Sometimes things seem like good ideas and aren't, really.
                                                    — Piglet

Ask for guidance first.

Self-will is a tricky thing. So are impulse behaviors.

We've heard of impulse buying—making purchases quickly and without thought, based on momentary impulse. It's easy to get caught up living our lives that way, too. So often, we run off in the heat of the moment.

Spontaneity is good. Saying yes to life is good, too. But impulse living can get us into trouble. We can overreact to a problem, then sit in a heap of regrets. Sometimes, the next step presents itself clearly, in a flash of inspiration. Sometimes, we're meant to go forward and not let our fears and negative thoughts hold us back. Sometimes, we're acting on impulse and may end up sabotaging ourselves.

Ask for guidance first. It takes only a second to check the map and see if the turn we're thinking of making is where we really want to go.

God, show me what your will is for me. Show me if the decision I'm about to make is in my best interests or if there is a better path for me to explore.

April 5   Just do what you can

Dear God,
I am doing the best that I can.

— Children's Letters to God

Sometimes all we can do is all we can do.

"Maybe my talent is being a good listener," said John. "Maybe I'm not supposed to be rich and famous. I'm supposed to be the person who just sits and listens."

The world needs listeners, too. If everyone were the storyteller, it would be a noisy place, and no one would ever get to hear the stories. Maybe you are a storyteller; maybe you are a listener. Maybe both. Maybe it will be your path to achieve recognition and fame; maybe yours is an anonymous path of service.

If you've done all you can—whether it's to pursue your dreams, work on that relationship, help someone else, or take care of yourself—then you've done your part.

Maybe all we *can* do is all we're meant to do, that day.

God, help me do what I can and not torture myself about what I can't.

April 6   The power of thoughts

In 1922, Egypt hailed the discovery of King Tut's tomb by archaeologist Harold Carter. On the walls of the tomb, the magicians in the king's court had scrawled that a severe punishment would befall anyone disturbing the contents of the burial site.

Over the next ten years, more than twenty people involved with the excavation died suddenly or mysteriously.

Whether you call it a curse or a hypnotic suggestion of sorts, what we're talking about is the tremendous impact that suggestions have on us. We're talking about the power of belief.

Many of us spend thousands of dollars in therapy and years of our lifetime disentangling our thoughts from the beliefs of our parents, beliefs that were passed on to them by their parents, and their grandparents, and even further on down the ancestral line.

Sometimes, the effects of other people's thoughts are less blatant, and even more controlling. We can react instinctively to the silent demands of a spouse or lover, or a boss. They smile or frown—or just look at us—and we know what they mean and expect. Sometimes a casual comment by a friend can send us into a tailspin when he or she suggests, *You can't do that; it won't work. Do it this way.* Months later, when the way we're trying to do it isn't working out and we still keep trying and wonder why, we look back and say, "Oh. My friend told me to do it this way. Maybe he was wrong."

An important part of living in harmony with others means we enjoy doing things that please them, and we don't unnecessarily or maliciously hurt those with whom we interact. An important part of being true to ourselves means checking ourselves from time to time to see if the things we're doing are really what we want, or if we're just a puppet and someone else is pulling our strings.

God, help me respect the power of belief.

Activity: Try a little experiment to prove to yourself how strong the mind is. Walk up to two people, whether you know them or not. Think something very positive and loving about them, but don't say these thoughts out loud.

April 7   Examine what others expect

"There's a difference between saying we're not going to live up to other people's expectations and actually not living up to them," a friend said to me one day.

Other people's expectations, or even what we imagine others expect from us, can be a powerful and motivating force. We can feel antsy, uncomfortable, wrong, and off-center when we step out of our *place*. These feelings can occur when we're not living up to what other people expect from us—even, and sometimes especially, if these expectations aren't vocalized.

Expectations are silent demands.

Not living up to someone's expectations can take effort on our part. What we're really doing when we don't comply with what others expect from us is standing our ground and saying *no*. That takes energy and time.

What do people expect from you? What have you trained or encouraged them to expect? Are they actually expecting this from you, or are you just imagining that expectation and imposing it on yourself?

An unexamined life isn't worth living, or so they say. The problem with living up to other people's expectations too much is that it doesn't leave us time to have a life. Take a moment. Ask yourself this question, and don't be afraid to look deeply: Are you allowing someone else's expectations to control your life? Examine the expectations you're living up to; then live by your own inner guide.

God, help me become aware of the controlling impact other people's expectations have on my daily life. Help me know I don't have to live up to anyone's expectations but my own.

April 8   Stop trapping yourself

"I found myself staying at home on weekends, not wandering too far from home," a woman said. "I was expecting myself to be there for my daughter whenever she wanted me, just like when she was a child. The problem was, she was in her mid-twenties and didn't even live in the same city anymore."

It's easy to paint ourselves into a corner with what we've grown accustomed to expecting from ourselves. Sometimes we can work so hard to build that career, get that relationship, or become a certain way that we start living up to an image of ourselves that has become outdated.

Stop trapping yourself.

Those goals might have been what we wanted then, but they don't work anymore. And just because we achieved them doesn't mean we can't go on and do something else. What do you expect from yourself? Have you taken a look? Do your expectations reflect the genuine desires of your heart, or do they reflect something else?

Are you grumbling and complaining about some aspect of your life—something you're expected to do but resent? Maybe the only person expecting you to do that is yourself. Expectations can be subtle little things. Take them out and examine them. If some of them are outdated or useless, maybe it's time to throw them away.

Can you feel the rush? Listen quietly. It's there. It's the sound of a life and spirit being set free.

God, help me set myself free from ridiculous and unnecessary expectations.

Activity: If this were the last ten years of your life, what would you be doing? Where would you be living? What would you be doing for fun, work, friendship, and love? If the answer is different from where you currently are, maybe you should be someplace else.

April 9   **You get to choose**

Don't forget that we get to choose.

I got my "A" license in skydiving. I continued to jump. But I was procrastinating on buying my own parachute and gear. I used the rental gear, even though it didn't fit my body comfortably and I was throwing money down the drain. I used the rental gear because the student parachutes were big.

A lot of sky divers start going for the smallest possible canopy as soon as they get into the sport. That didn't work for me. As safe as I try to be and as much as I concentrate on landing properly, I usually land on my behind.

The bigger the canopy over my head, the better my behind feels when I land.

Whenever I discussed buying my own gear, the other sky divers would start insisting that I had to buy a small canopy, not to waste my money going big. So I put off the purchase, wondering when I'd want to jump and land with a canopy that small.

One day Eddy, a sky diver with more than ten thousand jumps and no injuries in the sport, pulled me aside. He asked me if I had bought my equipment. I told him no. He asked why. I told him because everybody had told me that when I bought my first canopy, it should be smaller than the size I was comfortable jumping.

"Don't be ridiculous. Order the largest size you can. You're the one jumping. You're the one paying for the gear. Don't let other people convince you that you shouldn't have what you want. Do what's right for you, and you'll be in this sport for a long time."

I was comforted and surprised by his words. How easy it is to let other people's expectations control our thoughts and actions. Sometimes we just need a little reminder that it's more than okay to choose what's right for us—it's what we're meant to do.

God, help me set myself free from the limits that other people put on me.

April 10   Make the hard calls

Sometimes we make choices with relative ease. One option feels right. We have no negative feelings about the other choice. On some occasions, we may be faced with what one man described to me as a "hard call."

"I had raised my own children alone," Jason said. "And I did a good job. I enjoyed my independence, but I relished the idea of being in a relationship at some time in my life. A few years after my two children left home, I met a woman I truly liked. We spent time together, got right up to the edge of being committed, but I had to back off.

"I liked her, but she had two children of her own. They were teenagers. They didn't want me in their mother's life. I didn't want to lose this woman. But at a deeper level, I really didn't want to be involved in the teenage years of raising someone else's children. I knew I had to let her go," he said. "It was a hard call."

A hard call is when we don't like either choice, but one option is unacceptable. Hard calls can take many shapes and forms. We may love someone who has a serious drinking problem and simply decide we can't live with him or her—despite how we feel about the person. We may love someone who has physically abused us or displayed signs of violent behavior; while our feelings may be genuine, so is the danger. We can be faced with hard calls at work. At one point in my life, I could barely tolerate my supervisors. But I liked the work I was doing. I decided to stay; I'm still glad I did.

Hard calls are a part of life. They force us to examine our values and determine what's genuinely important to us. They insist that we choose the path that's in our highest good.

God, when I am faced with a tough decision, help me be gentle with myself and others as I sort out, with your help, what's right for me.

April 11   Let yourself change and grow

There are lots of hermit crabs in the tide pools near my house. They're interesting little creatures. A hermit crab will find a shell that fits him, put it on, and live in it. After a while, he grows and the shell no longer fits, so the crab scurries along the sea floor and finds another shell to live in. He crawls out of his first shell and into the shell that fits his new needs. This scene repeats itself again and again throughout his life.

Learn a lesson from the hermit crabs.

Just because a decision was right for you yesterday, doesn't mean it meets your needs today. People grow. People change. And sometimes we have to let our safe little places go, in order to grow and change.

Are you holding on to something that doesn't work anymore, just because it's safe and what you know? It could be a behavior pattern—such as feeling victimized in all your relationships or wearing yourself out trying to control what you can't.

Thank the lessons, people, and places of the past for all they've taught you. Thank your survival behaviors for helping you cope. There's nothing wrong with feeling comfortable and safe—having lifetime friends and a career that serves us well. But don't get so comfortable that you can't let go and move on when it's time. If the walls are too confining and limiting and you're feeling stuck and bored, maybe it's time to get out and find a new shell. There's another shell waiting that will fit you better, but you can't move into it until you leave this one behind.

God, show me the behaviors, things, people, and places that I've outgrown. Then give me the faith to let go.

April 12   Is it what you really want?

"Are you still in that relationship?" I asked a friend one day.

"If I were really sick, I could be," my friend said. "But I've decided not to do that to myself anymore."

Sometimes, a door is open. We can walk through it and into that room. We can stay there as long as we want and as long as we can stand being in that room. Many of us have learned to take care of ourselves so well that we can be in extremely uncomfortable situations and still comfortably take care of ourselves.

The question then becomes not, "Can I?" but, "Do I want to?"

There are many situations in life where we can insist on having our will and way, sometimes for an extended period of time. Stubbornness and persistence can be good qualities. We can stay with a thing until we learn it well. But we can also take that too far and stick with a thing—a project or relationship—when other weaker and wiser souls might have given up.

Instead of asking yourself if you can, ask yourself something different. If you've been hanging in there, trying harder, and diligently taking care of yourself, back off. Stop asking yourself if you're good enough to handle the situation. Ask yourself if the situation is good for you.

God, help me take the time to ask myself, "Is this what I really want?"

April 13   Let yourself make mistakes

There are times we don't know which way to proceed or what to do next. We can become so blocked and stymied trying to figure it out that we just sit and spin our wheels. In those situations, the solution may involve making some choice—even if it turns out to be the wrong one.

Ideally, we can meditate on our choices and one way will feel right and clear, and the other won't. But in those times when we can't get clear, sometimes we have to give things a try. Take that job. Move into a condo. Date that woman. If it's a mistake, you can correct it as honestly, quickly, and humbly as you can.

You don't have to live life nearly as perfectly as you think. Sometimes it takes making a mistake in order for us to get clear.

God, help me let go of perfectionism. Help me give myself permission to live.

April 14   What do you want?

"I went to the grocery store to pick up a few things," a friend said. "I stood in front of the condiments section, staring at the pickles and olives. What I really wanted was the olives. What I bought was pickles. It wasn't about the cost," he said. "It was about deliberately depriving myself of what I want."

Sometimes things happen in life. We've talked about that before. We start out with good intentions about what we want: a family, health, a modicum of success in our career. Then something unforeseen rips it away. Maybe our family life as a child was destroyed when someone in the family got sick or died. Maybe this happened later in life—when we were betrayed by a spouse.

We may not be able to have everything we want in life. And we may sometimes get things we thought we wanted, then change our mind. But we still don't have to torture ourselves by telling ourselves that we can't have what we want.

What do you want? Do you know? Or have you shut that part of yourself down? Yes, we all have times of discipline. And there's much to be learned by denying ourselves, at certain times, of certain pleasures. It's not good to want something or someone so much that desire runs and rules our lives. And sometimes wanting what we can't have can make life more interesting.

But it's okay to open our hearts to ourselves and be clear about what we want in our small and larger choices. Learn to master desire.

Open you heart to what you want. Then say it. Pickles or olives, which will it be?

God, teach me to master my desires. Grant me the wisdom to know when something needs to be off-limits for me, and when I am unnecessarily depriving myself of the pleasures and joys here on earth.

April 15   Say what you can't have

"Why is it," one man asked, "that if I walk into a room with one hundred women, the one I'm attracted to will either be engaged to someone else or live across the country? Will someone please explain that to me?"

I laughed when he asked the question, although he wasn't trying to be funny. Many people find themselves enamored with what they can't have. His question struck a chord because I'm one of them. Unavailability—and not being able to have what you want—although painful, can be deliciously enticing in many ways.

That miserable, deprived place feels so comfy and familiar to us. Even though we know where it leads—to letdown, loneliness, sitting by the phone—we'll let that feeling lead us around by the nose.

Wanting what we can't have is a universal dilemma. It's so easy to conjure up fantasies about how delicious it would be if we could only have *that*, even though we know we never could. Then we don't have to deal with what we have. And we don't have to face issues like intimacy, commitment, and love.

Learn to recognize longing and yearning for what we can't have. And ask for the courage and wisdom to learn about the true delights of available, requited love.

If we begin yearning for something we can't have, we don't have to take ourselves so seriously. We can see it for what it is and just enjoy a good laugh at ourselves.

God, help me stop sabotaging myself.

Okay, so you can't have what you want most in life.

What's next on your list? If you can't have what you really want, put that aside. It's a no. It doesn't mean you can't have other things. Don't let it contaminate the rest of your life. So you can't have that particular relationship. What do you want, a good healthy love relationship? Put it on your want list. So you can't live in that house. What did you like about that house? What would you like in the place you want to live?

Dig deeply. Look inside. I bet there's all kinds of dreams buried in you. Go ahead. Take a risk. Let them come out. Look—you're already thinking about something you denied yourself a long time ago.

Most of us have things in life we wanted more than anything or anyone else. Many of us have had to learn to let these things or people go. Put all the things you can't have on a different list. Or maybe add it to your list of questions to God, your "why's." "God, why couldn't I have that when it's what I wanted most?" Then let it go.

Now, make another list. Call it, "If I can't have what I wanted most, what would I want next best, after that."

God, help me come up with a next-best list. Show me what to put on it and help my dreams come true.

Activity: Make a wishes and dreams list. This is a very important list. We talked about doing it at the first of the year. If you made your list then and are satisfied with it, maybe this activity isn't for you. But if you think you may have held back, or you didn't make the list at all, the time is right for you to start pursuing your dreams. If you could have anything in life, what would it be? What places would you visit? What people would you meet? What kind of work would you do? Where would you live? What kind of spiritual growth would you experience? How would you treat others, and yourself? What ideals would guide your actions? What would your ethics be in life? Spice this list up. Don't hold back.

April 17   Keep your balance

Sometimes, our legitimate needs and wants run amuck.

We want something so badly—for instance our spouse sobering up, or that job, or that woman or that man—that we begin to obsess and dwell. We take ourselves out of that place of balance and end up in a no-win tailspin.

It's not that what we want and need is bad for us. It's just that right now, what we want isn't, obviously, taking place. Don't take it out on yourself by judging yourself wrong. Don't take it out on your needs by telling yourself you shouldn't have any.

Relax. Come back to center, to that clear, balanced place.

Don't let your needs and desires run away with you. Yes, passion is great stuff. Identify what you want. Then let it go. And ask God what your lesson is.

Today, I will come back to balance with any need or want that seems to be controlling my life. Instead of dwelling on it, I'll give it to God and focus on taking care of myself.

April 18   Say what you really want

What do you want? No, I'm not asking what thing you want, but rather what is it about that thing that you are seeking? Get to the root of your search. Do you want a new car? Do you want reliable transportation, or do you want the prestige that comes from driving a shiny new vehicle? Do you really want to do that kind of work, or do you just want the money and prestige you hope it will bring? Do you want a romantic relationship? Do you want a partnership based on equal ground, or do you want someone to take care of you? What is it that you're really looking for?

Get as specific as you can. When we examine our goals and dreams, we may find that they're motivated by a deeper desire. I want to reach this point in my career, we say. Look deeper. What's at the root of that goal? If what you're desiring is creative freedom, maybe you can gain it in other ways than by getting a promotion. If you want your spouse to quit drinking, perhaps what you're really seeking is a calmer home environment and relief from the pain. If you can't make him or her stop drinking, maybe there's another way you can achieve that dream. Or maybe you'll decide that you can contribute to that now, while waiting for your loved one to change.

Be honest in your search for the root of your goals. Some of the roots of your goals might not be so healthy after all; maybe the goal will need to change. But you could save yourself from heartache by discovering it now. Maybe the root is healthy, but you have placed too much value on following only one path to reach it.

Be aware of all the opportunities around you. Don't sell life short. There may be more than one way to get what you really want.

God, help me become aware of what I'm really seeking in life.

One day, I was at a restaurant with friends. Now, my friends knew—particularly one of my friends—that I don't eat pork. It's not a religious thing. I just get sick from pork, even the tiniest bit will give me a headache, and sometimes nausea. So no matter how good that bacon looks, or how much my mouth waters about pork chops frying in the pan, I stay away from pig.

So we're at the restaurant. I've looked at the menu. And the waiter comes over and rattles off the specials of the evening to us. The tortellini sounded pretty tasty. I knew he had used another word to describe the tortellini—*prosciutto*—but I skimmed over the word. The whole dish sounded interesting to me.

We sit and have small talk. Then, the meal comes. The waiter puts my dish down in front of me. I pick up my fork and begin eating.

"Do you know what prosciutto is?" my friend asked.

"Yes," I said lying.

"Point to the prosciutto," he said.

I picked out a vegetable that kind of looked like celery and stabbed at it with my fork. "There," I said, "that's it."

"You're kidding around now, aren't you?" he said. "Point to the prosciutto!"

I felt my face redden. "I don't like being tested this way," I said. "I know what prosciutto is."

"This," he said, stabbing a piece of something on the plate, "is prosciutto. It's ham. Italian ham. I just thought you'd like to know, being as you don't eat pork."

"Oh," I said, pushing my plate back. "I don't think I'm that hungry after all."

I know. This is an old lesson I've talked about before. I had to learn it again. Sometimes, we feel inadequate, but what we don't know can hurt us. And besides, if we say we don't know when that's the honest answer, we just might learn something new.

Today, if the true and correct answer is "I don't know," that's the reply I'll use.

God, help me let go of my belief that I have to know something I don't.

April 20   Flip a coin

Flip a coin. . . . This is a secret technique of many prominent executives. Because sometimes it doesn't matter what decision you make, as long as you make one. Then you just stick to it, having confidence in your having brought about the outcome.
                                                                    — Jay Carter

Sometimes, we are truly ambivalent. We don't know what we want. The scales are balanced, fifty-fifty.

Flip a coin.

If you don't like the decision the coin just made for you, at least you'll know you know what you want.

God, help me discover who I am and what I really want.

April 21   Discern what's important

Above all I had learned to distinguish what was important in life and what was not. The important was often a handful of water, sometimes a protected bivouac site, a book, a conversation.

                                                    — Reinhold Messner, Free Spirit

A friend of mine, desiring to pursue a life of adventure by joining the skydiving community, quit a good job, sold all of his belongings, and moved on to an airport with a couple of duffel bags and a parachute. Today, he has realized his dream. He's a professional sky diver, married, and living in a decent home close to his dream job—jumping out of airplanes. "I'll never get rich doing this," he explains. "But I get to wake up every day knowing that I get to do exactly what I want to do. And even more importantly, my years as a drop-zone bum taught me about what was truly important, and what's not."

We get attached to our things. We fuss when someone spills soda on the couch, get angry over the slightest ding on our leased Honda, and make up for lost time with loved ones by bringing them more things.

Look closely at your life. Decide what's really important to you. What would you genuinely miss, if you didn't have it? What would you perhaps not even notice, if it was missing from your life? What might you be better off without?

Learn to distinguish between the essential and that which you don't really need. You might find, like my friend, that you'd be happier with two duffel bags and a dream than you would be with a garage full of clutter that never gets used.

God, grant me the strength to pursue my dreams. Help me cut through the clutter and discover what's truly important for me and my family.

April 22   Solve the right problems

Are you solving the problems you want to solve, or the problems you think that you are supposed to solve?

— Thom Rutledge

Peter spent his days solving problems. He had attended the right college and found the right profession and worked for the right people. As a successful accountant, he counted other people's money and figured out what they owed the government. Peter was good at his job, but he wanted to take pictures. Still, accounting was an important job, and people needed him to help them with their taxes. Solving other people's money problems took up most of Peter's time, so much time that he gradually forgot about taking pictures.

One day, he picked up a magazine on photography and started reading. He bought a camera and took some pictures. Then he took a vacation and took some more pictures. He entered them in a local showing and received second prize.

Peter didn't stop being an accountant. But now he spends as much time solving problems of aperture and shutter speed as he does 401k's and 1099's.

Are you solving the problems that you want to solve? Or are you solving the same problem over and over?

Find the answers to the questions *you* have.

Then find more questions to ask.

God, give me the courage to follow my heart. Teach me how to experience more joy in my life.

April 23   Say what your intentions are

Have you ever done anything deliberately to hurt someone, to get even with that person, or to gain revenge? Have you ever done anything subconsciously with intentions that weren't noble?

"I dated a woman for three months," Kent said. "It took me that long to realize that I was simply getting even with my last girlfriend, who had broken up with me. I used this woman as a tool for revenge and a way to get even with my ex. I felt horrible when I realized what I had done. But when I looked more deeply, I saw that my relationships were a series of attempts at getting revenge and retribution. I never took time out to feel and clear my anger from the last relationship that hadn't worked."

Intentions are a powerful force. They combine desire, emotion, and will. They're stronger and more powerful than wishes or simple desires. They can be a profound force in our lives and in the lives of people we touch.

Take a moment before entering a situation. Examine what your true intentions are. Do you have a motive, an agenda, a strong expectation involved? Have you been as clear as possible with yourself, and with whomever else is involved, about what you really expect and want? Or are you operating with a hidden agenda, hoping that if you force your will long enough, you'll get your way?

Ask God to show you the intentions of the people you're involved with. Sometimes they don't know, themselves. Sometimes they do, but they're not telling you. In those circumstances, you're being set up for a manipulation and possibly some pain.

Be clear on your intentions. And stay as clear as possible on what other people want from you.

God, bring to light my intentions and motives, and the intentions and motives of those with whom I interact.

April 24   Put your intentions out there

Be clear on what you want. If you're starting a business, taking a new job, learning a new skill, or beginning a relationship, state clearly to yourself what you're looking for.

What level of performance are you hoping to reach? Stay realistic, but not pessimistic. What do you want? Be clear with the universe about what your intentions are. Be as specific as you can be.

If you're on the dating scene, what are you looking for? Some fun? A spouse? Be clear and specific about what you want.

After you've focused and clarified your intentions, then let your intentions go. Sometimes in life we can't get what we want. Other times, we can. And sometimes the journey to getting there is full of twists and turns, much more of an adventure than anything we could have planned.

Besides, the clearer we can be about what we want, the easier it will be to recognize and enjoy it when it comes our way.

God, help me be clear with you and myself about what I really want. Then, help me let go of my intentions and surrender to your plan.

April 25   Be as clear as possible

Marcia doesn't like to hurt other people's feelings. So when she doesn't want to date or see someone anymore, she doesn't tell them that. She lies. But she calls it "being nice." She either sets up some dramatic scene that justifies her getting mad and breaking up, or she gives them an excuse that leaves them hanging.

Let go of the drama. Tie up loose ends. If you know where you're at with someone, you can be diplomatic, but be as clear as you can be.

Be clear with yourself, too. Watch the behavior of other people. Are they making excuses to you why they can't be with you? Are you making excuses about why they don't call? Some of us wait a long time for someone who's not even thinking about us.

Stop telling others what they want to hear, when that's not the truth. Stop telling yourself what you want to hear, when what you're telling yourself isn't true, either. Don't leave other people hanging. Don't put yourself on hold.

Be as clear as you can be, with other people and with yourself.

It's the compassionate thing to do.

God, help me know that I don't have to create dramas to get what I want. Help me live my life from a place of centered, diplomatic honesty, even when that means I need to tell people something they'd rather not hear.

April 26   Practice diplomacy

Taking care of ourselves doesn't give us the right to be mean. Just because we're telling the truth, we don't need to tear people apart. Sometimes when we start to own our power after years—maybe a lifetime—of being timid and weak, we become overly aggressive trying to get our point across.

We can be honest with other people without being mean. We can be diplomatic in whatever we need to say, at least most of the time. And we usually don't have to scream and shout.

I've learned a little trick along the way. The weaker and more vulnerable I feel, the more I holler and the meaner I react. The more truly powerful, clear, and centered I am, the quieter, gentler, and more loving I speak.

The next time you feel threatened or start to scream and yell, stop yourself. Take a deep breath. Deliberately speak more softly than you normally would.

You can speak softly and still carry a great big stick.

God, help me be a diplomat. Teach me how to own my power in a gentle, peaceful way.

April 27   Stop reading between the lines

Chelsea dated Tom for five years. During the course of those years, Tom told Chelsea that he didn't want a serious relationship, and she shouldn't get serious about him. Chelsea didn't like what she heard. She thought Tom must care about her, because their times together were so good and because he kept coming back to see her.

Whether Tom was being manipulative isn't the issue. Whether he was keeping a door open for himself isn't the issue. The issue is, Chelsea wasn't believing what Tom said— until he left her for someone else.

Yes, sometimes people are coy. Yes, sometimes people are reluctant to get involved. But if people tell you they feel a certain way, don't read between the lines. Take them at face value. Correct your behavior to match the reality of the situation, not the fantasies in your mind.

Take people at face value. Say what you mean in your dealings with others, so they can take you at face value, too.

God, help me make a practice out of facing, dealing with, and accepting the truth.

April 28   Say what you did

"How do you think it went?" Rob, my flight instructor asked me after my one-hour flying lesson.

I was used to this part of the drill by now. After a skydive or after a flight lesson, the student usually takes the time to sit down with the instructor and review the session. I

131

reviewed the takeoff and landing, the maneuvers I had done, and objectively analyzed my fear and performance level. I critiqued where I needed improvement and what my goals were for the next session. Then came my favorite part. I had to pick out what I liked best about my flying that day.

I thought for a while. "I think I taxied really well," I said. "I'm really getting the hang of it."

Sometimes, in the busyness and exuberance of living our lives, it's easy to forget to take time to debrief. By the time we fall into bed at night, we're tired and done with the day.

Take an extra moment or two at night. Make room for a new habit in your life. The Twelve Step programs call it "taking an inventory." Some people call it "debriefing."

The purpose of an inventory isn't to criticize. It's to stay conscious and objectively analyze what happened. Go over the events of the day. What did you do? How do you feel about what you did? Where could you use improvement? What would you like to do tomorrow? And most important, what was your favorite part of the day?

Don't overanalyze. Don't use debriefing as a self-torture session. Simply say what you did, where you'd like to see improvement, and what you most enjoyed. You might be surprised at the awareness and power this simple activity can bring.

God, help me take the time to debrief.

Activity: If you have a spouse or a roommate, making a regular ritual out of doing a debriefing together can be a great intimacy-building activity. You can encourage your children to learn to debrief from the day at a young age. Or, you can debrief with a friend, on the phone, at the end of the day. You'll not only get to know yourself better, but will also become closer to the other person, too.

April 29   **Ask God what to do**

I was in treatment for chemical dependency. All I wanted to do was get high, cop some dope, do what I'd done for the past twelve years—obliterate myself. As a last-ditch, almost hopeless gesture, I looked at the ceiling in my stark room, the place I had been assigned to sleep. I prayed, *God, if there is a program to help me stop using, please help me get it.* Twelve days later, sobriety fell down upon me, changing me at the very core of my being, altering the entire course of my life.

I divorced my husband and took on the single-parenting and single-financing role, continuing to pursue my dream of being a writer. My kitchen cupboards were nearly bare of food. *I'm not that hungry, but the children are,* I prayed. "Don't worry," an angelic voice whispered in my ear. "Soon you'll never have to worry about money again—unless you want to." An immutable peace settled over me. No food or money fell from the sky. But the peace, a peace as tangible and thick as butter and as healing as the oils of heaven themselves, spread throughout my life.

Years later, my son was strapped to a hospital bed. I touched his foot, his hand. I knew, despite the whooshing of the breathing apparatus, that he was not in that shell anymore. Then the plug got pulled. "No hope, no hope, no hope," are the only words I can remember. Now, the whooshing sound turns to silence. I say good-bye, walk out of the room, just put one foot in front and walk.

"Just pick me up, and get me some drugs," I say to a friend, three days later. "I've got to have some relief from this pain." Driving around in the car, hours later, I look at the fresh box of syringes on the seat next to me. "Tell me what you want to put in them," he says. "Cocaine? Dilaudid? What?" His irritation is as obvious as my hopelessness. My mind runs through the routine. Cocaine? Unpredictable. Russian roulette with my heart. Dilaudid? A medical prescription. If I needed it, legitimately needed it, a doctor would prescribe it for me. No prayers. No hopes. Just simple words came out, this time. "Just take me home," I said. "I don't really want to get high."

Prayer changes things. Prayer changes us. Prayer changes life. Sometimes an event has been manifested that needs to be stopped, midair. Don't pray just when you're in trouble. Pray every day. Surround yourself with prayer. You never know when you might need an extra miracle.

Today, if I've tried everything else, I'll try prayer, too.

April 30   Use a gentle touch

There's a force out there, whether you call it destiny or use some other words, that brings people together who are meant to be together. It's the butterfly story.

If you hold a butterfly too tightly in your hands, you take all the oil off its wings and it can't fly. You can have the butterfly that way, but the butterfly can't be a butterfly.

If you really love a butterfly, you won't rub all the oil off its wings just so you can clutch it in your hands. If you really love something or someone, don't hold on too tightly. Let that person be free. Let people be who they are.

Don't rub the oil off the butterfly's wings. Let it fly back to you on its own.

God, help me learn to use a gentle touch with everyone I love.

May

Learn to Say When

Chip turned the rented four-wheel drive Chevy Blazer off the road and into an open field. The three of us, Chip, Andy, and myself, were in Florida on a spur-of-the-moment road trip. We had met Andy at the drop zone, where he'd been trying out for a skydiving team. Now the three of us were on our way to Orlando. It had rained the day before. We started to tear through the field, when the right wheels slipped into a ditch.

Chip rocked the truck, backward and forward. The right wheels sunk deeper. Andy hopped out of the truck, looked around, and then climbed back in. "We're stuck," he said.

"I've got my cell phone," I said. "I'll call for help. . . ."

Chip and Andy stared at me.

"You said you wanted an adventure," Chip said. "Well, this is it!"

We all got out of the Blazer. The right wheels were entrenched in a ravine, and a large log was jammed into the underside of the vehicle. Andy had a plan. We'd each go try to find boards or wood that could be placed under the wheels. We returned twenty minutes later. The guys propped the wood under the tires. Chip got in the truck. The engine revved. The wheels spun. Mud sprayed. The truck didn't move.

"I could call a tow truck," I offered again.

About one-quarter mile away from the field was an intersection that promised, at least eventually, some passersby. We tromped to the intersection and waited. Before long, we flagged down an old Cadillac with a man and a young woman in it.

The man promised to return in a few minutes with his truck and his brother.

About fifteen minutes later, the two men and the woman appeared in a truck. They hooked a chain to the Blazer. Then they got in their truck and drove slowly away. They revved their engine. Mud sprayed. Then *snap*, the chain broke.

We looked at their truck. We looked at the stuck, muddy Blazer. We looked at the broken chain.

"Sorry," the two men said.

"Thanks for trying," we said. "Try calling a towing place," the taller of the two men said. "They'll come and get you out."

Andy, Chip, and I got back into the stuck truck.

"Well," I said. "Are you ready to call a tow truck now?"

The truck arrived. The professional tower had us out in fifteen minutes, and we were on our way to Orlando. We had been stuck for more than six hours. The entire time, we all knew what we had to do to get out: call the tow truck. For a variety of reasons, we didn't want to do that until we got tired of being stuck.

Sometimes, getting stuck is the adventure at hand. We might not know what to do to move forward. Or we may be enjoying the drama of being stuck. We may be stuck in a grinding situation in a relationship. We may be at a plateau in our career. We may be stuck in our spiritual growth. We may have at one time liked and wanted to be where we've found ourselves, but now it's time to move on.

Learning to say *when*—whether it's when we want something more, or something else, or when we've had enough— is an important part of using in the language of letting go.

God, help me remember that I have the power to say when.

May 2   **Say when it's enough**

"Say when," my friend says as she refills my glass, meaning she wants me to tell her *when* I have enough juice.

Saying *when* is a simple idea that we can use in our daily

lives, as well. Sometimes there is no visible end to the troubles that beset us, and all we can do is seek shelter from the storm. But often, it's up to us to decide when we have had enough. An irritant might be just a minor inconvenience for a while, but the longer it lingers, the more irritating it becomes. Say *when*. Say that you have had enough, and refuse to let the irritant into your life anymore.

A draining person can latch on to a sympathetic ear. Know when that person is starting to take more than you are willing to give. Say *when*. The same can also be true of good things. Some of my friends like to make five, seven, and even ten or more skydives in a single day. I don't. I love the sport, but I also know when it becomes too much of a good thing for me. I say *when*.

Be aware of how much your cup can hold. When you have had enough, say *when*.

God, help me know and respect my limits.

May 3   **Say when it's too much**

I was sitting at the bus stop many years ago watching impatiently for the bus. I had been patient for so long—taking the bus to the grocery store, lugging big bags of groceries home. Whenever I found myself feeling irritated about not having a car, I'd be grateful. I'd be grateful that I was sober and that I could get around. I'd be grateful for all the good things in my life.

Yet, it was getting harder and harder to be grateful.

The bus finally arrived, and I bustled my way on with my heavy bags, then lugged them the two blocks to my apartment after the bus dropped me off. I didn't want to cry, but I couldn't help it that day.

"God, I'm getting sick of walking and taking the bus," I said. "I'm tired of this. How much longer do I have to wait to get a car?"

Within two months, I was driving an automobile.

It's important to be grateful. But sometimes, repressing our emotions and not saying how we feel about a situation is a form of trying to control the situation, too. We think if we hold our breath, don't complain, and do everything right, the universe will just benevolently give us what we want.

Is there some situation in your life that you've been hoping would magically get better if you bit your lip and wished long enough? If you've started playing the waiting game in a particular situation, tell yourself how you really feel.

Maybe it's time to say *when*.

God, help me forgive myself for having needs and desires.

May 4   **Know when to say *no***

Saying *no* is another way of saying *when*. For some of us, the hardest word in the language to speak is the short, simple word *no*. Instead of saying no, we toil on. *What will he think if I say no? Mary won't be my friend if I don't do this. The project won't get done unless I do it. I'm not a team player when I say no. A good Christian needs to sacrifice himself. Saying no is selfish.* And the list goes on. We abuse ourselves, take on more than we want, and find ourselves bitter and resentful. And we've done it to ourselves.

Know your limits. Know when to say *no*. There may be a few people who are offended by the limits that you set, but usually those are the ones trying to control or manipulate you. Some well-meaning colleagues may tell you that you're being selfish, but your ultimate responsibility is to yourself. That responsibility includes knowing how and when to set limits.

Look at your schedule. Are you so overloaded or booked that you can't see when you could have any time for fun, relaxing, or your own personal growth? It may be time for you to start setting limits. Remember, you get to decide what's best for you.

Learn to say *no* and stand by your choice.

God, help me to have the strength to set reasonable limits for myself and to tell others when I cannot help them. Help me learn to say no.

May 5   **Learn when to say *no* and *yes***

Read the following sentences out loud.

"No."

"No, this doesn't work for me."

"No, thank you. This doesn't feel right to me."

"No. This isn't right for me at this time."

Now, try this.

"I have to think about that first, before I can decide, I'll get back to you later."

"I've thought about it, and the answer is no."

Now, read this.

"I know I said yes and that this was what I wanted. But I've changed my mind. This isn't working out for me. It's not right for me anymore. I'm sorry for any inconvenience I might have caused you."

Now, this.

"Go away and don't call anymore."

See, you can say all those things you thought you couldn't.

Now, read these sentences out loud.

"Maybe."

"Maybe, but I'm leaning toward no."

"Maybe. It sounds interesting but I'm not sure."

"Yes. That would be nice."

"Yes, I like that idea. When?"

"Yes, I'd love to."

"Yes, but the time isn't right for me now."

Those are your basic choices, with a few variations. Learn them. Memorize them. Then ask yourself when each answer applies.

Learn to honestly tell people what your real answer is. Look into your heart to decide when a thing is, or isn't, right for you.

God, help me trust myself about when it's right to say no, maybe, *and* yes. *Then help me express myself in an honest, loving way.*

Activity: Do you have a difficult time expressing yourself? What is the most difficult thing for you to tell people—*no* or *yes*? Try giving yourself permission by writing yourself a permission slip, then carrying it around in your purse or wallet. It might read something like this: Dorothy has permission to say *no* whenever she wants. Or it might read: I have permission to say *no* ten times this week, and *yes* five times. Then sign the slip, and let it be a reminder to you to own your power by saying *no, yes,* or *maybe* whenever each of those answers is right for you.

May 6   **Say when it's worn out**

Throw it away when it wears out.

John and Al were talking one day about a mutual friend, someone they both knew and liked. "Mark thinks he has to be in pain all the time," John said. "He defines himself by his resentments. He's always angry, always upset, and so deeply concerned about how terrible and tragic life is that he's always pulling out his hair and wailing about life. I'm worried about him," John said.

"Let him go," Al said. "People need to wear things out. They need to take their time wearing out their beliefs and attitudes before they're ready to throw them away. You've needed your time to do this. So have I. Give Mark the time he needs—however long that is—to wear his beliefs out too."

Are you attached to any beliefs that are sabotaging your life—beliefs about your ability to be happy, joyous, and free? Life is a journey through places, through people, and through our beliefs. We wear these beliefs out one by one, shedding them and making room for a little more light.

Give other people the time and freedom to wear out their beliefs. Give yourself that freedom, too.

Right now, this moment, you're wearing out a belief. Look around at your life. Trust where you are. Trust what you're going through. Some belief is wearing thin right now, as you read this. Say when it's time to throw out that belief.

You are loveable. You are beautiful, just as you are. You have a purpose. There's a plan for your life. You can take care of yourself. You can think, feel, and solve your problems. Sometimes life is hard, but it doesn't have to be a struggle. And it doesn't have to hurt that much and that long. Not anymore. You can detach, and you can detach in love.

Look in the mirror for a few moments. Instead of just being honest with yourself about what you see, be honest with yourself about what you believe about who you see.

God, help me let go of my limiting and sabotaging beliefs.

In her book *Recovering from the Loss of a Child*, author Katherine Fair Donnelly writes of a man whose infant daughter, Robyn, died from SIDS (sudden infant death syndrome). The child had died in the stroller, while the mother was out walking her. The father had stopped to get a haircut that day and was given a number for his turn.

"It was something he never did again in future years," Donnelly wrote. "He would never take a number at the barber's and always came home first to make sure everything was all right. Then he would go and get a haircut. It became one of the ways he found of coping."

I hate "coping." It's not living. It's not being free. It reeks of "surviving."

But sometimes it's the best we can do, for a while.

Eight years after my son died, I was signing the papers to purchase a home. It was the first home I had bought since his death. The night before he died, I had also signed papers to buy a new home. I didn't know that I had begun to associate buying a home with his death, until I noticed my hand trembling and my heart pounding as I finished signing the purchase agreement. For eight years, I had simply avoiding buying a home, renting one less-than-desirable place after another and complaining about the travails of being a renter. I only knew then that I was "never going to buy another house again." I didn't understand that I was coping.

Many of us find ways of coping. As children, we may have become very angry with our parents. Having no recourse, we may have said to ourselves, "I'll show them. I'm never going to do well at music, or sports, or studies again." As adults, we may deal with a loss, or death, by saying, "I'm always going to be nice to people and make them happy. Then they won't go away." Or we may deal with a betrayal by saying, "I'm never going to open my heart to a woman, or man, again."

Coping often includes making an incorrect connection between an event and our behavior. It may help us survive, but at some point our coping behaviors usually get in our way. They become habits and take on a life of their own. And although we think we're protecting ourselves or someone we love, we aren't.

Robyn didn't die because her father took a number and waited to get his hair cut.

My son didn't die because I bought a new house.

Are you keeping yourself from doing something that you really want to do as a means of coping with something that happened to you a long time ago? Cope if you must, if it helps save your life. But maybe today is the day you could set yourself free.

God, show me if I'm limiting myself and my life in some way by using an outdated coping behavior. Help me know that I'm safe and strong enough now to let that survival behavior go.

May 8   Say when something triggers you

How do you defend yourself when you feel angry and hurt?

When Sally was a child, she lived with disturbed parents. They said mean, hurtful things to her much of the time. She wasn't allowed to say anything back, and she especially wasn't allowed to say how angry and hurt she felt.

"The only way I could deal with anger was by going numb and telling myself I didn't care—that the relationship wasn't important," Sally said. "Then I carried this behavior into my adult life. I learned to just go cold when I felt angry or hurt. I automatically shut down and pushed people away. One hint

144

of feeling hurt or angry, and boom—I was gone."

It's important to know our boundaries. It's even more important not to allow people to be reckless with our hearts. It's also important to know how hurt and anger trigger our defenses.

Do you have an instant reaction, not to other people, but to your own feelings of being betrayed, hurt, or angered? Do you shut down? Lose your self-esteem? Do you "go away" from yourself or others? Do you counterattack?

Feelings of hurt and anger will arise in the course of most relationships. Sometimes when we feel that way, it's a warning that we need to beware. Other times it's a minor incident, something that can be worked out. You may have needed to protect yourself once, a long time ago. But now it's okay to be vulnerable and let yourself feel what you feel.

Say when something triggers you and learn how you defend yourself.

God, help me become aware of how I protect myself when I feel hurt, angry, and attacked. Give me the courage to be vulnerable and learn new ways of taking care of myself.

May 9   Say when it's too much compassion

Sometimes, it's easy to step across that line and have too much compassion for the people in our lives. Although compassion is good, too much compassion can cripple the people we're trying to love. We understand so clearly how they feel that we don't hold them accountable for themselves. Too much compassion can hurt us, too. We can wind up feeling victimized by and resenting the people we're experiencing too much compassion toward. We're so worried about their feelings that we neglect our own.

Too much compassion means we don't believe in others enough to let them do what they need to do to help themselves. It's a way of telling them, "You can't." *You can't handle your reality. You can't learn your lessons. You can't handle the truth, so I'll treat you like a helpless child.*

Too much compassion can leave us prey to victimization and manipulation. We're so worried about how the other person feels that we neglect to take care of ourselves.

Here are some guidelines about compassion.

- If we're creating a problem for ourselves to solve someone else's dilemma, we've probably crossed that line.
- If we're so worried about another person's pain that we're neglecting our own emotions, we're probably over-involved.
- If guilt is the underlying motive for our behavior, maybe what we're practicing isn't compassion.

The lesson here isn't to stop caring about others. Instead, we need to respect other people's right to learn their own lessons.

Too much of anything isn't a good thing. If we've crossed that line into too much compassion, we can step back into the safe zone and use a lighter touch.

God, show me if I'm harming someone in my life—a parent, child, or friend—by smothering that person with too much compassion.

May 10   Say when it's time to stop sabotaging yourself

Jenny sat down in the comfortable armchair in the small, pleasantly lit office. The man sitting across from her looked like a normal, friendly man—not at all like she imagined a psychic would look. She relaxed and began to tell him why she was there.

"I don't usually visit psychics, but I'd like some information and guidance about the relationship I'm in now," she said. "The guy I'm seeing is a great guy. I'm really in love with him."

The psychic didn't have to be psychic to know that a "but" was coming next. He had heard the story many times before.

"But," Jenny said, "he's a drug dealer. But it's only marijuana. And he doesn't use himself. And he's just doing it long enough to make enough money to start his own business. Go legitimate, you know."

After rambling for a while, she stopped. "So," she asked the physic, "what do you think?"

"You don't need a psychic to tell you to get out as fast as you can," he said, giving her money back. "It's obvious. The relationship is doomed."

As in Jenny's situation, it's easy to see the ridiculously obvious faulty thinking in our friends and people we're close to. Sometimes it's harder to see our own faulty thinking and blind spots.

"I love her, but she's married." "I love him, but he's a cocaine addict." "I love him, but I know he sleeps around a lot."

While many people enjoy the benefits from seeking intuitive spiritual guidance at some time in their lives, there are many times we can easily tell our own future. Stop sabotaging yourself. Listen to what you're saying. Listen to the *but's*, to the words that come out of your own mouth. Yes, some drug dealers do reform. Yes, people recover from cocaine addiction every day. Yes, people with long histories of infidelity do stop sleeping around. And some married people do get divorced and marry those with whom they had affairs.

Some people win the lottery—every day. But more people never win the lottery.

Sometimes we're blindsided by events that couldn't possibly

be foreseen. Sometimes it's easy to predict trouble. Whenever possible, save yourself the pain and heartache inevitably coming around the bend.

Stop sabotaging yourself. Be your own psychic. Listen to what you're saying, and give yourself the same basic advice you'd give to a friend. You may be the exception to the rule, but probably not.

God, help me let go of my blind spots, the ones that cause me to sabotage my own happiness and well-being.

May 11   Say when it's time to disengage

"Run, duck, hide."

It's a motto that has served me well, particularly since I moved to California. "It takes money and a car to live here," a friend told me once. He was right. And those who don't have money or a car may try to take yours, I learned soon after that.

Manipulations, scams, and disturbed people abound.

They can be found anywhere. And sometimes these people are not all that disturbed. They're just going through their stuff, and it doesn't involve or pertain to us.

Sometimes, it doesn't make any sense to be therapeutic, helpful, or nice when other people are trying to dump their insanity on you. It will only get you in deeper. Using any rules of engagement will simply mean you're engaged. Disengage immediately.

Learn when to use your social skills. And learn when it's time to run, duck, or hide.

God, help me detach when immediate disengagement is what's required.

I jumped out of the plane, and my jump master followed close behind. This was going to be a fun jump. We were going to play Simon Says in the air.

He did a 360-degree turn to the right. I turned, too. He turned to the left, and I did the same. Then he did a back loop. *Okay*, I thought. *Here I go.* I jerked my knees up, but instead of back looping, I rolled onto my side and went into a spin. With each spin, I whirled faster and faster.

I tried to arch, the body position that would get me falling belly down and stable, and make it safe to pull my parachute, but my body movements weren't working the way they were supposed to work. *Maybe if I push my right arm out further, or maybe it's my left leg,* I thought.

My jump master watched me whirling like a fan blade. He tried to catch me each time I whirled around, but he couldn't get ahold. I kept focusing on trying to stop my spin. Finally, he yanked my hand, pointing to my altimeter.

My God, I was getting low. In less than thirty seconds, I'd hit the ground and my life would be done. I'd be dead.

The moral of this story is simple. I learned it when I joined my jump master back on the ground. "What are you going to do," he asked, "spend the rest of your life trying to gain control?"

Sometimes, it's easy to get caught up in a situation. We get so focused on the details of figuring out how to solve a problem that we can't fix, that we lose sight of the time. Our lives are whizzing by, and the ground is coming close.

Have you gotten caught up in trying to control something you can't? If you have, maybe it's time to stop trying to fix it and instead save your own life.

God, grant me awareness of what I need to do to take care of myself.

May 13   **Respect your own timelines**

"Do you have your 'A' license yet?"

I was getting sick of that question. Everyone I knew in sky-diving was pushing through the course, meeting all their requirements, and hurrying to get their license. I knew from the beginning that it wouldn't do me any good to push. This was a sport I needed to get right, and getting it right meant that I needed to learn at my own pace.

"It's the journey, not the destination," I kept telling myself as I watched my fellow sky divers progress, leaving me behind. "Everything happens in its own time."

Finally, I came up with my response. It was November. I proudly announced, whenever asked about getting my license, that I didn't plan on having it until June. I said it over, and over, and over. People left me alone. And I actually began to progress rapidly, after giving myself that much time.

In February, a series of events escalated my learning curve. I did my solo jumps, learned to pack my own parachute, and passed my written test. I had now met all the requirements for my "A" license. All that had to be done was submit the information and I'd have my license in hand.

After sending my material off, I waited an appropriate amount of time, then began checking the mail. Week after week, the license didn't arrive. I waited patiently and continued checking. Toward the end of May, I went into the offices at the skydiving school. I told them I was concerned because my license hadn't arrived yet.

They checked the records. "There was some confusion with the paperwork," they said. "But it's all been straightened out. You'll have your license soon."

When did that license arrive? In June, it came in the mail exactly when I said it would.

Some timing in life is out of our hands. Some isn't. Just as you have power to say *what*, there's a lot of power in saying *when*.

God, help synchronize my timing with yours. Show me if I'm pushing myself unduly or holding myself back.

May 14   **Say when it's time for a change**

Eventually, enough is enough. We have held on to our broken dream until it has become a weight on our back, held on to our broken relationship until we cannot find the strength to give it another go, and clung to expectations, fears, worries, and chains until we can't stand the strain any longer.

We're at a crossroads. One path leads further into familiar territory. The other path leads to a breakthrough. What lies on the other side, we can't see.

It's the void, the unknown, the unknowable.

This isn't death. It's a rebirth, an awakening as profound as that moment when sobriety first takes hold of the lifelong drunk. Or when the confused codependent takes those first steps of self-care.

Are you willing to risk it? Have you reached the point yet where enough is enough? Or will you take the other, more familiar path back to continue rehashing what you've already been through? Sometimes it's easier to stay with our limitations and with what doesn't work. At least then we know what to expect.

Take a chance. Try something new. Go ahead. Step on that new path, even though you're not certain where it will lead. See! Right around the bend is a glowing light. The new path may not be any easier to walk than the old path, but this new road will lead to joy.

For now it's enough to be willing to change.

To do that, step into the void.

God, help me see the things that I need to let go of to continue my growth. Help me walk away from what's comfortable and known into the unknown and what I can't see or predict.

May 15   Say when it's time for plan B

I exited the plane, enjoyed my free fall, then checked my altimeter.

Pull time.

I deployed my parachute, waiting for that sweet whooshing sound, the one that meant I had a working canopy open. I didn't hear the sound. I was leaning backwards and turning, instead of floating softly toward the ground. I didn't have to do my eight-point canopy check. I knew immediately that something was wrong.

Ever since I had begun skydiving, I had been aware that although things mostly go well, sometimes they don't. For a while, I dreaded the possibility that something wouldn't be right with my canopy on opening, that I might have to cut it away. To deal with the fear and dread, I planned on having to use plan B—cutting away my main and pulling my reserve—each time I jumped out of the plane.

It was time to execute plan B.

Whoosh. What a sweet sound that was, as the reserve canopy opened over my head.

Most of us have plans and ideas about how we think an activity, or a relationship, or a job, will go. We marry, and we expect the relationship to flourish. We date someone, and we expect that person to be at least a decent sort of being. We begin a friendship with someone because something about that person has attracted us, drawn us in. We accept a job or work offer—or hire someone to work for us—and we have some idea how things will proceed. We hope things will work out well.

Life is like skydiving. There are no guarantees. And while we may do everything right and properly, sometimes things just don't work out. While it isn't healthy or advisable to run from every problem, sometimes we need to cut away major malfunctions.

It's okay to have a plan. But take the time to develop a plan B, too. Know what you're going to do if plan A doesn't work out. Sometimes it's easier to come up with an option or an emergency procedure if we think it through before the crisis occurs. Then we don't have to panic. We can just institute the plan we rehearsed.

Have you reviewed your emergency procedures today?

God, give me the alertness to recognize when it's time to cut away a malfunction. Give me the presence of mind to save my own life.

May 16   Only you can assess what to do

It was about my fiftieth skydive. I was determined to master this spinning thing. When my turn came, I went to the door, pulled myself outside, then gave myself the count. Ready, set, go. I released my hold and let myself fall into the air.

At first, I fell stable, belly down. Then that dang spinning thing started. I tried to correct my body posture. That didn't help. The last time this had happened, I had spent so much time trying to correct the problem, I had lost awareness of my altitude. I had gotten obsessed with the problem and lost track of time—not a good thing to do on the ground, and even worse to do while falling through the air.

I remembered my jump master's words: *What are you going to do, spend the rest of your life trying to gain control?* Instead of making further attempts to solve the problem, I would stop it now. By pulling. I yanked my rip cord. Instead of hearing that sweet whooshing sound, the one the parachute makes when it opens correctly, I heard a heavy thud. I looked up. I had been spinning so fast when I opened that I had a knotted mess of line twists and a wad of material over my head.

I had experienced line twists before—a few twists that could be kicked out with a little effort. This was different. It looked like a Chinese braid over my head.

This just isn't working, I thought. I pulled my cutaway handle, freeing the knotted mass of stuff over my head, then immediately pulled my reserve parachute. It opened sweetly and immediately. I looked at my altimeter. I was at nine thousand feet. This was going to be a long ride down.

About five minutes later, I floated back to the ground. I threw my parachute over my shoulder and tromped back to the student room. When asked what happened, I explained my story. It was full of "should's." *I should have been able to stop spinning. I shouldn't have opened so high.* I apologized for what I had done and for the fact that my rented parachute, which I cut away so high, was going to be tough to find.

"This wasn't an ideal situation," said the manager of the school. "But it's your life. Only you can decide what to do to save it. It's up to you and you alone to decide what's right to do."

Some situations aren't ideal. Maybe we shouldn't be in them in the first place and maybe we should have known better. But the facts are what they are. Don't let shame stop you from taking care of yourself. What are you going to do?

Talk to other people. Get opinions. Read books. But it's your life—your relationship, your financial situation, your job, your home. It's up to you to decide what's best for you. You're the one who will ultimately live with the results of any decision you make. Assess the situation, and decide what's right for you.

Take responsibility for your decisions and for how best to live your life.

God, help me stop waiting for others to approve of what I do or don't do. Guide me in my decision-making and help me trust the choices I make.

May 17   Sometimes it takes a lot to say *when*

At times we say *when* with relative ease. We say, "No thanks, this isn't right for me," and we walk away. There are other times when it's harder to set a boundary or enforce a new limit or decision with people.

Jan and Patrick had a tough time saying *when* to their grown daughter, Elizabeth. Elizabeth had moved out of the house. She wanted her independence. But she still wanted her mom and dad's money. She would make deals with them—help me buy this car, or put this deposit on an apartment, then I'll pay you back. Then she wouldn't keep her part of the bargain. Mom and Dad continued to send money, even though they had threatened, warned, and tried to deal with the situation in a rational, loving way. They didn't want to alienate their daughter. And they didn't want her suffering, which is what Elizabeth claimed she would do if she was "cut off."

One day, Jan and Patrick sat down with the calculator. They figured out how much support they'd been contributing to

Elizabeth's life. They decided it was time to shut off the money supply. "The only time she called was when she wanted money anyway," Patrick said. "Jan and I figured that there wasn't much left of the relationship to lose."

They gave Elizabeth a three-month warning. The money faucet was shutting off on this date. When that date arrived, the money stopped. A few days later, Elizabeth called back, ranting and raving. She said not only she, but all her friends, thought her parents were despicable for not helping her out, the way good parents should.

"The guilt I felt was overwhelming," Jan said. "But I also knew that was one of Elizabeth's favorite tricks. She used our guilt to control us. It was painful. Setting this boundary, this limit, took most of our energy for that entire year—the year of cutting Elizabeth off financially, pushing her out of the nest."

It's now been a few years since Jan and Patrick set that boundary. Elizabeth has taken financial responsibility for herself. She didn't starve, nor did she go homeless. She was much more resourceful than her parents believed. Jan and Patrick still send her gifts, still take her out for dinner, but they no longer support their grown daughter financially. Their relationship with their daughter has shifted onto new ground. Conversations are no longer about money.

Saying *when* can be uncomfortable for the person saying it, and for the person hearing it. It sometimes involves more than an immediate decision or reaction; it involves a lifestyle change for the people involved. You may need to stand behind your *when* with focus, dedication, and commitment.

Don't expect it to be easy to say *when* and mean what you say. Leave room for other people to have their emotions about your boundaries; give yourself room to have some feelings, too.

God, grant me the energy and commitment to say when *and stand behind it.*

May 18   **Use your creativity in saying** *when*

Grace was the single parent of a seventeen-year-old son—Shawn. Shawn was charismatic, powerful, strong-willed, intelligent, and chemically dependent.

Grace loved Shawn deeply. But she also felt trapped by his rebellious teenage years, coupled with his drug and alcohol usage. Shawn had been through treatment once, did well for a while, then had relapsed. Shawn had a driver's license and a car. In his sober times, Shawn handled the responsibility of the car well. And the agreement was, if Shawn relapsed, he would relinquish the keys.

The problem with chemical dependency is that denial and lying go hand in hand with the disease. When Shawn began using again, he also began lying to his mother. It didn't take long for Grace to see and understand what was going on. She knew what her boundary was. Take away the car.

Grace was clear about what she could and couldn't do. She couldn't make Shawn stay sober, but she could refuse to allow him to drive.

Grace took action. She grabbed a screwdriver, went outside, removed both license plates from Shawn's car, and drove directly to the post office. She then mailed the license plates to a friend of the family and asked that friend to keep the plates until Shawn sobered up.

Shawn knew a boundary had just been clearly set. Six months later, when his plates were returned to him, he was sober and ready to respect the responsibility involved with driving an automobile.

Sometimes, it's not enough just to say *when*. We need to get creative in how we say it, too.

God, help me know that you will always be there to guide me in set-ting limits, when it is my responsibility and in my best interests to enforce a particular boundary.

May 19   Tell yourself how long you'll wait

Use deadlines as a tool.

Sometimes, we find ourselves in an uncomfortable situa-tion. We don't know what to do next. We don't know how to solve the problem. We don't know the course that's going to unfold. Maybe we're seeing someone, and the relationship isn't gaining any momentum, but it's not time to push the issue. Maybe all we need to do is give the other person a little space and time to work through his or her stuff. Maybe the business that we're pursuing isn't gaining any momentum, but things may change course. Part of us, the obsessive part, says, "I need to know right now." But the other part of us, the serene, wise part, says "Relax. It's not time. You don't have all the information yet."

Create a deadline, a private one, with yourself. Tell your-self you'll give it six weeks or three months or maybe a year to change course. Then you'll evaluate the data and make a decision about what to do next.

Sometimes, setting a deadline is all we need to do to help ourselves relax. We know we're not trapped. We're not being a victim. We're making a conscious decision to let go and let things unfold.

God, grant me the serenity to not try to force outcomes and solu-tions too soon.

May 20 **Say when it's time to get something done**

Yesterday we talked about using deadlines to help ourselves let go. Self-imposed deadlines can also be a way to focus our energy on a task at hand, especially one we've been putting off.

"I'm going to get up and have the house cleaned by 10:00 A.M." "I'm going to lock myself in the house and have this report written in two days." "I'm going to get the yard cleaned up by the end of the week."

There are many times in life when it's appropriate and healthy to listen to our internal clock about what to do and when to do it. Going with the flow can be a spiritual process, but there are other times when it's helpful to use self-imposed deadlines to help us get the job done.

Do you need to set a deadline for yourself?

God, help me set appropriate deadlines for myself.

May 21 **Say when it's either/or**

A deadline is different from an ultimatum. Deadlines involve the use of time to get something done. Ultimatums use power.

Ultimatums involve two ideas: an *either* and an *or*. Use ultimatums sparingly in your life. Sometimes, however, an ultimatum is the only way to get a person's attention.

Here are some examples: "Either you get sober and stop using drugs, or I'm going to put you in prison." "Either you start working and stop drinking, or I'm going to take the children and leave." "Either you show up for work on time, or I'm going to find someone else to do your job."

Ideally, an ultimatum is not used to control the other person.

It is an expression of our limits—a powerful way of indicating to the other person that we're on the verge of screaming *when*.

Sometimes people use ultimatums as power plays. They use them to play on our fears, particularly our fear of abandonment: "Either you do what I want, or I'll go away." "Either you keep quiet and don't confront my behavior, or I'll get angry and punish you by being mad." This may work for a while, but ultimately, it can backfire.

Don't use ultimatums as power plays, or devices to control the people around you. Don't let other people use ultimatums to control or manipulate you. Use them as last-ditch warning notices that you're about to say *when*.

God, help me be aware of ultimatums, both the ones I dish out and the ones other people use on me.

Activity: Recall a few times people have used ultimatums on you. Did they work? Why or why not? Are you allowing someone to control you now with a spoken or unspoken ultimatum? What's the *either*? What's the *or*? Are you using or overusing ultimatums to control the behavior of the people around you? Be aware of the use of spoken and unspoken ultimatums in your life. Respect their power.

May 22   Say when the price is too high

The cost of a thing is the amount of what I call life which is required to be exchanged for it, immediately or in the long run.
— *Henry David Thoreau*

Consider the young man who was doing great in his high school studies, then suddenly started to fall behind. One day, a teacher pulled the young man aside and asked him what happened. The student told him that he had asked his father for a car, and the father told him that if he earned the money, he could have one. The student, being industrious and hard working, went out, got a job, saved the money, and bought the car. But then the car needed insurance, gas, and maintenance, so the student kept the job to keep up the car. The job took up more and more of his time, until finally he began to fall behind in his studies.

"Why don't you just get rid of the car?" asked the teacher.

"Get rid of the car?" came the reply, "but how would I get to my job?"

How often we feel that if we just get that new car, that new boyfriend or girlfriend, that promotion, or the condo in the good neighborhood, we will find happiness and contentment —only to discover that the thing just brings with it more pain, more costs, and more bother than it's worth. The new sports car runs only half the time, the new partner needs more care than your dog, the promotion eats up your weekends, and the new condo won't allow pets.

Things don't bring true happiness. Instead, they often sap your strength and leave you emptier than you were before. Think about the true cost of a thing before you pursue it—in time, lifestyle changes, energy, maintenance, and money. Can you really afford the amount of life that the thing will take from you in return for the happiness it brings? Are you willing to pay the price?

God, help me be aware of the true cost of the things in my life.

If you wait for the perfect moment when all is safe and assured, it may never arrive. Mountains will not be climbed, races won, or lasting happiness achieved.

— *Maurice Chevalier*

"I'm just waiting for the time to be right" is a common excuse we use. We can sit on the sidelines, waiting for the perfect moment, but never get in the game. Sometimes, the time doesn't feel right. I was too old when I started to sky-dive, too poor when I started writing, too enmeshed with an alcoholic husband when I began recovering from codependency, and too involved with my addictions when I began recovery. The time may never be right. You can choose to wait until someday arrives, or you can begin now.

Is there a dream hidden away in your life, something you wanted to do but put off for so long that you've almost forgotten what it is? Maybe the time is right to pull it out again. Get the college course guide and sign up. Go to a local gym and start working out. Take a chance.

The right time for the journey is when you begin it. Why not today?

God, motivate me to live a fuller, richer life.

Activity: Pull out your wish list. Choose one thing on your list that has been quietly waiting for the time to be right. Decide that the right time is now. Then begin.

I have a friend who is always planning to start a writing project "as soon as she gets organized." She has read nearly every book, attended every seminar, and bought all the tapes on the subject. She has closets full of organizers, drawers stuffed with folders, and several related computer programs. There's only one problem. Instead of starting, she hides behind a mask of "firsts." "I'll start writing, but first I've got to learn this program." "I'll listen to that tape, but first I've got to read this book."

Are you hiding behind a mask of firsts? Is there always something that keeps you from beginning? Take off the mask. Start the project. Ask that special person for a date. Do that Fourth and Fifth Step. Stop making excuses. Eliminate them.

Learn to say when it's time to begin.

God, please help me eliminate excuses from my life. Show me how full my life can be when I pursue my dreams.

May 25   Say when it's time to do that difficult thing

Sometimes, true windows of opportunity open in our lives. We get a chance to make that amend. The perfect time to end or resolve that relationship arises. It's like a gift from God when that window opens up. All we need to do is gently step through. But sometimes, we need to help God open the window—especially when we're working up the courage to do a difficult thing.

Maybe we're waiting for just the right moment to end a relationship. Maybe we're looking for an opportunity to make an amend, tell someone we're sorry about something we've done that's caused that person pain. Maybe we have a new project we'd like to begin. Sometimes, we can passively wait, and wait, and that window just seems painted shut and stuck.

Ask God to help open the window, but do your part, too. Make a decision that you're going to do it—whatever it is. Then let go, but not too long. Remember your decision. Remember your commitment to opening that window. Don't force it, but focus your attention. You may begin to feel the slightest crack in the energy, that opening you need. Or you may have to wiggle the window frame, push on it just the slightest bit, to crack it open yourself. Then you'll see it. You'll feel it move. There. It's open.

Help God open that window in your life by deciding to do it.

God, help me remember that the time doesn't always feel right. Help me honor my deepest urges to do what I must to take care of myself.

May 26   Go through the door that's open

Sometimes, doors close in our lives. No matter how badly we want something, no matter how hard we've tried, no matter how much we want to pursue a particular course in our lives, the universe says no.

Many years ago, I wanted passionately and desperately to write a book on codependency. All twenty publishers I queried said the same thing: No. Some said it politely. Some said it by refusing to respond at all. That door just wouldn't open up, no matter how hard I pushed.

One publisher came back with a counteroffer. "We don't want the book on codependency," the editor said. "But how about writing something for us on denial—why people do it, what part it plays in their lives, and how they can become more aware and accepting of reality."

I accepted the offer. I needed the work. But I wasn't thrilled. I diligently did my research and wrote the manuscript. About a year later, that same publisher came back to me and asked me to write the book on codependency. I pulled out all my notes and research, including a large notebook in which I had jotted down all my ideas and questions on the subject. As I went through this notebook, I noticed a question written in such large letters it took up the entire page: "What about denial—what part does this play in codependency?" I had written on the next page: "Why do people do it; how can they stop? Help me understand," I had written, almost as a prayer.

I reused the denial concepts in my codependency book. I had long forgotten about my question to the universe. But God hadn't.

Sometimes when doors shut, it's because we're not ready to walk through the one we want. Maybe the door that's open in your life is the one you need to walk through. Go ahead, step in. Look around. It might not appear to be as exciting as the one you'd hoped would open, but maybe it's exactly where you need to be.

Are you trying to push through a door that's closed in your life? Make life easier on yourself. If you've diligently tried to open a door and it's not budging, look around. Push on a few other doors. See which one opens. Then walk through that one.

God, help me trust your timing in my life. Help me understand that sometimes you know more about saying when *than I do.*

May 27   Say when it's not right for you

Not all doors that open up are good for us to walk through.

Sometimes, we're in that dark corridor, and no doors or windows are open. Then, a crack of light appears. We get an offer—for a job, for a relationship, for a place to live. Our gut goes off. We know this isn't right for us. If we weren't desperate, we wouldn't consider it.

You're not desperate. Even if you are, act as if you aren't. If it's not right for you, it's not right for you. Back off—even though you may be burning with impatience and desperation.

You don't have to do anything that's not right for you.

God, grant me a spirit of serenity and patience. Help me take a moment before making any decision to ask for guidance first.

May 28   **Say when it's time to focus**

I was getting ready to make a skydive. I had a lot going on at the time—problems with construction workers, some phone calls I needed to make.

"Put it all aside for right now," Andy, my jump master, said. "The only thing in the world you're going to focus on for the next hour is the skydive you're going to make. You don't want to be jumping out of that plane with other stuff going on in your mind."

I did what he said. I deliberately pushed aside all other thoughts of people, what they were feeling, what I had to do, and how they were going to respond.

"That's one of the benefits of skydiving," Andy said. "It's really taught me to focus my mind."

Sometimes we get interrupted. Sometimes it's good to let our consciousness flow and our minds wander. Sometimes it's time to focus on one task and let other cares and ideas slip away. We have so much power in this marvelous world. One of the powers available to us is dedication, commitment, and focus on the task at hand.

Learn to focus on one thing you want to do. If you've been

struggling with and procrastinating about something, make a commitment to focusing on that task until it's done.

God, help me learn to focus my energies on the essential tasks at hand.

May 29   **Say when it's time to seek shelter**

There's a saying that a boat may be safe when it's in harbor, but that isn't what boats were made for. But let's not forget the value of safe harbors either. A wise sailor knows the limits of each boat and will seek shelter if the weather becomes more than it can bear.

Seeking out new experiences, meeting new people, living life to its fullest is one of the best reasons for being alive. The purpose of recovering from addictions and learning to take care of ourselves isn't to keep us stuck perpetually in therapy. It's to free us to live our lives. But we need to be aware of our limits. And there is no reason to put yourself into a situation of unnecessary risk.

Only you can be the judge of that in your life. We each have different levels of freedom and similar but unique needs. A strong ocean liner can weather much stronger storms than a small powerboat. You may be able to withstand more or less pressure than someone else. Push your limits occasionally; that's how we grow and change. But know what those limits are, and be willing to seek shelter when the storms come.

You are not alone. Whether through meditation or prayer, secular or religious support groups, Twelve Step or self-help meetings, a harbor exists in which you can ride out the storms and remain strong to sail the exciting waters of life another day.

Do you know where your harbors are? Lives are meant to be lived, so live yours as fully as you can. But remember that you cannot live fully when you're recovering from storm damage. Be bold, but be safe.

God, help me be aware during times of stress that a safe harbor exists.

Activity: List your safe harbors. Examples of this might be friendships that are completely safe and supportive, support groups, prayer, meditation, and places of worship. How often do you need to connect with these harbors to keep yourself in good shape? Be aware that when you go through periods of stress and distress—and these times appear frequently in our lives—you might need to seek extra shelter to keep yourself safe from the storm.

May 30   Give yourself time

Set deadlines. Say *when*. Stop waiting for that perfect time. But be gentle with yourselves and others.

Too much waiting is a trap. Waiting, counting the days, months, and years, waiting for someone or something outside of ourselves to make us happy and magically bring us what we want is a pit. If you fall into it, climb out.

But be gentle with yourself, too. If you're tackling something new—whether it's learning a new craft, beginning a new relationship, or recovering from alcoholism or codependency, give yourself time to reach your goals, to begin to get it, to understand.

Some revelations, insights, and illuminations are received in a moment, a second. But the work of assimilating new ideas and translating them into lifestyle changes takes time.

A friend of mine called me one day. He had lost his best friend and roommate to a sudden illness three months earlier. "What's wrong with me?" he said. "My spiritual beliefs are intact. I work hard on myself. Yet I break down crying, for no reason. I'm a wreck. Why aren't I over this yet?"

"Because it takes time," I said. "Give that gift to yourself."

The seeds of change grow gently, sometimes almost imperceptibly. Birth takes time. Transformation takes time.

You are being transformed and reborn.

Give yourself and others the gift of time.

God, help me let go of unrealistic expectations of how quickly I, or others, need to grow and change. Help me know that I have all the time I need.

May 31   Let go of timing

"Melody, it just isn't time yet," my friend Virginia said to me one day. "You wouldn't be out on your lawn trying to pull the blades of the grass up, forcing them to grow."

"Yes, I would," I said, "if I thought it would help."

Persistence, determination, clarity, and commitment can be our greatest assets. We gather energy, we use our determination to get things done—whether it's cleaning our house, visiting a therapist for help with an issue that's become more than we can handle alone, looking for a new job, or beginning a relationship.

Goals are good. Setting our sights on the task ahead is helpful.

So is letting go, and working with the seasons of our lives.

We are one with everything that is. The same energy and spirit that permeates the ocean, the mountains, the forest, and the creatures also permeates us. Who are we to think that we don't have our rhythms, seasons, and cycles?

Who are we not to trust the rhythms of life?

Plant the seeds. Water them, if there's a drought. But let it go. The grass will grow itself.

God, help me let go of impatience. Help me align myself with the natural cycles of my life. Help me trust your timing in my life.

Activity: Pick one segment of nature and study it. Maybe you'll choose the sunrise and the sunset. Or choose a favorite park. Or the ocean. Even a lake will do. Don't just think about it. Actually do it, for your meditation time today. Spend ten minutes to half an hour just sitting with and contemplating a segment of nature that speaks to you.

June

Learn to Say Relax

In skydiving, there is a position called the arch. It is a body position where the body is specifically arched from the neck down. The theory behind this is that gravity always works, and if the hips are arched, the sky diver will fall facedown toward the earth in a balanced, stable body position.

The trick to this body position is that it must be maintained in a relaxed way. If the sky diver doesn't relax enough, the body will bounce around, maybe even flop over. Or, legs and arms won't be in the right position, and the sky diver may start spinning out of control.

It is a deliberate, assertive, yet relaxed posture. It's a place sky divers call "home."

"You have to practice your arch," my jump master had instructed. "And you have to learn to relax."

"How," I said quietly and sincerely, "do you expect me to relax when I'm falling through the air at 120 miles an hour to my certain death if everything doesn't work out right?"

"Practice," he said. "Get out of your head and let your body remember how it feels."

During free fall, I was stable. I grinned at my instructor. This was fun. Then for a second, I tensed up. I started wobbling through the air, feeling like I was out of control. Finally, I took a deep breath and let myself relax.

There it was again. I had finally found home.

Whether we're chasing our dreams, trying to let go of a relationship, trying to raise our family, trying to get to know ourselves better, recovering from a dependency, healing from a loss, or just plain going about our lives, we can find that place called "home," too—even when it feels like we're falling to the ground at 120 miles an hour.

Part of the language of letting go is learning to say *relax*.

God, teach me to relax inside, even when it feels like the last possible thing I can do.

June 2

I think that change often slips in when we're relaxed inside of ourselves.

— Sark

Relax. Calm yourself down. Breathe consciously.

You don't have to take a nap to relax, but sometimes it helps. So does taking a hot shower, walking through a forest, wading in a stream, drinking a cup of tea, going for a swim, watching a movie, listening to music, saying a prayer, meditating, getting a back rub, looking at the moon, or hearing a good joke.

Become conscious of how your body feels when you're relaxed inside. How do you stand, walk, sit, breathe?

Become conscious of how you feel and what you think when you're relaxed. It's almost like nothingness, only you're awake and aware. There are no angry thoughts and feelings. No frightened thoughts and feelings.

Practice relaxing until you can take that relaxed feeling with you no matter where you go or what you're doing.

When's a good time to relax? When you can't do anything about whatever's bothering you. When you're afraid. When you're certain that you have to do something, but you don't know what that something is. When you're meeting someone for the first time, obsessing, feeling guilty, grieving, feeling lonely, telling someone how you feel, balancing your checkbook, falling in love, getting a divorce, climbing a mountain, or learning to do something new.

When you practice relaxing inside, you're practicing peace.

Practice peace until you can do it perfectly.

God, help me learn to consciously relax inside of myself.

June 3   **Say *relax* when you start to worry**

Sometimes we tire ourselves out before we have even begun. We struggle and wrestle with our spirit before finally consenting, giving in, and deciding to walk our path. Then when we start, we wonder why we're so tired.

Why do these things happen to me? What will happen if I try this idea? Where will I go if she leaves me? How will I live without him? What if I don't do it right? What if?

The path is sometimes uphill. Walk up the hill. Sometimes we have to go around an obstacle. Go around it. When we spend time and energy fussing, complaining, and questioning the road before us, we rob energy from ourselves—energy that could be better spent on the journey.

Relax. Accept the path before you. A flat path would be boring. If we could see all the way to the end of the road from where we are standing, then what would be the point of walking it? Quit fighting the journey and start enjoying it.

God, keep me from the exhausting practice of worry and resentment. Let me trust in you and the universe.

June 4   **Stop trying so hard**

Stop trying to force and make things happen. Don't you see that by pushing so hard, you're sabotaging yourself?

There's another way, a better way.

Surrender—not to the way you want things to be, but to the way things are, right now. Sometimes that means we surrender to loneliness, defeat, confusion, and helplessness. Sometimes that means we don't get what we want today. Instead we get what we have today.

We're not in control of many things and circumstances in this world. By forcing things, we often disconnect from our true power, instead of aligning with it.

Maybe something has to happen first, before you can get what you want or do what you want. Maybe there's an important lesson you're trying to skip. Maybe it's not time. Stop trying so hard to push and force, to make it happen. Stop trying to do the impossible, and instead do what you can do—surrender to the way things are.

Then watch how naturally the impossible falls into place.

God, help me stop trying so hard to force things into place. Help me remember that all is well.

June 5   You don't have to exert that much control

"Hey Killer, how about relaxing the old death grip there."

Why did he always say that? Probably because I always got nervous and held the yoke too tightly. Rob, my flight instructor, was teaching me basic maneuvers in the little Cessna 172 trainer again. He wanted me to put the plane into a steep turn. The only problem was that every time I tried, I felt as though the little plane would fall out of the sky. I know. It's crazy. But knowing didn't help my feeling very much.

"Here, watch this. I have the controls," Rob said. And taking the controls, my instructor put the plane into a sharply banked turn. Then he let go of the yoke. "Aaaaah!" I yelled. Nothing happened. The little airplane kept turning with no further input from anyone. "You see," Rob explained, "when you have the trim settings adjusted right, the airplane will do what you tell it to do. There's no need to force it. Now relax and try again."

I did, and the turn was better this time. Maybe the plane wouldn't fall out of the sky after all. And another small piece of the puzzle got filled in.

There are many things that we can do to keep our lives on course. We can talk to our mentors and sponsors, read positive books, attend support groups, listen to positive music, pray, meditate, work a recovery program if we're in one, and grow. We don't want to become complacent. Safety consciousness is important. But once we have set ourselves on course, it isn't necessary to constantly be worried about falling out of the sky.

Set your plan in motion. Get on the right track. But remember that if saving your life is important, it is also important to have a life worth saving. Relax a little. The plane will keep on flying as long as you give it the right input.

God, grant me the grace to relax, to let go of worry and self-doubt, and to let myself enjoy life and the experiences that it has to offer.

June 6   Let go of tension

In *Find and Use Your Inner Power*, author Emmet Fox used the metaphor of trying to force a key into the lock to unlock the door. When we're tense and afraid, Fox explained, we fumble. Sometimes the very key that is the right key doesn't work because we're trying to force it, because we're so tense and uptight.

Relax. See! The less control and force you use, the better.

Maybe the key you've been trying to use all along is the right one. Maybe it was your fear and panic that was keeping you from unlocking the door. Maybe you were trying to force it, after all.

See how easily and naturally things work out when you just simply relax and let go. You will tap into your true power and the power of the universe when you move, love, work, and play from a place of relaxed and calm inner peace.

Move from your center. Let things work out.

God, help me stay serene, confident, and joyful as I go through my day.

June 7   You've got all the time you need

If we believe our relationships or jobs are finite situations, then it becomes easy to feel stressed if things don't go the way we planned in the time frame that we expected. The promotion doesn't come in time, and now our careful career plan is off track. And relationship problems become huge, dramatic monsters—a series of issues—that eat away every spare minute.

But if we believe that we are living in an infinite time frame, stress begins to dissipate. If I don't get the promotion this week, maybe it will come next month and who knows, I may not even want it by then. Some of those big, monstrous relationship issues just sort themselves out if they're not constantly held under a magnifying glass. And the moments spent with our loved ones become more enjoyable because we're not continually *working* on the relationship.

When we behave on a finite scale, we can get so wrapped up in the details of a few moments that we cannot free ourselves to enjoy the next moment. When we start living on an infinite plane, it is easier to relax and let the universe carry us down the river, bringing us to all the lessons and joy that we need.

God, help me relax and know that if a situation doesn't come to pass today, eventually it will work itself out. And I've got all the time I need.

June 8   Let go of judgments

We can't relax when we're being judgmental. As soon as we decide that a thing or situation is either good or bad, we place ourselves in the situation of having to do something about it. For example, if someone is good, we begin to compare ourselves to that person: *Am I better or worse? What can I do to improve?* If we decide that a thing is bad, then our conscience tells us that we must try to get rid of it.

Either way, we get so busy thinking about our judgments and allowing our minds to create scenarios that we cannot relax and enjoy things the way they are.

Drop your judgmental mind today and relax. If blessings or good people have come into your life, let them be. You do not have to be better or worse than they are.

If a thing is damaging or hurtful to you, you will know that and you can deal with it when the time comes.

Be aware of the people and things in your life. Relax and enjoy them without passing judgment on them.

God, help me learn to enjoy the people and experiences in my life.

June 9   Manifest your life

Today, try this activity: Go down to the local hardware store and buy a patio stone. Get one of the nice flat round ones, one that will fit into your briefcase or backpack. Take that patio stone home and look at it. Then take out a marker and start to think about one of your goals that you wrote on the list at the start of the year. Think about all that is keeping you from reaching that goal—all your fears, excuses, and pre-requisites. Each time you think of a reason why you are not walking down that path, write it on the stone in marker. Keep writing until you can't think of another reason.

Then carry the stone with you. You did write down a fear of looking ridiculous, didn't you? Carry the stone to dinner—hold it on your lap while you eat. Hold it while you watch TV, while you go to the bathroom, in the shower, and even to bed this evening. Tomorrow, spend the day with your stone. Let it be a reminder of both your dream and your fear. Feel how rough, heavy, and cumbersome it is. Makes it kind of difficult to get anything done, doesn't it? Now, at the end of the day, sit down again with your stone. Look at all of your excuses written there. Make a conscious decision to let them go. Put down the stone—put it right next to the front door. Feel how much lighter your step is, how much easier it is to do things. Now, as you leave for your day each morning, look at the stone sitting there on the step—heavy, rough, cumbersome—and leave it there. Let life and the elements wear your fears away.

You have dreams, hopes, ambitions. All of your fears and excuses are stones, which fill your hands and weigh you down. Leave them behind. Start to manifest your dreams in your life.

God, help me let go of everything that is blocking me from fully and joyfully living my life today.

June 10   Let go of guilt

Guilt is a rock. It lies in the pit of our stomachs and keeps us awake at night. All of our muscles work overtime just to carry it around, and yet we still hold on to it.

Yesterday, you stumbled. That was yesterday. But you also righted your wrong and vowed to do better today. So why are you still carrying that guilt around with you?

If you're in recovery, you probably did some terrible things before you got sober. How can you ever move on? But you got sober. You made amends. What happened yesterday belongs to yesterday. Today, you can let go of your guilt and relax in the peace that comes from walking a path with heart.

Have you made a list of people you have harmed and made amends to them, as suggested in the Eighth and Ninth Steps of the Twelve Step programs? That's an excellent way to begin clearing and releasing guilt. If you're not in a Twelve Step program, there are other options. Most religions offer rituals to clear guilt. Sometimes, we've taken all these steps and we still feel guilty. What's wrong? We're hanging on to our guilt, and we're being hard on ourselves.

You will find it easier to relax and flow through the experiences of your life if you let go of the weight of yesterday's guilt.

God, today I give you all of the guilt from my past. Take it from me, and allow me to begin fresh right now. Help me make the amends I need to make, then let my guilt go.

Activity: If you've taken steps to make amends and clear away your legitimate guilt, and your guilt is still haunting your every move, try this: First thing in the morning and last thing in the evening, look in your mirror. Look yourself in the eye. Then say out loud seven times, "I now release all my guilt, earned and unearned." Try this for a week. See if your guilt doesn't disappear.

Do you walk around wearing a suit of armor? Often, if we were hurt as children or hurt frequently as adults, we put on a suit of emotional armor to protect us from being hurt more. We lower our visor to avoid seeing the pain and block out all hurtful sights. We pick up weapons, sharp words, manipulative behaviors, acting out—anything to help us defend ourselves against those who would hurt us again. We get used to being in battle and soon all of life is a struggle.

Stop fighting. Yes, you have been hurt. Many of us have. But when you project the characteristics of one person onto everyone you know, you don't allow their true selves to shine through. All you can see is the limited view from your visor.

You are growing and gaining strength every day. You're safe now. Why not put down the weapons for a little while, lift the visor on your suit of armor, and see the people around you for who they are—mostly kind, good-hearted ordinary people just like you. They have been hurt and healed; they have won and lost. They laugh and they cry. Open up to them, and allow the sharing to begin to heal you and your heart.

God, help me to lower my defenses today, to be open to the good in the people around me and to the good that I have to offer them.

June 12   **Relaxing will help your work**

Joe is a professional chef. He started working in kitchens before he was in his teens. Gradually, he worked his way up from washing dishes until he found himself running a successful catering operation. The only problem was, the more successful the business became, the less time Joe had for the rest of his life. Joe reveled in the knowledge that he was the hardest-working guy he knew. In his mind, the company existed solely because he was there.

Joe was surprised when his wife left him for someone less successful.

"How could she do that to me?" he moaned to friends. "I worked my tail off so she could have nice things and this is how she repays me?" Then one day while catering a wedding, he realized what had happened. He hadn't been present for his marriage. He had fallen victim to his own success, imprisoned by the company he had created. He took a day off. Then a weekend. Then he trained an assistant to help run the company. It cost him money at the outset, but he discovered life in the process. "I was so busy being a success," he says, "that I didn't realize how miserable I was." When he took a vacation to the Southwest, his culinary instincts got the best of him and he spent half of the vacation learning new recipes, but he had fun. "For the first time in years, I was playing in the kitchen again rather than just working," Joe says.

Today Joe has discovered the joy of balance. He no longer feels that he alone must bear the weight of the world, and is stronger for it. His business is growing and he has gotten a reputation as an innovator, largely due to things he has learned while not in the kitchen. When we're successful, it's difficult to take time away from our work; it feels like the success that we worked so hard for will slip away if we're not there tending to it every moment. The truth is, we get so busy earning a living that we forget to have a life.

Take some time to see if you could spend a little less time at the office and a little more time with yourself and the ones you love. You might be pleasantly surprised at the effect a break can have on your motivation and the joy you have for what you do.

God, teach me—and help me learn—to have fun in my life, my work, and my relationships with the people I love.

June 13   Relax and flow

I visited the Hoover Dam in Nevada some time ago and marveled at its construction and purpose. Here was a huge structure that had been built into a canyon to harness the power of thousands of tons of moving water.

The water flows through the machinery, and the energy of the moving water is transformed into electricity that powers thousands of homes and businesses. But it wouldn't work if you dammed up a lake, because the water has to be moving for it to have power.

The secret to the power is in the flowing.

How often we try to stifle the flow of events in our lives with control. We think that if we could only get things to go the way we want, then everything would be all right. We take the energy of the universe and bottle it up. And we kill its energy.

Let go of control.

Let the energy of life flow through and around you. You can learn to direct the flow, but you don't need to control it. Become open to the energy that is flowing around you, and rather than trying to bottle it up, let it flow. Energy is useful only when it is flowing.

Relax and go with the flow of the universe. You'll be better able to harness its power.

God, help me let go of my need to control. Help me let go of my fear.

"I like skydiving with Todd," Pat said. "He's got such a good attitude. When you're in the air with him, no matter what happens, you just get the feeling that everything's okay."

Being relaxed is contagious. Just as someone who's miserable, frightened, and negative can affect the people around him or her, being relaxed, clear, and humbly confident can affect the people we touch, too. Have you ever known anyone like that—someone with a sense of humor, someone who's surrendered, full of joy, and at peace with himself or herself? This is someone who not only knows things are going to be okay—that person knows things are okay now.

Today, if you are going to spread anything, let it be joy and goodwill.

God, help me lighten up. Make my joy contagious.

Activity: Today, watch yourself as you go through your day. If you were a neutral observer of yourself, how would you describe yourself? What words would you use? Which words would you like to use to describe yourself? Watch your interactions with other people—people you know and strangers, such as clerks in stores and banks. Don't judge yourself, just observe. Awareness is the key. Become aware of who you are, how you respond to other people, and how they react to you. Decide what attitude you'd like to share with the people in your world.

June 15   **Live in harmony**

When I began practicing aikido—a martial art based on nonresistance and harmony—I discovered how much resistance I still had. The more I tried to relax and practice nonresistance, the more resistance I experienced. I lived, moved, breathed, worked, lived, and loved from a place that was not relaxed.

My immediate reaction to any feeling I had was, "Oh, no. I can't feel that."

My first reaction to any problem that arose was, "No, this can't be taking place."

If someone disagreed with me, I responded with an attack or by trying to force my will.

And if I had a task to do, I prepared myself by getting tense and afraid.

One of the biggest challenges and biggest rewards we can discover in our lives is to live in harmony with ourselves and the people in our world. We do this by learning to tell ourselves, "Just relax."

From that relaxed place, which some call surrender, we'll tap into our true power. We'll know how to deal with our feelings. We'll be guided into what to do next.

God, show me the areas of my life where I'm in resistance. Help me let go and learn to consciously relax as I go through my life.

June 16   Deal with manipulation

A few years ago I was in Jordan on an excursion through the Middle East. I wanted to go to Pakistan, but when I got to the Pakistani embassy in Jordan, an official ordered me to go to the American embassy, miles away, saying, "You have to get a piece of paper from your government vouching for you. That's the only way the government of Pakistan will even consider your request."

I went to the American embassy in Jordan and stood in line

there all day. Finally, when it was my turn, I told the gentleman why I was there. "That's ridiculous," he said. "There's no such thing as an international voucher for people in the United States. That's what a passport does. It says the American government is vouching for you, declaring you worthy and reliable to travel abroad."

He began to speak more quietly. "He's just messing with you," he said, of the government official at the other agency. "Sometimes they like to play games with people, show them how much power they really have."

I went back to the Pakistani embassy. When I returned, there was an elderly Muslim man sitting in the waiting room. He wore a turban. His head was bowed. He was reciting the Koran and rubbing his string of prayer beads.

He helped set the tone and reminded me of what I needed to do: calm down, be peaceful, stop resisting, and harmonize with the situation. It didn't matter if the visa man was wrong and I was right. He had the power. I needed to go to him. I sat quietly waiting for my turn. When I went up to the counter, I deliberately acknowledged his point of view. Then I gently explained that I didn't get the piece of paper he asked for from the American embassy, because that paper didn't exist. I explained it was probably the only time in my life I'd be in this area of the world. I pointed to the poster on the wall. "The Himalayas are so beautiful there," I said. "If I don't go now, I don't know that I ever will. You have the power to say yes or no. And I have no choice but to go along with whatever you say. It's in your hands."

He told me to go sit down. I did. Five minutes later, he called me back to the stand. "Here," he said, handing me my passport. "Enjoy your visit to Pakistan."

We have a right to get as mad as we want, but sometimes harmonizing can achieve so much more than yelling in indignation or even fighting back. Next time you find yourself in a situation where you're being manipulated, let go of your resistance and practice harmony instead.

God, teach me the power of moving gently, with humility and respect, through the world.

June 17   Relax when things don't go as you planned

So, the boyfriend calls, says he's going hiking with his buddies for a week, cancels his date with you, and says he hopes you won't be mad.

Or the bank calls and says you're overdrawn, and you don't know how that can be. You've been trying to carefully watch your deposits and checks. You've gone out of your way not to mess up. This can't be right!

What do you do when life seems to force you to react? You can panic, become anxious, yell, and respond with a counterattack. But that probably won't solve the problem. And it may turn things into a brawl.

Or you can calm down. Breathe deeply. Tell yourself to relax. Say as little as possible, if that's possible, while you're upset and disturbed. If a problem or disturbance that's not fair interrupts your life, try responding by saying "hmmm." Then calm down and decide what you need to do.

There's a time to get upset, yell, scream, and shout. But that time isn't when you're trying to sort out problems. Before you take action, get centered, calm, and clear.

You will discover that when you're centered and calm, you're more powerful than you think.

God, help me start sailing through life with more ease by learning to relax and let life be.

June 18   **Relax even when you're being attacked**

Attacks can come in many shapes and forms. They can be emotional attacks, where someone pelts us with anger and rage. We can be attacked physically, too.

Self-defense is important. But it's easy to get confused, when we're being attacked, about what it means to take care of and protect ourselves. It may be a boss, a spouse, a child, or a friend who turns on us in anger and rage. We might be dating someone, someone we don't know well, who suddenly starts spewing venom and rage. Instinctively, we may attack back.

If someone yells at us in anger, says something mean, or physically hurts us, we usually don't think twice. We tense up and fight back. Then the situation escalates. The other person's fear and anger contaminate us. We become afraid, angry, and mean, too. Our intense and volatile emotions feed and fuel the situation. Things can easily get out of control.

Instead of escalating the situation into an all-out brawl, try harmonizing and restoring the situation to peace. You might be surprised with the results that learning to relax and harmonize brings. And you'll be closer to connecting with your true power.

God, fill me up with so much peace that my presence neutralizes and deflects attacks, no matter where I might be.

June 19   **Relax enough to face reality**
                   when life twists and turns

Sometimes in life, no matter how deeply we intend to make the best decisions possible for ourselves, things happen. Marriages end, jobs turn sour, friends wane. For reasons outside our control or understanding, the situation twists and turns into something other than what we bargained for.

Have you been waiting for a situation to revert to what it originally was—or what you hoped it would be when you got in? Are you telling yourself that there's something wrong with you, when the reality is, the situation has changed into something other than what you thought it was? Things often don't go as smoothly as we planned. Sometimes, we need to endure and get through the rough spots. But I'm talking about those grindingly difficult moments when life suddenly twists on us.

These are the times we need to quit torturing ourselves. Let go of what you thought would happen. If life has twisted on you, don't turn on yourself. Don't try to make things be the way they were. Come up to speed. Return to now. Let yourself accept the new situation at hand.

The road isn't always a straight course. Sometimes, even a path with heart unexpectedly twists and turns.

God, help me relax and trust myself enough to deal with reality, not my fantasy of what I hoped it would be.

June 20   Relax and face the truth

Sometimes, we have to face things we'd rather not see.

That person we've been dating just isn't someone who is good for us. Our spouse isn't just a social drinker; he or she has a serious problem with alcohol. Our child isn't just being a cute little child anymore, making up silly stories; that child is lying and stealing from us.

Sometimes, these moments of truth are big bombs in our lives. Other times, we run from those smaller moments of truth—we've done something that hurt someone, no matter how defensive and innocent we pretended to be, and we need to face up to that. Maybe our children have grown up and left home and we've been running from that truth, pretending that we still need to center our lives around them. Or maybe the truth is, we are feeling angry, abandoned, or hurt.

We all have moments of truth in our lives.

I was talking to a friend one day. He had been complaining that his air purifier didn't work. I was going to the repair shop, so I offered to take his machine in and get it fixed.

"It's plugged in," he said. "I got it to turn on, and I can't afford to be without it."

"You've got it turned on, but it's not working right?" I asked. "You're without it now."

Relax. Let your illusions go. Turn and face whatever you're running from. Not facing the truth doesn't make the truth go away, no matter how much we hope it will.

If you've been running from the truth in some area of your life, gently begin to face what you've preferred to avoid. The power is in the truth.

God, help me let go of my illusions. Help me understand the power that comes when I take the time to see clearly and have my moments of truth.

June 21   Calm yourself first

Calm yourself.

Many incidents will come to pass in our lives. Sometimes, things happen to get our attention, to point the next lesson out, to help guide us along our path. Sometimes, things just happen.

Our emotional responses to the world are important. How do you feel? What do you like? What don't you like? Have you been denying something, something taking place before your eyes? What we sense, what we feel, and, more important, *what we know* deep inside is an important part of our spirit, our connection to the Divine.

It's important not to underreact. It's important not to overreact.

When something comes up, calm yourself. Feel your emotions. Don't move into denial. Feel each wave of each feeling. Allow your thoughts to pass through you. But the key is not to act on these emotions. Let them pass through you first.

Your power comes from being centered and clear. That's where your answers, insights, and lessons will come from, too.

The first thing to do when something happens is feel what you feel.

The second is calm yourself. From that place of calm, you'll be guided into your next step.

God, teach me to take guided action, not action motivated by turbulent emotions.

June 22   Relaxing is how we heal

Stopping, calming, and resting are preconditions for healing. When animals in the forest are wounded they find a place to lie down and rest completely for many days. . . . They just rest, and get the healing they need.

— *Thich Nhat Hanh*

We hurt. We suffer. We wrong our loved ones and they do wrong by us. Reaching desperately for an answer will not help us. Pretending we're not hurt doesn't help, either. When we are wounded, the wound needs rest in order to heal. So it is with our souls. If we poke at our hurt, pick at the sore, rub it in the dirt of others' opinions, we do not allow it time to heal.

If you've been hurt, accept that. Feel the hurt. Be aware of it. Let it heal. Maybe it would be better if you didn't talk to that person for a while. Maybe you need to let go of the relationship. Maybe you just need some quiet time. Whatever the answer is, find a safe place and allow yourself to heal.

If you're feeling pain, be aware of it. Feel the pain, and then quit picking at the wound. Lie low. Quit fighting. Relax. Give your wounds time and enough rest to heal.

God, help me relax enough to stop, calm down, and heal.

June 23   Relax and enjoy the ride

One of the good things about jumping out of airplanes is that there is at least one aspect of the sport that is impossible to mess up. When you choose to open the door and get out of the plane, one thing is certain: You will fall. There will be wind that you can use to control your movement through the air, and you will get back to the ground. So relax. Enjoy the ride.

Some things in life are that way, too. We can be as tense or as relaxed as we want to and the *thing* will not change—other people, the weather, the driver in front of you on the freeway. Often there is nothing that we can do to affect a situation, and yet we will fight with the universe, tense up, and try to control things rather than just relaxing and learning to use *what is* to the best of our ability.

There is no need to change the universe. It was before this lifetime, and it will be long after you have passed. You can choose to spend your life fighting it, or you can relax, let go of your control, and learn to work with and within it.

Have you been fighting against gravity, trying to get back into the plane? Let go of the uncontrollable situations in your life. Let them be what they are. Relax and learn to work with them rather than against them. You will have more strength and success when you do. You might even have some fun.

God, show me the areas of my life where I'm still trying to exert control over the impossible. Help me let go and enjoy the ride.

June 24   **Find ways to relax**

Recovering alcoholics—and many people who choose not to drink or use drugs—need to find ways to relax that don't involve alcohol, drugs, or medications.

Many of us remember daily that we are choosing not to drink or use drugs. But we may forget that it's important to learn ways to relax our bodies and our minds. Maybe it's time to assertively pursue options for helping us to unwind.

I can tell you things that help me: Hot water—whether it's taking a long shower, sitting in a hot tub, or resting in a bathtub; meditation and visualization; being near a large body of water and if that's not possible, looking at a good picture of the ocean or a beautiful sea; drinking hot herbal tea; massage; music; meditation tapes; a good movie; laughter; deep, conscious breathing; playing the piano; and being outside in the sun.

We each have our own needs, our own methods of calming ourselves down. Do you have a list of what works for you? If you don't, today is a good day to make one.

Today and each day, do at least one thing deliberately that relaxes you. Begin allowing your body to memorize how it feels when it's relaxed; then consciously duplicate that feeling throughout the day whenever you feel yourself become tense.

God, show me ways to relax.

Activity: Begin making a list of the things that help you relax. This is an important part of your self-care list. If it's a long one, great. If it's a short one, pursue other methods of relaxing that are available to you, and add them to this list. Whenever you feel yourself becoming tense, take out your list and actually do one of the things on it—the one that most appeals to you at that moment. Part of getting to know yourself better means becoming acquainted with things that help your body relax.

June 25   **Surrender to God's will**

It was a stressful time in my life. I didn't know what to do. I had pressing business decisions to make and painful relationship issues to face. Everything felt like a mess.

I gathered up a few favorite books, the Bible, a journal, and some clothes. Then I headed for the mountains, a resort that was a favorite place of mine to hide out in and gather my thoughts.

I told myself, "I'm going to stay in there. Write in my journal. Pray. And meditate. I'm not coming out until I know what to do."

After forty-eight hours of writing about my problems, praying about my problems, and meditating about my problems, I remembered something a friend had said to me.

"What are you doing?" he had asked.

"I'm trying to surrender to God's will."

"No you're not; you're trying to figure it out."

Within six months, each of the problems I was wrestling with worked themselves out. I was either guided into an action that naturally felt right at the time, or a solution came to me. The immediate solution to each problem was the same: let go. Just surrender to the situation taking place.

Sometimes, what we need to do next is surrender.

If you don't like the word *surrender*, try calling it *making peace*.

God, help me surrender to your will, especially when I don't know what to do next.

June 26 — Take a time-out

"Tickets! Tickets!" And you give yours to the big man in the beard and the T-shirt at the gate and step onto the carousel. So many choices! Horses and carriages of every color. The white one with the golden tail? The green one with fire in his eyes? Yes, he looks fast—but no, someone else got there first. You settle for the black-and-red horse with the sparkling silver saddle. Someone bumps past, leaving sticky cotton candy on your arm. And then the music starts—loud, creaky organ music blaring through old blown-out speakers. The lights flash on and off, and the world spins around you. Children shriek in delight while you tug on the reins, guide your mount around the course, and try to let go of the nagging suspicion that the green horse would have been more fun. You vow to get back in line and get that one next time.

Step off of the carousel.

Take a break for a moment and watch all the horses go hurrying past. The green one is no better than the red one, just different, and certainly not any faster. All your frantic pulling on the reins is wasted effort, too. See, they come right back again. They keep right on going around whether you are there or not. Let them.

Sure, it's fun to be on the ride, to be right in the middle of all the action, up and down, 'round and 'round, lights flashing, music blaring. Just remember that you have a choice.

You can be on the ride, or you can get off. Be where you want to be, and occasionally, relax.

God, help me remember that I have choices, and relaxing and letting go are two of them.

June 27   Relax inside

Meditation does not have to be hard labor. Just allow your mind and your body to rest like an animal in the forest. Don't struggle. There is no need to attain anything. I am writing a book, yet I am not struggling.

                                                        — *Thich Nhat Hanh*

Life does not need to be a struggle. Yes, there are busy times and slow times in all of our jobs. Deadlines and time-frames, budgets and schedules. But when we struggle, we burn up all of the energy in the fight and have nothing left to give to the project. How much better it is to relax, to work on the project and let go of the deadline. The project will be done when it is done, and we will most likely finish it much faster if we focus on the project, not the deadline.

Are you spending valuable energy fighting and struggling with yourself? *How will I get this done? What if I do it wrong? What if? What if?* Relax. The answers will take care of themselves. Just concentrate on the task at hand—calmly, easily, smiling. The Buddhist have a saying: "If you are finished with your rice, then wash your bowl." The beauty of life is relaxing and being aware of the task at hand. Relax. Enjoy the work you're doing today.

God, help me give up resistance and learn to relax.

"Only two more weeks until vacation," we say. "Two more weeks until I can relax." Then we return to our stressful lives of running here, hurrying there, and scrambling to get this or that done.

Why wait? Why not relax today? Part of living fully in the moment is taking a break when you need it. If you are tired, take a nap. Plan an afternoon away from work. Go to the park on a Saturday morning by yourself. Take a bubble bath; order dinner out; take the kids the zoo.

So often we feel that we are running, running, just trying to keep up with the rest of the world. It's an illusion. Much of the time we're running in place. Stop. The only one keeping you on the treadmill is you. Yes, we all have responsibilities. But taking time to take care of ourselves is one of our responsibilities, too.

God, grant me the peace and grace to listen to my own needs.

A mind too active is no mind at all.

— *Theodore Roethke*

It's possible to learn to relax into the ordinary aspects in your life. Be aware of those normal moments; relax; allow your mind to be quiet. Allow your spirit to speak to you in those moments.

Look at the family sitting at breakfast, the birds gathered around the feeder, the dew on the grass when you step outside to pick up the morning paper, the pattern of the shadows on the walk in the moonlight. Be aware of the beauty of the ordinary. Be aware of these soothing moments and make the most of them. When you learn to be aware and relax into the ordinary, it will be easier to relax in the stressful moments when you need clarity and focus.

The practice of meditation is a practice of mindfulness. It is a practice of becoming aware of and in tune with our bodies, our spirit, and the spirit of God. One of the goals of meditation is to reach a point when we can carry this mindfulness with us throughout the day. When we can still the noise of our chattering minds, we can see the path with heart that we are to follow.

God, help me to quiet my noisy, worrisome mind in my ordinary world. Help me to relax in the familiar and to be aware of and appreciate it.

June 30   **Make yourself at home**

It was night, only a few months after I'd begun my skydiving adventure. It was too cold to stay in my tent; I had rented a cabin near the drop zone. Now I'd come back to hang out for a while, before retiring for the night.

One of the sky divers I'd met recently was sitting in a lawn chair, under the tarped area between the rows of trailers that had been turned into team rooms and student training areas. The evening lights had been turned on. He was wrapped up in a sleeping bag, reading a book under the hazy glow. He was one of the full-time sky divers, who had been attracted to the gypsy lifestyle of the skydiving community as much as the sport itself.

"What are you doing?" I asked.

"I'm in my living room, reading a book," he replied. "Do you like the view of the backyard?" he asked, making a gesture toward the rolling hills that cascaded gently in the background. "That's my patio," he said, pointing to a small area just around the corner. "The morning sun hits there. It's a warm place to sit and eat breakfast. Sometimes I sleep in that tent," he said, pointing off to the side. "And sometimes I take my sleeping bag and curl up under the stars in the landing area, over there."

I looked around, almost envious of his freedom.

Sometimes, we get so busy and involved creating a "home" for ourselves that we create a structure that's too safe, limiting, and confined. We forget about our real home, the planet earth. It's good to sleep indoors. It's nice to make ourselves comfortable in our home. But don't let your cozy nest become a locked, confining box.

Stretch your arms. Push the lid off the box. Get out into the world. Walk around. Move about. See the hills, the lakes, the forests, the mountain peaks, the valleys, the rivers.

See how big your world can be. See how connected everything is. See how connected you are, too—to all that is. Make yourself comfortable, wherever you are. Make yourself a home and be at home in the world.

God, help me relax and make myself at home in your bountiful world.

July

Learn to Say How It Feels

He no longer dreamed of storms, nor of women, nor of great occurrences, nor of great fish, nor fights, nor contests of strength, nor of his wife. He only dreamed of places now and of the lions on the beach.

— *Ernest Hemingway*

Many teachers of our time attribute consciousness—energy not just matter—to all the creations that exist in God's marvelous world. Many teachers from ancient times espoused this philosophy, too.

How does it feel when you sit next to a sprawling oak tree? How does it feel when you lie in the hot sand at the beach, listening to waves splashing on the shore? How does it feel in your kitchen in the morning? How does it feel when you're with your best friend? Or your spouse?

How does it feel to go into a store filled with beautiful objects, stuffy salesclerks, and signs that scream: DO NOT TOUCH?

Many of us are survivors. We learned the art of leaving our bodies early on, perhaps in our childhood or maybe later, as a way of coping with situations that didn't feel good and that didn't feel right to us. We learned to deny how a situation felt—and often how it felt to be with certain people—in order to cope with situations we found ourselves in that we didn't have the tools or the power to escape. We trained ourselves to ignore how things felt because either we told ourselves we had no choice, or we truly didn't have a say in the matter.

We don't have to survive anymore. That time is past. Now, it's time to live.

Come back into your body. Stretch your senses, so that they fill up all of you—your sense of taste, smell, touch, sight, and sound, and your intuitive senses, too. How do you feel emotionally? If you can't put words to it, just describe it as best as you can. Then go to the next level. Tune into the feelings and moods of the world around you, but not so much that you take these feelings on as yours. Tune in just enough to recognize how the energy of each situation feels to you.

Don't judge your responses and feelings as either good or bad. And you don't have to do anything to control how it feels—to you or anyone else. Just allow yourself to experience and recognize how it feels to be you.

Part of speaking the language of letting go means learning to delight and revel in all our senses, including our inner knowing.

Learn to say with trust and confidence, *This is how I feel.*

God, help me come fully to life.

July 2   It's good for your heart

"I know I've got some emotions up, just brewing right beneath the surface," Jake said one day. "I'm edgy, irritable, and definitely not centered. But I don't want to look. I don't want to go into the emotions. I don't like feelings. Whenever I give into them, I end up feeling like a piece of cooked spaghetti—for days."

Emotions can take a lot out of us. Feeling them, whether it's anger, fear, or sadness, can leave us exhausted and drained.

Not feeling our emotions, however, can keep us edgy, irritable, and off-balance. Not feeling our feelings for an extended time can drive us to acting out, whether that means overeating, obsessing, staying in bed and hiding from the world, or staring at the television every night until we pass out.

Be gentle with yourself. Don't force it. But don't run away from your feelings, either. You might feel like cooked spaghetti for a while, but what's really softening up is your heart.

God, help me face and feel any feelings.

July 3   Say what's up today

What's up?

I don't mean the events. You most likely are extremely aware of the events taking place—or not occurring—in your life. What's up emotionally?

Do you feel anxious, scared, ambivalent, wishy-washy, or fiercely determined? Do you feel clever, powerful, blissful, curious, or relieved?

There are many shades and colors, *nuances* of emotions. Some emotions get our attention quickly. They clearly present themselves and we immediately name them and claim them as ours. Sometimes the feelings are not that easy to identify. Those are usually the ones we need to pay the most attention to; those are often the ones that can be controlling our lives.

An important idea to remember about feelings is that they are just emotional energy and we're allowed to feel *however* we feel. There's no right and wrong about emotions; the names are just words we use to identify that particular emotional energy burst.

There's another way we can feel, another space we're each entitled to. That space is called "centered, balanced, and clear." When we identify, feel, and release whatever feeling is *up* each day, we'll easily and naturally return to that quiet, peaceful, centered place.

Sometimes, if the emotional burst is big—of the volcanic size—it might take a few days or a week to return to that clear, centered place. Other times, just an acknowledging nod in the direction of the emotion that's up is all we need to do.

Don't resist. Give in. Give in all the way to what and how you feel. Then just let that feeling float away. The more you give in to whatever you're feeling, the less it will hurt and the more quickly it'll disappear. The more specific you can be about the event or person that's triggering the emotion, the more you'll help yourself slide gracefully through the emotional burst.

Mastering your emotions means taking responsibility for how you feel. Feelings are important, but remember, they're *just* feelings, too. Don't let them define reality, control your life, or color your world. Mastering your emotions means clearing out your emotions so you can live, move, love, work, and play from that peaceful, centered place.

Take a moment today and each day of your life.

Ask yourself, "What's up?"

God, help me become fluent with my emotions. Help me learn to feel whatever I feel, then regularly restore myself to that centered, balanced place.

July 4   **Celebrate your freedom**

Today in the United States, we celebrate our nation's independence. Why not take a moment to celebrate your independence as well? Whether you've found freedom from an addiction or from codependency, or you've discovered the freedom to live your life as fully as possible, take a moment to honor and acknowledge how much that freedom means to you.

It's good to identify our problems. Through the awareness

of what's wrong and what's broken, we learn what to repair and fix. It's good to focus on the health and the goodness in our lives, too. Becoming aware of what's right and what's working is how we discover joy.

Look back along the winding road of the path of your life. See how far you've come? It looks good to me. How does it look to you?

Hurray! We're finally free!

God, thank you for setting me free.

July 5   Balance

In Western medicine, the practice has long been the correction of problems. We have a pain; the doctor identifies its source and treats it. The Eastern approach is different. Many of the Eastern medicines operate from the idea that a healthy body is one that is in balance. When we are sick, it is due to an imbalance in our bodies. The practitioner then seeks to identify the imbalance and restore the body to balance.

Instead of just treating the symptoms of pathos, Eastern medicines seek to maintain balance as a way of life.

That's a good way to approach taking care of our souls.

Perhaps your heart has been injured through the carelessness of another, or maybe your mind is troubled by distressing, uncomfortable, and sometimes wrong thoughts. When we seek to restore balance, our hearts and our souls will heal.

Be aware of the imbalance in the thoughts in your mind and the emotions disturbing your peace. Then listen to your spirit. Let it tell you in its still quiet way what it needs to regain balance. Maybe you need some time alone, time in meditation or prayer, a quiet walk, a day at the zoo, or some sleep.

Give your body and soul what you need to regain balance, and then healing can begin. Learn to lovingly listen to and take care of yourself.

Maintain balance as a way of life.

God, help me listen to my spirit so I can restore myself to balance each day.

July 6   Let the feelings go

Sometimes we get stuck on a feeling. We don't want to acknowledge it and give it its due. So we tell ourselves we're too intelligent or busy to feel that way. Maybe we're scared of that feeling, afraid of what it might mean. We think if we feel that way, we'll have to do something we don't want to do. We're afraid that feeling might mean we have to change. Or we think the feeling will mean we have to face a loss of something we value in our lives and don't want to lose.

Sometimes we feel guilty about our emotions. We think it's wrong to have that feeling; it makes us a bad person. So we tell ourselves we *shouldn't* feel the way that we do.

We can become so used to a particular kind of feeling—such as anger, resentment, or fear—that it becomes a comfortable and familiar way to view our world.

We can use our feelings to control people: *I feel this way when you do that, so don't do that anymore.* Some people call this using emotions to manipulate other people. It's not a good thing to do. But some of us convince ourselves it's the only way to get what we want.

Learn to say how it feels. Then learn to let that feeling go.

God, help me flow in the stream of my feelings.

Sometimes things need to feel worse before they get better. Feelings are one of those things.

When a feeling comes to the surface, it presents itself boldly. Usually the feelings being stirred up are ones we label unpleasant—fear, hurt, rage, guilt, shame, or deep sorrow and grief. They will feel intense, for a while. Some feelings take a moment to come to the surface and clear. Other feelings take more time.

Feeling the emotion that intensely means it's finally clearing out of your system. Even though it may feel like it, it's not really getting worse. It's healing; it's getting better. You're cleaning out that old wound. To do that, you have to reopen it, but just for a little while. But finally, after you do that, it will truly heal.

What do you need to do with feelings? Acknowledge them. Feel them. Give each one its due. They like to be honored that way. Once you identify and feel them, then they'll go away. And each time you do this, the pond becomes clearer and cleaner, until finally the water is pure.

Notice how you react to yourself when a feeling comes up that needs attention and care. Do you spend as much time resisting the feeling as you actually do feeling the emotion? Do you expend more energy than necessary worrying that the feeling won't leave, that you won't be able to handle it, or that the feeling will take over your life? Consciously and deliberately relinquish your resistance to your emotional world. In March we learned to say *whatever* as part of speaking the language of letting go. Now practice saying *whatever* in love to your feelings.

God, give me the courage to face what I feel now, and what I felt before and didn't have the resources to feel. Help me trust that this process will help me feel better than I did before.

July 8   Dump it

Sometimes, we don't have one clear feeling to express. We have a bunch of garbage we've collected, and we just need to dump.

We may be frustrated, angry, afraid, and sick to death of something—all in one ugly bunch. We could be enraged, hurt, overwhelmed, and feeling somewhat controlling and vengeful, too. Our emotional stuff has piled up to an unmanageable degree.

We can go to our journal and write this whole mess of feelings out, as ugly as it looks and as awkward and ungrateful as it feels to put it into words. We can call up a friend, someone we trust, and just spill all this out over the phone. Or we can stomp around our living room in the privacy of our own home and just dump all this stuff out into the air. We can go for a drive in our car, roll the window down, and dump everything out as we drive through the wilderness.

The important idea here is to dump our stuff when it piles up.

You don't always have to be that healthy and in control of what you feel. Sometimes, dumping all your stuff is the way to clean things out.

God, help me understand that sometimes the only thing preventing me from moving forward in my life is hanging on to all the stuff that I really need to dump.

You don't have to be an emotional sponge, picking up every feeling around you. Learn to distinguish whether what you're feeling belongs to you or to somebody else.

Linda has a grown son. Whenever her son is going through a difficult time, Linda takes her son's emotions on, as if those feelings belonged to her. She'll talk to her son on the phone for a while. He'll express himself intensely and powerfully about how he really feels about everything in his life. After all, Linda's his mom. It's safe to tell her how he really feels, even if he can't tell anyone else. Linda may feel fine when she begins talking to her son. But by the end of the conversation, Linda doesn't feel that good anymore. She may feel angry, upset, or worried—or whatever her son was feeling before he talked to her.

Sometimes we soak up other people's feelings because we forget to protect ourselves. Often, we do this because of the depth of feeling we have for this person. The remedy for this is the same as it is when we're dealing with our own emotional stuff. We recognize what we're feeling. We give that feeling its due. Then we let it go. We squeeze out the sponge.

Sometimes, it just takes the act of recognizing that we've taken on another person's emotions to clear those emotions out. If we strive for awareness, we'll begin to recognize when the feelings we're feeling aren't our own.

Children are often open and unprotected. If we're going through a lot of feelings around them, they may absorb our emotions, too. It's important to share our feelings with others and let people talk about their feelings to us. But we need to pay attention. If we've picked up someone else's emotions, we need to let those feelings go.

God, help me know that part of being close to people and loving them means I sometimes take on their feelings. Show me how to protect myself so I can keep my heart open to the people I love without taking on their feelings.

Activity: As children, we may have absorbed emotions from our parents. These emotions can linger with us long into adulthood, shaping our beliefs and our general attitude toward life. These emotions can be tricky. We think they're our own, but they're not. They belong to someone else. Ask your Higher Power to show you whether you've absorbed any emotions from your parents or other people in your life. Then stay open to the responses you get to this prayer. If any emotions or memories begin popping into your consciousness, go to your journal and write about them. Just document the scene or memory that comes to mind. Then release the emotions. Set them free and let them go. Carrying around someone else's feelings doesn't help the other person and it doesn't help us. You deserve to be free and clear.

July 10   Let the drama go

Actors in movies or on television often must exaggerate their feelings in order to create drama on the screen. If they are hurt, they cry with a special intensity. If afraid, they scream and cower in a corner or curl up on a sofa. They may grab a person trying to leave and beg for that person to stay. In rage, they may stomp around hollering in a dramatic storm.

We can learn to separate what we're feeling from what we do. If we're feeling fear, hurt, anger, or any other emotion, we need to experience the emotion until we become clear. Sometimes beating a pillow helps release our anger. But we don't have to stomp around and slam doors. That's letting our emotions control us.

You don't have to revel in your emotions. And you can separate your behaviors—what you do—from what you feel.

Stop being a twentieth-century drama queen. It isn't necessary, anymore. We are more conscious than that now.

God, help me let go of the unnecessary drama in my life.

July 11   Stop building cases

You don't have to build a big drama around your life. We may need to end a relationship or explore a new career. Instead of simply saying, *This is what I'm going to do,* we build a case.

Like a lawyer getting ready to go to court, we prepare our arguments. We take one feeling and build a hundred-page document around it, prepared to battle our case.

You can build cases if you want to. But usually, there's a hidden feeling underneath all that case-building that's asking to be cleared. It could be a tinge of guilt or fear. Or it could just be the belief that it's not okay to clearly express ourselves, say how it feels to us, and do what we need to do to take care of ourselves.

Let go of the drama. Just say what you need and how it feels to you.

Be as simple and clear as you can in expressing yourself. If you find yourself building a case or creating a big dramatic scene, take a moment. Why are you making such a fuss?

God, help me keep it simple, especially when it comes to expressing myself.

Inside me is a wheel, constantly turning from sadness to joy, from exultation to depression, from happiness to melancholy. Like the flowers, today's full bloom of joy will fade and wither into despondency, yet I will remember that as today's dead flower carries the seed of tomorrow's bloom, so, too, does today's sadness carry the seed of tomorrow's joy.
— *Og Mandino*, The Greatest Salesman in the World

Honor your emotions; they are an important part of you. They hold your connection to love, passion, joy, healing, and intuition.

Not having emotions would make us cold robots. Emotions are part of the glory of being human, and they're our connection to our hearts.

Respect and treasure your emotional self. Learn to cherish your variety of emotions.

God, help me become the passionate, vibrant human being you created me to be. Help me feel all my emotions, and embrace the glory of being alive.

July 13   **Say it like it is**

Acknowledge your pain. Then you can begin to identify the source of it, and in identifying, you can begin to heal. When we open ourselves to emotions, we don't just get the good ones, like happiness or relief. Feelings are a package deal. We get the entire emotional range.

Pain and suffering are part of the experience of being alive. Things go wrong. Lovers leave us, parents and sometimes children die. We fall, we fail. Don't hide from your pain.

Don't bury it under a shell of drugs, alcohol, or shallow achievement. If you hurt, then hurt.

Recognize what you're going through. Then learn to tell it like it is.

God, help me acknowledge the pain in my life instead of trying to mask it with mood-altering substances or mindless busywork. Teach me to say what hurts. Show me what it is that I need to do to heal; then give me the strength to do that.

July 14   Take care of yourself, no matter what

Some days, we wake up in the morning, and by the time we go to bed that evening, our life has twisted, changed in a way that we couldn't predict and don't want. Our worst fears have come true.

Life as we have known it will never be the same again. The problem isn't just that this tragedy has come along and knocked our lives for a loop, although that alone would be enough. To complicate matters, we now know how vulnerable we are. And we wonder, in that vulnerability, if we can ever trust God, life, or ourselves again.

Many years ago, the founders of Alcoholics Anonymous, a spiritually based program designed to help alcoholics recover, cautioned people not to base sobriety and faith in God on the false notion that any person is immune from tragedy. They knew that life would continue to be life.

You are not alone, in your joy or in your sorrow. You may feel that way for a while. But soon you'll begin to see that many others have experienced, surrendered to, and transcended a similar misfortune or loss. Your pain is important. But you're not being singled out. Don't use your misfortune to prove that you were right all along—you're a victim of circumstance, fate, and God.

"God must really love me," a young man said one day after walking away from a motorcycle accident that should have been tragic.

God loves all of us, whether we walk away pain-free or not.

Keep taking care of yourself, no matter what.

God, transform my pain into compassion for others and myself.

July 15   Expect grief to be a lot of grief

Your grief will take more energy than you would have ever imagined.

— Therese A. Rando,
How to Go on Living When Someone You Love Dies

Grief is more than one feeling. Depending on the nature of the loss, it may become a temporary way of life. It may last eight weeks or eight years.

Let go of any judgments you have about grief and about how long you think it *should* take to get over that loss. Instead, practice compassion for other people and for yourself.

Keep your expectations realistic. Give anyone who's grieving, whether it's yourself or someone else, more latitude than you think could possibly be needed.

God, there's a lot of broken hearts on this planet. Please help heal them all, including mine.

"I'm not disconnected from my emotions," said Jan. "But what I am is frightened. I go so deeply into some feelings that I think that how I'm feeling now is the way I'll always feel. I get frightened, especially with sadness, that there's no end, no bottom, to what I'm going through."

Some feelings are just plain big. It feels like we've fallen into an emotional well with no bottom.

We haven't. There is a bottom. It may take a while to get there, but there is a bottom. And there are ways we can take care of ourselves when we're feeling this way. Some people get professional help. Others make a decision to go through it, giving special care to themselves. If you're going through an emotionally exhausting time, you may want to design your own care routine. Here are some suggestions that have helped some people get through these times.

- If you're involved with a support group, go to your meetings, even and especially if you don't feel like going out.
- Let a trusted friend know what you're going through. Ask that person for support; be clear in asking for what you need.
- Get plenty of rest. It takes a lot of energy to go through feelings this big.
- Make yourself get up and get out sometimes, too. Just the sheer act of being around people, in a park or at the mall, reminds us that life goes on when it feels like our life has stopped. Ask yourself what might feel good, and listen to any positive ideas you get.
- Exercise, even if you don't want to. Move your body around. It'll help move those feelings around, too.
- Make daily goals, a list of things you want and need to

do each day. Give yourself room to feel your feelings, but exercise your will and volition, too.

- Don't let your environment reflect what you're feeling; let it reflect how you want to feel. Tidy up your living space.
- Give yourself time deadlines for emotions. For instance, give yourself half an hour to thoroughly and completely give in to the feeling, then go do something else for a while. Go for a walk, watch TV, go to a movie, read a book. Tell yourself you're not running away from the feeling. You're just going to take a break for a while.
- Journal. Write about how you feel. Few things in life can substitute or work better than actually making a connection with ourselves.
- Then pray. Connecting with God always helps.

God, help me accept and get through all my feelings, even the big ones.

July 17   Relief is around the bend

I needed to go into the city for errands. It was a chilly morning at the beach, not even 70 degrees. I put on my jacket, got in the car, and headed out. I made the turn onto the canyon road and was struck by the beauty of the fog burning off, playing peekaboo with the canyon walls. It was 94 and sunny when I arrived in town.

I ran my errands and stopped at In-and-Out Burger for lunch. When I got back in the car, the thermometer read 102. It was hot. Traffic was bad, the temperature reached 106 on the freeway, and even the air conditioning didn't help much.

Finally, I turned back onto the canyon road. The grass was brown and I worried about wildfires—they get so bad here.

Soon, I noticed the temperature was down to 94° again, then 90°, then 88°. The hills turned green. I rounded a corner and could see the Pacific Ocean. The temp was 82°. By the time I made it home it was back to 74°.

I was surprised at the big difference a few miles made.

Sometimes, a small change can impact the way we're feeling—a lot. Feeling overwhelmed or pressured? Do something else for a while. Give yourself a treat. Sometimes, the smallest change in our routine can do wonders to change the temperature in our lives.

God, help me see any changes I can make that will have a positive effect on my energy and on the way I feel.

July 18   It's our lesson

When you learn your lessons, the pain goes away.
— *Elisabeth Kübler-Ross,* The Wheel of Life

Sometimes, we wait and wait for a painful situation to end. *When will he stop drinking? When will she call? When will this financial stuff get better? When will I know what to do next?*

Life has its own timeline. As soon as we get the lesson, the pain neutralizes, then disappears.

And the lesson is always ours.

Examine your life. Are you waiting for someone or something outside of you to happen to make you feel better? Are you waiting for someone to learn his or her lesson for your pain to stop? If you are, try turning inward. See what the lesson really is.

God, please show me what I'm supposed to be learning right now.

Be careful what you say you'll *never* do again. You might be building a wall between you and the good in your life.

He hurt me, so I'm never going to speak to him again. She hurt me, so I'm never going to get involved with women again.

Sometimes, our hurt feelings can be accurate and reliable warnings that we need to back off and stay away. But usually when we say *never*, it's because we don't want to be vulnerable and feel the hurt that came our way.

Saying *never* may be an indication that we've closed our hearts.

Have you built a wall with your "never's"? Look. Peek underneath. Is there a feeling of hurt you need to feel, instead?

You got burned when you touched the hot stove, so you're never going to go near a stove again? You'll miss out on some tasty meals.

God, help me be vulnerable enough to feel my pain and learn my lesson, instead of saying never *and building a big wall.*

Frank was a happily married man, or so he thought. Then one day, his wife of ten years came home and told him that she didn't feel like being married anymore. "I love you. I'm just not in love with you," she said, walking out the door.

Frank was devastated. He got mad at his wife, mad at his church, and mad at God. He got mad, and he stayed that way. He fumed and he generalized. He decided that all women must be this way and sooner or later anyone who got too close would hurt him.

Many of us experience hurt in life. It comes with the game.

It's okay to hurt, to be angry, even to be bitter for a while. But no one is interested in hearing our lost love story ten years after it happened.

We even get sick of hearing it, ourselves.

Sometimes it's time to nurture our pain. Sometimes it's time to get over it and get back in the game.

We all fall. Most people change their minds. We all make mistakes.

We don't have to let a bad experience in life prevent us from having positive experiences in the future. Walls are indiscriminate. While they may protect us from being hurt again, they'll also prevent us from experiencing joy.

God help me let go of self-sabotaging attitudes formed in a moment of hurt. Open me to the beauty that awaits when I approach life with an open heart.

July 21   Maybe it's not supposed to feel good

Every night for months, Laurie went home from work, turned on her computer, and wrote and rewrote the same thing: *I hate my job. I hate my job. I hate it, I hate it, I hate it.*

For six weeks in a row, Jonathan complained daily to his friends about his roommate: *I can't stand him. He's driving me nuts. I don't like him.*

For years, right before falling asleep at night, Mindy calculated the number of years she thought it would be until her husband died and she was free from her wedding vows: *Just fifteen more years, then he'll be gone and I can have a life.*

None of these three people were going through what we call a "love-hate" relationship with their spouse, roommate, or job. All three were involved in hate-hate relationships.

They all had one thing in common: they felt guilty for how they felt. Laurie kept trying to make herself like her job; Jonathan turned himself inside out trying to get along with his roommate; Mindy continued trying to be a better wife.

Be patient with yourself if you have moments and times of not liking someone or something, whether it's your job, your roommate, your home, or your spouse. But if you're consistently and blatantly not liking someone or someplace, maybe it's time to move on.

Watch for patterns in your emotional responses to your life. If you're consistently responding to something or someone in a particular way, entertain the possibility that that person, place, or thing might have outworn its usefulness in your life.

God, grant me the wisdom to discern when my feelings are urging me to move on. Help me let go of my guilt about how I'm feeling and find a path with heart.

July 22   Stop depriving yourself

Stop depriving yourself of what feels comfortable, right, and good to you.

Some of us grew up in environments that were emotionally deprived. Being happy and enjoying life wasn't allowed. Emotional deprivation was the theme.

Many of us learned to continue this pattern in our adult lives. We chose relationships with people who didn't feel good to us. We chose jobs that felt uncomfortable.

Many of us have heard stories of people who are addicted to feeling miserable. It's easy to see when other people are fostering deprivation and misery in their lives; it's more difficult to discern when the person is us.

We may be so used to feeling bad that we genuinely don't know what feels right to us.

You won't know what feels right to you until you relax and learn to identify how you feel. Let go of your attraction to misery. Walk toward what feels comfortable to your heart, mind, body, and soul.

Lighten up. Let yourself get comfortable with what feels good to you.

Do you know what feels good? Do you know what you like? One day, a friend was getting his back rubbed, "That feels good," he said. "It's supposed to," the person rubbing his back said to him.

Become conscious as you go through your daily life. Go on a treasure hunt. Find out what feels good to you. You just might discover that there are more treasures and pleasures in this world than you thought.

God, help me stop depriving myself of the good things in life.

July 23   Fill up your life

I merely took the energy it takes to pout and wrote some blues.
— Duke Ellington

One of the good things about the blues is their power to make me feel better. No matter how bad it gets in my little world, I can be pretty sure that B. B. King, John Lee Hooker, or Stevie Ray Vaughn has seen worse. Sometimes, it just feels good to vocalize all those bad feelings.

Bad things happen in life. Sometimes they are small annoyances; sometimes they are the major grief mongers. What matters is not what happens to us, but how we react to it. He left you. That is a fact. Now, after you get done with the quart of Breyers' rocky road that you are drowning your sorrows in, what are you going to do about it? You can sit around and complain to your friends about how unfair life is, or you can get up, put the empty bowl in the dishwasher, and go fill up your life.

Feelings are one of the blessings of being human. All of them. Sometimes we feel good; sometimes we feel bad. Take some time. Take some energy and be upset. Be aware of the feeling of being upset. But then get up, go out, and make positive use of your life.

God, help me put to positive use all of the feelings in my life.

July 24   Let go of fear

Sometimes, we say we want to go to the next level in our lives—in work, in play, or in love. But it feels like the door is shut. Fear can disguise itself behind many different faces: we want to do it our way; we're not interested; or it's just not time. What we're coming up against isn't a closed door, it's the fear we're repressing and holding inside.

If you're confused about why you're not moving forward naturally in some area of your life, take a closer look. See if you've got some hidden fears that might be holding you back. If you're blocked and trying to move forward, remember to feel and release your fear first. Then see if that wasn't just the key you needed to unlock and open that door.

God, help me see, feel, and release my fears about moving forward in my life.

Everyone is in awe of the lion-tamer in a cage with half a dozen lions—everyone but a school bus driver.

— *Unknown*

You may not be a great warrior. You might not lead explorations to the North Pole or climb Mount Everest. But you still need courage.

Courage lies in the simple things as well as the grandiose. It's fun and easy to speculate about how we would respond in our fantasy lives—climbing that mountain or leading knights into battle—but what about now?

Do you have the courage to live your life, to walk your path every day, right where you are?

Sometimes, it takes more courage to do the ordinary things in life than it does to walk to the door of the airplane and jump.

It takes courage to get sober, to stay sober, to get up every day and go to your job, support your family, pay the bills, and walk the path that you have been given to walk. We all need courage to do the thing that scares us and sometimes to do the thing that doesn't scare us, over and over again.

God, please grant me the courage to do the right thing in my relationships, in my job, and in my spiritual growth. Please give me the courage to live my life.

"French Valley traffic, Cessna 80809 taking active runway one-eight for left crosswind departure. French Valley."

I turned onto eighteen, pushed the throttle in, then held my breath as the little gold-and-white plane sped down the runway, then lifted off the ground. I pulled back on the yoke, lifting her gently, but not too gently. She needed to clear the trees, houses, and towers in front of me. But if I lifted her nose too fast, too high, we'd lose speed and go into a stall.

There was a lot to think about, trying to do this right.

We began to ascend, just past five hundred feet, when the plane began hopping about in the air. It was just the wind, but it was those same burbles of air, the lifting and the dropping and the being bounced around, that made me feel like we were going to suddenly fall out of the sky.

"You've got the controls," I screamed at Rob.

"No, you've got the controls," he said, placing his hands resolutely in his lap.

"Rob, I'm scared," I said. "I feel really uncomfortable."

"Then breathe."

I couldn't breathe, at least not the way he meant—consciously, breath in, breath out, calming myself down. Holding my breath was a habit, one I'd acquired early in my life. Holding my breath was how I responded to my fear.

I got the plane up to one thousand feet, then two thousand. I wasn't comfortable, but I climbed to five thousand feet so we could do the maneuvers we had planned.

I tried to relax and breathe, but I still felt overwhelmed. I couldn't relax.

Rob was fidgeting with something; I wasn't sure what. I kept watching outside the plane for other traffic, then watching inside the plane at the gauges. I was about to give up trying when suddenly, Rob began sticking pieces of paper over each of the dials.

"What are you doing?" I asked.

"Teaching you to trust yourself," he said. "Tell me when it feels like we're going at sixty-five knots," he said.

Now, I had to relax. "About now," I said.

He uncovered the dial. We were at sixty-five knots.

"Now, do a coordinated turn of thirty degrees—without checking the instrument panel," he said. "Tell me when it feels right to you."

I relaxed even more deeply, gently guiding the plane into a slow, coordinated turn.

"Perfect," he said, showing me the gauges.

"See," he said, confidently. "You're just scaring yourself by confusing yourself in your head, with all these dials and all you think you have to do to get it right. All you really need to do is relax and trust what feels right to you."

Let go of the fear and confusion. Stop overwhelming yourself with all you have to do, and trying to get it right. Get information. Read books. Get help. Then relax. You know more than you think.

You'll know when you're getting it right.

Trust what feels right to you.

God, help me learn to let go of my fears and trust when it feels right to me.

July 27   Say how it feels intuitively

The first time intuition clonked me over the head is a story I've told many times in my writing. I was in treatment for chemical dependency at the time; I needed a job to get out. I had searched the ads and applied for every opportunity I thought I deserved. No job was too small, meager, or humble to overlook in the application process. No one wanted to hire me. I looked for weeks, months, without success.

One day, I was at the end of my resources. I was waiting for a bus to take me back to the hospital, where the treatment center was located, when a small voice in my heart urged, *Look behind you.* I did. I was standing in front of a bank. Next to it was a stairway leading to an attorney's office, on the second floor.

Go upstairs and ask to talk to the head of the law firm. Tell him you want a job, were the words I heard next.

That's crazy, I thought. *It doesn't make any sense.* But I did it anyway. That still, small voice kept urging me on. When I talked to the attorney, I told him where I lived and what was going on in my life. He said he understood; someone in his family had experienced problems with chemical dependency, too. Then he looked at me and said, "It's funny you came in. I was thinking about creating a new position for a legal secretary in my office, but I haven't gotten around to advertising yet."

Two weeks later, he called me. I got the job. It was better than any I had applied for, it paid more, and it made the best possible use of the skills I possessed at that time.

We all have a special source of wisdom and guidance available to us, in times of trouble and in the day-to-day workings of our lives.

When faced with a dilemma, take a moment. Feel out the situation. Get out of your head. Make at least one decision intuitively today.

God, help me trust my intuitive powers.

July 28   Turn the switch on

Many of us have turned off our intuition switch, our sense of knowing the truth. We may have turned it off when we were children, because our parents lied to us. Or we may have turned the switch off later on in life to be in relationship to people who were lying to themselves and us. Our inner voice, our sense of knowing the truth, had to be turned off in order for us to remain in the situation.

It is time to turn the intuition switch back on. Go into your circuit-breaker room and turn it on. You know and can feel it when somebody is lying to you. You may not know it right away, but you can tell before long. You know if you trust or mistrust somebody. And you probably know the truth right now about how you feel.

Can you trust yourself? Stop doubting. Begin trusting and listening to what you know is the truth.

You know when a thing feels right to you, and you know when it doesn't. The problem isn't that your intuition doesn't work. The problem is that sometimes you choose to ignore it.

God, help me listen when you speak. Help me trust the radar you've built into me.

Activity: This is a meditation to help you activate your intuitive powers. Get yourself in a relaxed position, either sitting in a comfortable chair or lying on a couch. Spend a few minutes consciously relaxing your entire body, starting with your head, your face, then moving downward to your toes. Then picture yourself at the bottom of a staircase, standing in front of a door with your name on it. Open the door and go into the room. In this room are a lot of switches, similar to a circuit-breaker room. Look for the switch marked "Intuition." See yourself going over to the switch, then turning it on. If it needs any repairs, see yourself making those repairs. If you're having difficulty turning it on, ask what the problem is, what you need to clear up before you can turn it on. Once the switch is turned on, leave the room. Lock the door behind you; then walk back up the stairs and slowly move back into awareness. Whenever your intuition falters, check the switch in your switch room to make certain your switch is on.

July 29   **Let your intuition help guide you**

*Paying very close attention to your intuition is perhaps the
most important rule of all.*

— *Lynn Hill*

For many years, I used intuitive or spiritual guidance only
in times of deep need, crisis, or despair. It was a last resort. I
didn't know the word *intuition*. What I knew then was to
plow forward, figure things out in my head as best as I could,
then proceed. Occasionally, I would find myself backed into a
corner or at a dead end. Then, and only then, would I go to
intuition.

And I didn't go to it. It came to me.

Over the years, intuition has become critically important. I
recently made a friend who is a highly intuitive woman. She
would encourage me to learn to go with the flow and relax.

"Practice at the grocery store," she said. "Practice using
your intuition in the small details of your life, those times
you don't think it matters. If you practice using your intuition in the smaller details, you'll begin to be able to trust
your intuition in important matters, too."

"I can't," I said.

"Yes, you can," she said. "Just practice."

Over the years, I slowly moved toward intuition, and away
from solely rational thought. It was an awkward journey. I
was propelled along the road after Shane died. For a long
period, I was deeply into my emotions. I came to rely on my
intuition, more and more.

Now, intuitive guidance is a regular part of my daily life.

But for those who feel as awkward and stymied about

accessing intuition as I once did let me give you a few ideas that have helped me.

- Consciously relax. When an issue or a decision needs to be made, small or large, relax first. Do not panic or become tense. Responding with panic will block our connection to intuition.

- Ask yourself, *What feels right?* This answer will arise from a peaceful, nonemotional place, not a place of urgency or fear. If more than one choice or solution comes to mind, feel out each solution. Does one feel bland and lifeless? Does one feel heavy and dark? Does one solution feel lighter and right?

- If you don't know what to do, let it go. Go do something else; occupy your busy, rational mind. Often, an intuitive thought will pop into our minds later, when we stop trying to force the answer.

As with most other areas of our lives, practicing to relax and learning to trust ourselves is the key. Often, the intuitive answer is something that feels like the natural thing to do. Sometimes our intuition tells us to do something that looks absurd at first glance.

Honor this connection we all have to information beyond the scope of rational thought. You'll make silly mistakes from time to time. Most of us do. And don't discount the power of rational thought and plain common sense. But in times of indecision, let intuition be a regular, not a last-resort, resource you rely upon.

God, help me relax and listen to that still, small voice. Help me remember that when I listen to my intuition, I'm listening to one of the ways that you speak to me.

"Let's turn here," he said, turning down a short road. We had been looking for a new restaurant to try, and lately they had all been disappointments. The sign at the start of the road was weathered, and I remembered eating at the place it advertised years ago. I didn't like it very much.

The restaurant had changed some inside. We sat at a walk-in table next to a window looking out on the Pacific Ocean. Our server was gracious and genuine. We ordered crab cakes for breakfast. They were the best crab cakes that I ever had, and we ended up going back for dinner that same night.

The restaurant has become a regular place for us because we ignored what we thought we knew and went with a feeling instead.

After all of the omelets, waffles, and crab cakes that we've eaten at that restaurant since then, I'm glad that my boyfriend trusted his intuition and his intuitive whim. Both men and women have been given the gift of intuition. It's not a gender-specific thing, though sometimes we encourage men to focus more on the logical than the intuitive.

Open up. Trust your heart when it whispers quietly to you. Start small. Go for a drive and on a whim take a road you've never traveled before. Gradually, as you become more tuned in to your intuitive feelings, they will guide you along your path. Sometimes your intuition will help you find a nice place to eat; sometimes they'll guide you to a winning career path and sometimes to a best friend.

Listen to your heart. Sometimes you need to ignore what you think you know, and go with your intuition.

God, teach me to listen to my heart.

And it came to pass. . . .

— *The Bible*

We can't always be sure that things will always work out, but we will always have the strength to make it through. We can trust that eventually both the bad and the good will come to pass.

I've had the good ripped away from me and felt sorrow until I could drown. But it passed.

All I'm saying is that sometimes the bad guys win and the good guys lose. Sometimes it's the other way around. Sometimes nothing that we do seems to swing the decision one way or the other, but we can always come back tomorrow. There's always another chance to play the game, dance, sweat, and cry. And maybe it's the experience, not the outcome that is the true prize.

If you're feeling a loss of strength or confidence, let go of the desperate need for a positive outcome in your life. Realize that this, too, will pass. Gain your strength from knowing that whether an event is good or bad, we're enriched by our experiences. Only we can choose to learn from them or allow resentment and foolish expectations to destroy their value.

Dust yourself off. Pick yourself up. Step up to the plate and get back in the game.

God, give me the hope, faith, and courage to live my life today.

August

Learn to Say Thanks

This is my favorite story about letting go. Although some of you may already be familiar with it (I told it in *Codependent No More*), I'm going to tell it again.

Many years ago, when I was married to the father of my children, we bought our first house. We had looked at many houses with nice yards, family rooms, inviting kitchens. The house we actually bought wasn't any of those. It was a run-down three-story that had been built at the turn of the century and used for rental property for the past twenty years.

The yard was a sandlot where there should have been grass. There were huge holes in the house that went clear through to the outside. The plumbing was inadequate. The kitchen was grotesque. The carpeting was an old orange shag that was dirty, stained, and worn out. The basement was a nightmare of concrete, mildew, and spiders. It wasn't a dream home. It was more like a house you'd see in a horror show.

About a week after we moved in, a friend came to visit. He looked around. "You're really lucky to have your own house," he said. I didn't feel lucky. This was the most depressing place I had ever lived in.

We didn't have money to buy furniture. We didn't have the money or the skills to fix up the house. For now, that rundown barn of a house needed to stay just like it was. My daughter, Nichole, was almost two, and we had another baby on the way.

One day, right before Thanksgiving, I vowed I would take some action to fix up this house. I got a ladder and some white paint and tried painting the dining room walls. The paint wouldn't stay on. There were so many layers of old peeling paper that the paint just bubbled up, and the paper—at least the top three layers of it—came loose from the walls.

I gave up, and put the ladder and the paint away.

I had heard then about practicing gratitude. But I didn't feel grateful. So I didn't know how gratitude in this situation could possibly apply to me. I tried to have a good attitude, but I was miserable. Every evening after I put my daughter to bed, I went downstairs into the living room; then I sat on the floor and looked around. All I could do was feel bad about everything I saw. I didn't see one thing I could possibly be grateful for.

Then I ran into a little paperback book that espoused the powers of praise. I read it, and I got an idea. I would put this gratitude thing to a deliberate test. I would take all the energy I had been using complaining, seeing the negative, and feeling bad and I'd turn that energy around. I'd will, force, and if necessary fake, gratitude instead.

Every time I felt bad, I thanked God for how I felt. Every time I noticed how awful this house looked, I thanked God for the house exactly as it was. I thanked God for the current state of my finances. I thanked God for my lack of skills to repair and remodel the house. I deliberately forced gratitude for each detail of my life—those areas that really bothered me, those things I couldn't do anything about. Every evening, after I put my daughter to bed, I went down and sat in the same spot in the living room. But instead of complaining and crying, I just kept saying and chanting, *Thank you, God, for everything in my life, just as it is.*

Something began to happen so subtly and invisibly, I didn't notice when it first began to change. First, I began keeping the house cleaner and neater, even though it was truly a wreck. Then people, supplies, and skills began coming to me. First, my mother offered to teach me how to repair a house. She said we could do it for almost no money. And she'd be willing to help.

I learned how to strip walls, repair holes in walls, paint, texture, plaster, hammer, and repair. I tore up the carpeting. There were real wood floors underneath. I found good wallpaper for only a dollar a roll. Whatever I needed just began coming to me, whether it was skills, money, or supplies.

Then, I began looking around. I found furniture that other people had thrown away. By now, I was on a roll. I learned to paint furniture, refinish it, or cover it up with a pretty doily or blanket. Within six months, the house I lived in became the most beautiful home on that block. My son, Shane, was born while I lived there. I look back on it now as one of the happiest times in my life. My mother and I had fun together, and I learned how to fix up a house.

What I really learned from that situation was the power of gratitude.

When people suggest being grateful, it's easy to think that means counting our blessings and just saying thank you for what's good. When we're learning to speak the language of letting go, however, we learn to say thanks for everything in our lives, whether we feel grateful or not.

That's how we turn things around.

Make a list of everything in your life that you're not grateful for. You may not have to make a list; you probably have the things that bother you memorized. Then deliberately practice gratitude for everything on the list.

The power of gratitude won't let you down.

Being grateful for whatever we have always turns what we have into more.

God, show me the power of gratitude. Help me make it a regular, working tool in my life.

One day, a friend called me on the phone. He was going through a difficult time and wondering if and when things would ever turn around and improve. I knew he was in a lot of pain; I didn't know then that he was considering suicide.

"If you could give a person only one thing to help them," he said, "what would it be?"

I thought carefully about his question; then I replied, "It's not one thing. It's two: gratitude and letting go." Gratitude for everything, not just the things we consider good or a blessing. And letting go of everything we can't change.

A few years have passed since that day my friend called me on the phone. His life has turned around. His financial problems have sorted themselves out. His career has shifted. The two very large problems he was facing at that time have both sorted themselves out. The actual process of facing and working through these problems became an important part of redirecting the course of his life.

Someone once asked the artist Georgia O'Keeffe why her paintings magnified the size of small objects—like the petals on a flower—making them appear larger than life, and reduced the size of large objects—like mountains—making them smaller than life.

"Everyone sees the big things," she said. "But these smaller things are so beautiful and people might not notice them if I didn't emphasize them."

That's the way it is with gratitude and letting go. It's easy to see the problems in our lives. They're like mountains. But sometimes we overlook the smaller things; we don't notice how truly beautiful they are.

Identify problems. Feel feelings.

But if you're going to make anything bigger than life, let it be the power and simplicity of these two tools: gratitude and letting go.

God, teach me to use gratitude and letting go to reduce the size of my problems.

August 3   **Push against the wind**

One day at the drop zone, I began working with a new skydiving coach, John. We were on the ground, rehearsing the moves we were going to make during free-fall time. He knew that I was having trouble controlling my body during free fall.

John noticed something about me, then suggested we try an exercise.

We stood up.

He pushed me, on the shoulder.

Instead of pushing back, I let my body go where he pushed it. I was practicing nonresistance, the skill I had acquired in martial arts. He pushed me again. Again I demonstrated non-resistance. I let my body naturally move in the direction it was pushed. This act of not resisting had served me well, both on the mats and off the mats. Not resisting people when they wanted to argue—learning to say, "Hmmm," instead of engaging in battle—kept my life and environment calm. Not resisting when problems or experiences came into my life enabled me to go with the flow and be calm and centered enough to tackle these problems much more efficiently than if I was resisting them.

I explained this to John.

"Nonresistance is good to practice many times in your life," he said. "But sometimes you need to fight back. You need to assertively push against what's pushing on you if you want to get where you want to go. Pushing against the wind—directing your body assertively—is what you need to do if you want to learn to fly."

Practicing nonresistance is good in our lives. Surrendering is an invaluable tool. Both these activities take us immediately into the flow of life. When we're relaxed, we tune into God and our inner selves. Once we surrender, we automatically know what to do next, and when to do it.

But sometimes we need to assert ourselves, too. Surrendering and practicing nonresistance don't mean we turn into pieces of paper being blown about by every wind. Sometimes we need to push against the resistance coming our way.

That's how we assert ourselves; that's how we guide and direct our course. That's how our Higher Power guides and directs us, too.

We've learned to surrender. Now it's time to learn to assert ourselves, too. Have you surrendered so much that you've stopped asserting and expressing yourself? Assert yourself. Make the moves your heart leads you to do. Know where you want to go and what you want to say.

Once you've admitted powerlessness, learn to connect with your power. Learn when it's time to practice nonresistance, and learn when it's time to push against the wind.

God, help me align with your power in my life. Teach me to express and assert that power as I go through my day.

August 4   Be grateful for the wind

"It'd be easier to skydive without all that wind trying to push me around," I said to my jump master.

"No, it wouldn't," he said. "Without the wind, you wouldn't

be able to move around at all. If you didn't have resistance, you wouldn't be able to fly your body. That's what the wind is there for—to push against."

It's easy in our lives to think that we'd be so much happier without that problem, that situation, those people disturbing our peace. *What a bother,* we think. *Why can't my life just be calm and serene, peaceful, with no interruptions and bothersome events?*

Sometimes, resistance is necessary. While it's important to live in a calm, nurturing environment, sometimes resistance is essential to our growth. Take a moment. Look at how your problems have shaped you into who you have become.

When problems and challenges arise, they force us to examine our ideals, become alert, and often learn something new about others and ourselves. Even our enemies, rivals, and competitors give us something to push against. They help us define who we are and challenge us to become our best.

Instead of complaining and grumbling about that problem or circumstance, thank it for being there. Right now, this moment, the resistance in your life is giving you something to push against.

Be grateful for the wind. You need it to learn to fly.

God, help me be grateful for all the problems and circumstances in my life. Help me remember that you're teaching me to fly.

August 5   Stop fighting it

I go to the refrigerator and open the door. The food in it smells bad; the air feels warm. I decide that the power must have gone off for a while and close the door. My friend comes over later that day and opens the refrigerator, to get himself a soda.

"Whew," he says. "There's something wrong with your refrigerator."

"No, the power just went off for a while," I said.

I don't *want* anything to be wrong with the refrigerator. I'm busy with too many other things. I don't want to take the time to call a repair service, be interrupted when they come to the house, then be interrupted again and again, as they come back to fix it.

Later that night, I open the refrigerator again. I look for a moment, then slam the door shut. *Dang, it is broken,* I think. I take all the frustration about the inconvenience and use the energy to surrender to the problem, then get it fixed.

There's a difference between fighting with a problem and pushing against the resistance it offers in our lives. When we fight with the alcoholic to sober up, we're fighting with the problem. When we get hurt and angry enough to push against it, we use that frustration to motivate us to surrender, then go to an Al-Anon meeting, or a therapist, and begin to learn how to detach and take care of ourselves. Life gets better. Instead of fighting with the problem, we're pushing against it and using the resistance to move down our path.

Are you fighting with a problem in your life right now, instead of using the resistance it offers as a challenge to grow? Instead of depleting your energy fighting with that problem, surrender. Then use the frustration and upset as motivation to assert yourself and take positive action.

God, thank you for the resistance in my life. Help me to stop fighting with it and to use that energy to truly solve the problem.

August 6   **The lesson may be a test**

Sometimes, problems and challenges come to move us to the next place in our lives. Sometimes, they come to challenge and reinforce what we already know and believe.

Maybe that problem in your life has come along to teach you something new.

Maybe it's an opportunity to remember and practice what you already know to be true.

Push against that problem. Push your ideals and beliefs against what's going on. Examine what you think, believe, and feel. Stay open to change. But remember that, sometimes, it's not about changing what you believe. It's an opportunity for you to validate yourself and your beliefs.

We're not always learning something new. Sometimes, the lesson is to remember and trust what we already know.

God, help me to be open to change; help me also to stand fast by my beliefs when they are right.

August 7   **Stop second-guessing yourself**

Often in life, when an incident arises, we know what we want and need to do. It's clear. We've already got that lesson under our belt. Our hearts and inner guides are clearly speaking to us about what we want or don't want to do.

But I should be open to change and new ideas, we think. *Maybe what I want is wrong. Could it really be that what I want is right? Probably not. Maybe I don't know what I'm talking about.*

Like Winnie the Pooh says, "Oh bother. Oh angst."

We're creating this bother and angst ourselves.

Be open to new ideas. We're not always right in what we believe. Stay open to examining and changing your beliefs and ideals. But don't spend all your time second- and third-guessing yourself. Your life will whiz by. You won't get anything done. And chances are, those second, third, and fourth guesses will lead you back to the place you started from.

God, help me stop wasting my time and energy second-guessing myself. Help me learn to trust you and to trust myself.

August 8   You're being protected

It's easy to be thankful for answered prayers, easy to be joyfully grateful when the universe gives us exactly what we want. What's not so easy is to remember to be grateful when we don't get what we want.

John wanted an executive position in the company he worked for. He worked hard for the promotion. He prayed daily for his promotion, while giving a hundred percent of his energy and dedication to the position that he was in. But when the time came, he was passed over for his dream job. He left the company shortly after that. Today, he runs his own company with more responsibility, success, and joy than he could have ever hoped for at his old firm.

Susan, a recovering addict, wanted to date Sam more than anything. They got along great those times they ran into each other at work. He was charming, handsome, and sober, she thought. For months she tried to arrange a date with him, prayed that God would bring him into her life. But things never seemed to work out. She didn't know why. He seemed so interested in her. She was positive that the relationship was divinely ordained. She was stunned when she arrived at work one morning to find that Sam had died the night before of a drug overdose. He had been using drugs and lying about it the whole time.

Sometimes we get what we ask for. Sometimes we don't. God says, "No." Be grateful—force gratitude; fake it if you must—when God answers your furtive prayers by saying no.

Take the rejections with a smile. Let God's "no's" move you happily down the road. Maybe you're not being punished, after all. Maybe God is protecting you from yourself.

God, thank you for not always giving me what I think is best.

August 9   Be thankful when you get something else

Dear God,
Thank you for the baby brother, but what I prayed for was a puppy.

           — Children's Letters to God

Sometimes we look around, assess the situation, and decide what we think we need. So we go to God and begin praying.

Out of the blue, our prayers get answered. But the answer isn't what we requested. We were so specific, we think. Now, this—this *thing*—has come along. We didn't get what we asked for. Our prayers were answered, but we got something else.

Don't get bitter or so involved with feeling blue about not getting what you requested that you miss out on what you did receive. Wants and needs are closely connected. And all our needs, even the ones we're not completely aware of yet, will be met. Be grateful that God knows more about what we need than we do.

Sometimes when we pray, we get what we want. Sometimes we get what we need. Accept both answers—the yes's and the something else's—with heartfelt gratitude. Then look around and see what your lesson and gift is.

God, help me remember to be thankful even when the gift is not quite what I expected.

August 10   It's all a gift

Men are not angered by mere misfortune but by misfortune conceived as injury. And the sense of injury depends on the feeling that a legitimate claim has been denied.
            — *C. S. Lewis*, The Screwtape Letters

Oh, the grousing about we do, especially when we feel denied of one thing or another—some reward, or achievement, or position that we felt belonged to us.

How enraged we may become when a wish, a hope, a dream, or a want is blatantly denied.

How easy it is to be jealous of the success or happiness of another, even convincing ourselves that the person has laid claim to something that rightfully belonged, instead, to us.

The lesson here is simple.

Remember to be grateful. God doesn't *owe* us anything. All of it is a gift.

God, thanks for everything, just as it is.

August 11   Pray for those you resent

My favorite story about praying for those I resent is one I told in *Playing It by Heart*. Here it is again:

Years ago, when I spotted the *Stillwater Gazette*, the oldest family-owned daily newspaper in existence, I knew I wanted to work there. I could feel it—in my bones and in my heart. When I went in to the offices to apply for the job, however, the owner didn't have the same feeling I did. He had an opening for a reporter, but he wanted to hire someone else. Abigail, he said, was the right one for this job.

I prayed for Abigail every day. I asked God to take care of her, guide her, and bless her richly and abundantly. I prayed for her because that's what I had been taught to do—pray for those you resent. Sometimes I prayed for her three or four times each day. I prayed for her this much because I resented her that much.

God, I hated Abigail.

For the next months, almost half a year, I tromped down to the *Gazette* once a week, begging to be hired. Finally, I got a job there. But it wasn't the one I wanted. Abigail, bless her heart, had mine.

She got the best story assignments. She worked so quickly and with such journalistic ease.

So I kept praying, "God bless Abigail," because that's all I knew to do.

Over the months, as I got my lesser assignments from the editor—lesser than Abigail's, that is—I began to watch her work. She wrote quickly and efficiently. Got right to the point. She was a good interviewer, too. I started pushing myself to write better, and more quickly. *If Abigail can do it, so can I,* I told myself. My enemy began to inspire me. Over the weeks and months that transpired, I spent more and more time around Abigail. I listened to her talk. I listened to her stories. Slowly, my enemy became my friend.

One day, Abigail and I were having coffee. I looked at her, looked straight in her eyes. And suddenly I realized, I didn't hate Abigail anymore. She was doing her job. I was doing mine.

Soon, I got an offer from a publisher to write a book. I was glad I didn't have Abigail's job; I wouldn't have had time to write that book. Then one day in June 1987, that book hit the

New York Times best-seller list.

Years later, I wrote the story about Abigail in *Playing It by Heart*. The book got published. I returned to Minnesota to do a book signing. I was in the bookstore's bathroom, washing my hands, when a woman approached me.

"Hi, Melody," she said. I looked at her, confused. "It's Abigail," she said. Abigail wasn't her real name; it was a name I had given her in the story. But with those words, I realized she had read the story. She knew she was Abigail, and she knew how I once felt.

We joked about it for a few moments. I asked her how her life was. She said she had quit writing and had become a wife and mother. I said I was still writing, and my years as a wife and mother were for the most part over.

Resentments are such silly little things. Envy is silly, too. But those silly little things can eat away at our hearts. Sometimes, people are put in our lives to teach us about what we're capable of. Sometimes, the people we perceive as enemies are really our friends. Is there someone in your life you're spending energy feeling envious of or resentful toward? Could that person be there to teach you something about yourself that you don't know or to inspire you along your path? You'll not know the answer to that question until you get the envy and resentment out of your heart.

God, thank you for the people I resent and envy. Bless them richly. Open doors for them, shower them with abundance. Help me know that my success doesn't depend on their failure; it's equivalent to how much I ask you to bless them.

Earlier in this book, I suggested that you write your memoirs. Even if you don't sit down to do that, I'm going to suggest that you review your life.

Reading my mother's memoir was a profound experience, one that touched my heart and brought compassion into it in a way I hadn't been able to experience from all my family-of-origin work. As a child, I'd shut down when my mother would talk about her experiences. I'd turn off my listening device. It sounded like grumbling and complaining to me. I didn't want to hear about her pain.

But when I read about her life in story form, I experienced a different response. I was able to read it objectively, not as her daughter or a person feeling guilty because I wished she hadn't had all the pain she did. I saw how directly her experiences had created and shaped who she was. I saw the desires of her heart. I saw her tragedies, her broken dreams. I saw her heroism, too.

My snippy little reactions—the irritating mother-daughter stuff—vanished in this new light. She was no longer a mother who had issues. She was a human being nobly living her life. Like the rest of us, she had her frailties, her vulnerable areas, and her strong points.

The point here isn't for you to read about my mother. It's for you to take a new look at your life and all the experiences you've been through, endured, survived, and then transcended. When I wrote my life story, I resisted at first. I hadn't enjoyed it that much going through it. I didn't want to relive all those experiences.

But something happened in the actual writing. It was similar to what happened when I read my mother's account of her life. I began to see myself and what I'd been through differently, in a new, more compassionate light.

Each experience, each decade, each chapter in the book taught me something valuable. From each experience I'd been through, I reclaimed or discovered new insight and power. Maybe much of what I had preferred to forget or turn my back on wasn't the wasted life I thought it was.

What a beautiful story each one of us has. Whether your experiences ever make it into a book, it's still your book of life. Are you grateful for each chapter you've lived? Are you grateful for each experience you've had? Are you grateful for the story you're living now?

The good news is, the story of our lives hasn't ended yet.

There's still more to come.

Touch the experience of being human in all of its sorrow and joy.

Be grateful for the story you're living now.

God, help me to laugh, cry, love, be aware, and be thankful with all my heart for every moment and each experience that I've been given. Thank you for my life.

August 13   Thanks for the lessons

People say everything happens for a reason and God has a Plan for it all. I believe things do happen for a reason. And I believe in God's Plan. But if we don't learn the lesson from the circumstance and let ourselves completely heal from it—whether it's the past or today—the things that happen for a reason will just keep happening over and over again.

— Playing It by Heart

"I learned something today," a woman said to me. "Before I can completely let go of anything or anyone, I need to thank the person and the experience for what it taught me."

Sometimes, the last thin cord binding us to that person or experience, that part of our lives that we're trying so valiantly to be free from, can be effectively snipped with the shears of gratitude.

Are you hanging on to a resentment for that ex or a friend from days long past? Are you still harboring bitterness about a job or business deal gone bad? Are you holding on to a part of your life that was painful with bitterness and resentment? Are you holding on to a particularly good time or cycle you had with someone, afraid that if things change and you let the past go and come into now, things won't be quite as good?

Maybe you needed that relationship to teach you about a part of yourself. Maybe you learned compassion or more about what you wanted from life. Maybe that friend, even though he or she isn't in your life anymore, helped you open up a part of yourself that was shut down and needed to be activated and set free. What about those painful experiences? You learned something, probably a lot, from them, too. And that experience that was so fulfilling? That, too, needs to be let go of if we're going to open our hearts to the new.

Apply a dose of gratitude. Thank the experience for being in your life. Thank that ex, or that friend, or that business, or that boss. Thank them over and over again in your mind. Deliberately sit down and figure out what the lessons and gifts were. If you can't see them, ask to be shown.

Move a step closer to letting go and becoming free by being grateful for how that person or experience enriched your life.

God, thank you for the past. Help me let go with gratitude, so that I can live more fully and joyfully now.

August 14   **Be grateful for where you are now**

"It doesn't take as much faith to believe that everything happens for a reason as it does to embrace the belief that I am who and where I am now, today, for a reason—even if I don't know what that reason is and even if I don't particularly like who or where I am today," a friend said to me. "When I can take that in, my dissatisfaction and negativity disappear, and I can proceed calmly and gratefully with my life. To me," he said, "that's what spirituality is all about."

Faith and hope aren't just for the future. Try using them on today.

Could it be that you're who you are and where you are now for a reason? Thank God for your life, exactly as it is, right now.

God, give me enough faith to believe in today.

August 15   **Make a gratitude box**

One day, years after I discovered the power of gratitude, I was feeling stuck, stymied, and ungrateful. Again. After a few minutes of this, I knew what to do. I understood clearly what the remedy for my situation was.

I went to a shop in town and picked out the most beautiful little box I could find. It was silver, with engraving on it. About four inches tall and six inches wide. Then I went home and took out a pad of paper. I tore it into tiny little strips. On each piece of paper, I wrote one thing that was bothering or troubling me—from finances, to work, to love.

When I had finished writing out my troubles list, I started on another one. Now, on each slip of paper, I wrote down the names of people I wanted to pray for, the people I loved, the people I wanted to ask God to bless.

When I finished, I put each little strip of paper in the box.

Then, I held the box in my hands and thanked God for everything inside.

I still have my gratitude box. I keep it in plain view. People think it's just a pretty decoration, but it means a lot more than that to me. From time to time when I feel down, I open the box. I take out one slip of paper, and I practice gratitude for whatever slip I happened to pull out. Sometimes, I pull out a name of someone I want God to bless. For that day my mission is to surround that person with my prayers.

Most of the troubles I put in that box have long since been resolved. But the box is still around to remind me of the power of gratitude.

Do you have some problems in your life today, areas that you can't seem to resolve? If you don't already have one, consider making a gratitude box. Remember, there's a difference between knowing about the power of gratitude and actually applying gratitude in our lives.

God, help me do the things I know will help me to feel better.

Activity: Take the time to make a gratitude box. Put one slip of paper in it for every problem or trouble you're currently experiencing, one slip of paper for everything and everyone you're worried about, and one slip of paper for people you'd like God to bless. The blessings include your loved ones and those whom you resent. Then spend two to five minutes each day either thanking God for everything and everyone in that box, or take out one slip of paper at a time, and thank God for that. Leave the box in plain view as a daily reminder that practicing the power of gratitude will change your life.

August 16   **Thanks for my heart**

"Last Thursday, I was able to find the courage to end a relationship I had been struggling with. I knew there was nowhere for it to go, and I was seeing some scary character traits in this person. Now, I am dealing with a lot of sadness. That tells me that the urge we humans have for bonding with each other, and the desire for companionship, must be incredibly strong. I am grateful even more than I am sad."

It was just a short message on the on-line bulletin board I maintained at the hazelden.org Web site. That's all the woman needed to say. For me, the lesson was clear and complete: be grateful for our hearts.

God, thank you for the ability and desire to love. Love is a cherished gift from you.

August 17   **Get out of the nest**

The mother eagle teaches her little ones to fly by making their nest so uncomfortable that they are forced to leave it and commit themselves to the unknown world of air outside. And just so does our God to us.

— Hannah Whitall Smith

Sometimes, the pressure comes from within us. Sometimes, it's external. That job folds. The relationship stops working. Alcohol and drugs stop working. *What am I going to do?*

Oh, I see. God's teaching me to fly, again.

Thank you, God, for pushing me out of the nest.

There's so much do-it-yourself talk. So much self-help talk. Healing is a gift.

Yes, we participate in our gifts. If we're recovering from chemical dependency, we go to our meetings and work the Steps. The same is true if we're recovering from codependency or other issues that we might face.

We stand at each gateway and protest, "I don't want this. I don't want the problem. I don't want the healing. I want my life back, the way it was—or the way I imagined it to be." And we resist and struggle, but the changes fall upon us anyway.

We do our part, whatever that means to us, each day. Bit by bit, the next step becomes clear. A healing begins to settle in.

We receive our medallions for the number of days we've stayed straight or gone to Al-Anon. Or we go through an important holiday without breaking down and crying, because we focus on who is there, instead of who isn't there.

We can feel good about the things we've done, the part we've played in taking care of our lives. But remember, healing is a gift. So is love. So is success. Feel good about doing your part in helping yourself. But a gentle thank you may be in order, too.

God, thanks.

My friend was talking on the phone to his sister one day. They had a little sibling rivalry going on, but it was the good, motivating kind.

"I'm going to Asia," he said.

"Well, I've been to Africa and helped build a hospital there," she said.

They bantered back and forth about the places they'd been and where they hoped to go next. Then they decided that you got points only for how cool the trip had been—and what you learned and what you did with the experience after you were there.

"You helped build that hospital for kids. You get a lot of points for that," he said. "But you don't get any points for Denmark. All you did was change planes. You didn't even look around and enjoy the sights. We'll have to talk again, in a few years, and see how many points we each have."

It's been said before, but it's important enough to say again: It's not just where you go; it's what you do with it that counts. Are you having great experiences, but keeping them to yourself? Are you bothering to get out of your chair and see the sights in your world, or are you staring at your TV? Are you trudging your path, but not gleaning any insights along the way? Are you doing anything of value with what you've learned, even if it's sharing your experience, strength, and hope with a close friend?

How many points do you have for really cool trips?

Part of saying *thanks* is sharing our lives with the world. The other part is learning to enjoy our lives, ourselves. Live and love and learn and see things; then pass those things on.

Don't just say *thanks*. Demonstrate your gratitude for life by living as fully as you can.

God, help me commit to doing something of value and service with the gift of my life, even if that means simply enjoying what I'm experiencing right now.

Celebrate the abundance that comes into your life. So often, we spend so long in the "do without" stage that we don't know what to do when we're given the opportunity to "do with." We can get so used to the suffering—we can even come to expect it—that we feel guilty when we're given the good things in life and when we finally have enough.

We may have become conditioned to believe that to have success and abundance, we must have done something wrong. We're just not sure we deserve this newfound happiness.

What do we do now that we don't have to struggle to make each step and beg God for the money to pay for each meal?

Celebrate. Enjoy it. Abundance is a gift of the universe. It's important to learn to be a healthy, cheerful giver. It's important to receive cheerfully, too.

If you've been given much, be thankful. Use your abundance wisely. Enjoy it. Share it with others. Be thankful for the gifts in your life.

God, thank you for the gifts.

Activity: Make an inventory of your gifts. This is separate from the gratitude list of things we're striving to be grateful for. Exactly what are the gifts you've received? Sometimes we get so busy trying to get more, we forget to be thankful for what we've got.

August 21 Practice an act of gratitude

None of our success comes without the help of others. Time after time, it seems that there is someone standing at the crossroads waiting for us, pointing the way down the path with heart.

They may be friends, family members, ministers or mentors, or even police officers or judges. I think they might be angels sent to help us through those tough spots and point us back to the path with heart.

They're in the right place at the right time with the exact words and help we need.

Have you thanked them yet?

Practice an act of gratitude. Find one of your guiding lights or guardian angels and tell that person what he or she meant to you in your life. Your guides may not even be aware of the impact that they had on you. And who knows whether your kind words may be just the light that they need today to push them gently down their path with heart.

Then, take it one step further. Take the kind, loving thing they did to or for you and pass it along to someone else.

God, remind me to give thanks where thanks is due.

August 22 Be grateful for your families

I walked into the kitchen at the Blue Sky Lodge one afternoon. I looked around at my group of friends. "I feel really blessed," I said. "You know we're more like family than friends."

They agreed.

My house is full of friendship, and at the risk of sounding mushy, it's full of love. There's almost always someone home to take care of the place, though we do forget to take the trash out from time to time.

I've learned and laughed with my housemates, and I hope that they have learned from me as well. Are you grateful for the people you live with? Or if you live alone, are you grateful for your friends? Someone once told me that the great thing about being independent is that we get to choose our families. Be thankful for your family today, whether it's the one that you were born with or the one that you've chosen.

Our families are a gift.

God, thank you for my families.

August 23   Celebrate the gift of friendship

Celebrate the gift of friendship.

Get a piece of paper and a pen. Now write down:

1. The name of a good friend.
2. A lesson that you have learned from him or her.
3. Something about the friend that makes you smile.
4. Your friend's favorite meal. (This might take a little research.)
5. An activity that he or she enjoys.

Now, pick up the phone. Call your friend and invite him or her to a celebration with you. Do the activity that he or she enjoys: go for a walk, go to a ballgame, sit at home and watch videos, whatever this person likes to do best. Then prepare your friend's favorite meal or take your friend out to eat at the restaurant he or she likes best. Tell your friend specifically, and from your heart, the lesson he or she helped you learn.

Then tell your friend what he or she does that makes you smile. Tell your friend the things that you genuinely appreciate about her or him—those things that make your friend uniquely who she or he is.

Friendship is another important gift from God. Don't just tell your friends how much they mean in your life. Show your friends how much you care with an act of gratitude.

God, thank you for making each of us unique. Thank you for my friends.

August 24   **Celebrate who you are**

Today, celebrate who you are. Yes, you have much in common with other people. But you're also uniquely you.

Grab a piece of paper and something to write with. Now write down:

1. A lesson that you have learned in life.
2. A talent that you have, no matter how quirky.
3. Your favorite meal.
4. The name of a friend who respects and likes you for who you are.
5. An activity that you enjoy.

Now, pick up the phone and call your friend. Invite him or her to a celebration with you. Do the activity that you enjoy—go for a walk, go to a ballgame, sit at home and watch videos, whatever you like to do. Then prepare your favorite meal or go to a restaurant and have them prepare it. Show your friend your talent—remember this person likes and respects you for who you are. So if you can balance a Ping-Pong ball on the tip of your nose, go ahead and do that. Show him or her how good you are. Talk to your friend about the lessons you have learned, and invite him or her to share a lesson learned from you.

Instead of fussing and worrying about how different you

are, be grateful that you're unique.

Celebrate being you.

God, thanks for me, too.

August 25   Show your gratitude

Why wait? Show your gratitude today.

If someone has been kind, thank him or her today. Yes, we can wait and buy that person dinner next week. But how about writing an e-mail this afternoon or leaving a message on a telephone answering machine telling how much you appreciate the kind words or deeds?

We cannot show gratitude without sharing it with someone. When we show our gratitude, it's a way of sharing our joy with that person. Even when we do something as simple as burning a candle to show gratitude to God, it shares our joy with everyone who sees the flame of the candle. It strengthens their faith and reminds them to show their gratitude, too.

Make showing and sharing your gratitude a part of your life. If someone does something nice for you, share your happiness with that person. Send a card or make a phone call. If you believe that a prayer has been answered by God, share your gratitude with God. Tell someone, or thank God publicly at your worship service. If you have had a victory in your recovery, show your gratitude by sharing it with others in your group. Then share your gratitude with them for the help they've given, too.

Demonstrate gratitude in your actions every day. Gratitude is more than just a thought process and more than just a Sunday-morning church activity. Demonstrate your gratitude through your compassion, and your tolerance. Gratitude strengthens and supports our relationships with God and with other people. Make a commitment to show your gratitude by sharing it with others whenever you have the opportunity.

We can show our gratitude for life in even our smallest actions. Find a way to demonstrate your gratitude to the universe. Feed the birds! Action gives life to ideas. When we start to look for ways to show our gratitude, we will find more and more to be grateful for.

Gratitude is a form of self-expression that must be shared. We cannot have an attitude of gratitude without having an object of that gratitude.

Why wait? Show your gratitude today by sharing how grateful you are.

God, today I will show you how grateful I am.

August 26   Find the gratitude

Here's an interesting phenomenon about gratitude: it's difficult to feel too bad when we're feeling grateful. Your mind has room for only one thought at a time. If you fill it with gratitude, there isn't room for negativity.

Today, be grateful for your life. Allow that gratitude to carry over into your activities and to flavor all of your interactions. Think of one thing to be grateful about in each activity you do, with each person you interact with, and in each task that you do.

Find the gratitude in your life, and you'll find joy standing right next to it.

God, help me look for the good in my life.

Stop comparing and judging. Those two behaviors can drain all the joy out of a perfectly good life.

We compare this time in our lives to another time. Then we decide that this time is worse, not as much fun. Or we compare our life to someone else's, and we decide the other person is having more fun and success than we are.

Comparison is judgmental. We judge this to be better than that, and this to be worse than the other. By comparing and judging, we deny ourselves the beauty of the moment and the wonder of the life that's in front of us now.

Instead of deciding if a situation is good or bad, just be thankful for it—the way it is. Most things are neither good nor bad, unless we attribute those judgments to them. Most things simply are, and they are what they are, at this moment in time.

Go into the moment. Let it be what it is—free of judgments and comparison. Can you believe how beautiful it is, right now, right here where you are? Why didn't you see that before?

If comparing and judging is draining all the joy out of your life, start putting some fun back in it by applying a little gratitude, instead.

God, help me put the fun back in life by letting each moment be what it is, without comparing it to anything else.

Don't overlook the wonder of the ordinary.

The extraordinary, the amazing, the phenomenon are daily glorified in the movies, the news, and on television. Our senses become bombarded. We become addicted to drama. The only things that get our attention are the big, catastrophic, knee-jerking events.

Take a closer look at your life, your everyday world, and the people and activities in it. If it were all taken from you in one moment, what would you miss? What sights, what sounds, what smells? Would you miss the view from your kitchen window? If you were never to see that scene again, would you nostalgically reminisce about it, wishing you could see it one more time, remembering how beautiful it was, and how much that familiar sight comforted you in your daily life?

What about those toys strewn about or the baby crying, because he's hungry or wet? What about the sounds of the city you live in, as it comes to life each morning? Or how about how your child smells after her bath? Or when she comes in cold from playing in the snow?

What about the way your friend smiles, or that little thing he says all the time and it's not funny but he thinks it is, so you laugh?

Look closely at the ordinary in your life. While you're being grateful, don't forget to express pure, sheer gratitude for how beautiful the ordinary really is. We can easily overlook the ordinary, take it for granted. The sun rises and sets, the seasons come and go, and we forget how beautiful and sensational the familiar really is.

God, thank you for every detail of my ordinary, everyday world.

August 29   Spiral up

I was flying the airplane one day, practicing my turns, when I turned to my instructor, Rob. "Something doesn't feel quite right to me," I said. "The horizon looks a little bit off."

"That's because you've got us in a graveyard spiral," he said. "If you keep going like this, we'll keep spiraling faster and faster until we lose control and crash into the ground."

"Aaaah!" I said. "You've got the controls. Get us out of this mess."

The spiral had just begun. Rob easily restored the plane to coordinated flight, with a slight twist of his wrist. I was greatly relieved.

Sometimes in life, we can get a little complacent. We begin grumbling about a few little things. We start seeing the negative things about our jobs, our families, our romantic relationships, our friends. Or we get weary and tired of being alone, and not being able to meet anyone we want to date. Maybe nothing is really wrong in our career, but it just isn't giving us the pizzazz we'd prefer. So we start grumbling and complaining about how bad it is. We see other people making more money than we are, getting better breaks, and doing something that looks like more fun to us. It's not that anything is wrong; it's just that things don't seem good enough.

Than we find more things that irritate us about our friends, our co-workers, and our boss. Soon, most of what we see looks depressing and wrong. The negative is accentuated in everything we see.

That's a good indication that we're in a graveyard spiral, too.

Some people in this world need a special technique to get peacefully, joyfully, and harmoniously through their lives. I'm not saying this applies to everyone, but I know it applies to me. Every day in my life, I need to deliberately, consciously apply large doses of gratitude to everything I see.

Look! If instead of seeing the beautiful horizon or the

clouds, all you can see is down, apply gratitude and humility to each aspect of your life. In a few moments, you'll restore yourself to coordinated flight.

God, help me use the powerful remedy of gratitude as a tool for daily transformation in my life.

August 30   Turn your day around

I got up and checked the calendar. The car had to go in for servicing. I hated driving it in, getting someone to follow me, then standing in line at the service garage. Besides, I was busy. My friend followed me to the garage, and I climbed into his car. Geez, it was hot. I wished I was at home, in the air-conditioned lodge.

"Want to go out to eat breakfast?" I asked.

"Not really," he said.

"But the window washers will be at the house. We might as well wait until they leave. Even if we go home now, I won't be able to write."

"You're right. Where do you want to eat?"

"Do you have any cash on you?" I asked. He didn't. "Well then, we can't go to our favorite restaurants. They don't take checks or credit cards."

We chose a restaurant neither of us liked. His waffle was pasty. I could taste the grits in my soggy pancakes from the premade mix that hadn't been stirred. The syrup was imitation maple flavoring. The grapefruit juice was weak. I pushed my food around the plate, then stopped eating. My stomach already hurt.

We went to the cashier to pay for our food. We waited and waited while he did some other work, ignoring the fact that we were the only ones waiting in line. Finally, he turned to us and smiled. "Good news," he said. "You've won a prize."

"What it is?" I asked.

"A free sundae. You'll get it when you come back to eat here next time."

I started to tell him to give my surprise to the next child who came in, when he turned to me scowling. "Ma'am, we have a problem," he said. "Your credit card was denied."

"That's impossible," I said. "I pay my bill in full each month. Try again."

He did. The card still didn't go through.

My stomach really hurt by the time we got home. The bank had screwed up. The automatic payment to my credit card company had mysteriously been sent someplace else. By the time that problem got solved, it was time to go pick up my car.

There was a long line ahead of me at the service garage. It had been 104 degrees in the car. I was almost passing out. And everyone ahead of me was ordering tires. I sat down on the bench to relax. Finally, my turn.

"Here's your keys," the man said. "Just a minute." He turned and asked the mechanic, "Did you check the brakes?"

He said, "I forgot."

"Sorry," the man said. "It'll just be another half hour."

An hour later, on the way home, I stopped at the bank. I really needed some cash. The regular line was long, winding its way from the tellers to the door. The business line was long, too, but not as bad. I took my place. Fifteen minutes later, it was my turn. "This line is for people who have a business account," the woman snapped.

"I do," I whispered. "Look at the check."

Much later that evening, when I finally started to write and my stomach began settling down from the pancake mix, a vision popped into my head. "What about two eggs, cooked in real butter, with mushrooms, a ground beef patty, and some toast?"

A few minutes later, he disappeared out the door. "Going to the store," he hollered. "Be right back."

We sat at the counter at 10:30 that night. The eggs were perfect. The mushrooms were stuffed with cream cheese. The toast was soft from butter. And the hamburger patties were done perfectly and smothered in A-1 sauce.

A peace settled in. I felt grateful and blessed. I remembered a conversation I had heard a long time ago. "Oh, I see it's going to be one of those days," a woman had snapped to her boss. "Not unless you make it that way," he said.

Stuff happens. But no matter what time it is, it's never too late to say *thanks*, and have a good day.

God, help me know that between you and me, we have the power to eventually turn any day around.

August 31   Be a good guest

Guests come and go at the Blue Sky Lodge. Sometimes a sky diver comes to the drop zone for the weekend from a nearby town and needs a place to shower and sleep for one evening. Often, people come from around the world to train and jump at Skydive Elsinore, and it is a particular pleasure to offer our international friends a bed, showers, and the amenities of the Lodge.

Martin was one such guest.

After spending years in the military, he decided to have some fun with what he had learned. He now recruits skydiving trainees from the United Kingdom and plans training excursions at Lake Elsinore, staying for several weeks at a time. He frequently brings his wife with him, but occasionally comes here alone. On one such solo visit, we invited him to stay at the Blue Sky Lodge and were thrilled when he accepted our invitation.

All Blue Sky Lodge guests are told the same thing: Make yourself at home. The pool, hot tub, miniature golf course, DVD player, stereo, showers, food, beverages, books, prayer room, stunning mountain view, musical instruments, and contents of the refrigerator are here for your enjoyment. Help yourself!

"Martin was a good guest," Chip commented recently. "He swam, used the hot tub, ran, and sat outside and enjoyed the view."

I agreed. It gave us both pleasure to see Martin make himself at home and enjoy the gifts the Lodge has to offer. He was respectful and grateful—a delightful humble air—but he was also confident, and confidently enjoyed the pleasures and gifts available and offered to him.

What kind of a guest are you? Are you making yourself at home on this planet, whatever the circumstances you find yourself in? Are you taking delight and pleasure in the gifts and moments available to you, each day? Or are you sitting uncomfortably on the edge of a straight-backed chair, wondering if it's okay to help yourself?

We each have different gifts and pleasures available to us at any given time in our lives. Sometimes, we have to look to see what these gifts are. The pleasures may be as simple as a view of an old oak tree from our kitchen window, a big bath tub that fills up with hot water and comforts our body and soul, or a walk around the city block surrounding the apartment we rent.

Sometimes, the best way to say *thanks* is to simply enjoy with humble confidence the gifts and pleasures that are offered to us today.

Are you a good guest? Make yourself at home. It's your world, too.

God, teach me how to enjoy and savor the pleasures, gifts, and talents that are spread out before me. Help me learn to make myself at home, wherever I find myself today.

September

Learn to Say **I Am**

September 1   Learn to say *I am*

We hear a lot about becoming whole. "Become a complete human being." "Start on the pathway to becoming whole." "You won't find romantic love until you know you're complete." Frankly, these kinds of comments often confused me. But then I decided that wholeness relates directly to the process of detaching and letting go.

It's admirable to go after our dreams and know what we want to accomplish. But after we identify what it is we're after, we need to let it go. We need to know in our hearts and souls that we're okay whether we ever get what we're after or not.

Another friend described it this way. "It's the old Zen Buddhist thing," he said. "When you're one with yourself, life becomes magical. You can get whatever you want."

The most powerful and magical words we can say in the language of letting go are these: *I am.*

Then we step it up one notch by learning to say, *I am complete just as I am.*

God, help me know the power of the words I am.

September 2   Coping devices

We may do less-than-logical things to cope with tragic events. We don't do these things because we're silly. We do them because it's the only way we know to survive.

One of the silliest things we do to cope with life is devaluing ourselves when bad things happen to us.

We might have experienced a lot of pain while we were growing up. So as a child we looked around and said, "Yup. This must be my fault. There's something wrong with me."

Or, "I know if I would have kept my room cleaner, my daddy wouldn't have gone away."

Low self-esteem—and all the ways it manifests—becomes a way of coping with painful events. We look around and see all the people who don't appear to have our level of problems, so we may conclude, "There's something wrong with me." Although adapting a posture of low self-esteem might have been a way of surviving pain, that time has passed. It's time to replace low self-esteem with new perspectives.

Stop coping with events by devaluing yourself. Instead, respond to life by loving and taking care of yourself.

Love yourself just as you are.

God, help me love myself for who I am now.

Activity: Do a review of your self-esteem. Go back over past events from your childhood, teenage, and adult years. What painful events occurred? Did you give away your self-esteem to certain people? Now is a time to claim your self-esteem and take it back. Write down positive areas of your life. Write down what your friends and family members appreciate about you.

September 3   Let go of low self-esteem

"Self-esteem is so illusive," said Amanda. "I've been working on my self-esteem for years. The harder I work at it, the less I seem to have."

I believe we can let go of low self-esteem. We can turn around lack of belief in ourselves. We can become willing to forgive ourselves. We can stop tolerating treatment that doesn't feel good to us. We can look at the dangers of defining ourselves by money, power, or prestige, or by whom we know and what we have. Ultimately, we can become willing to take care of ourselves and nurture ourselves through whatever experiences life may bring.

Twelve Step programs offer two Steps that can help us build self-esteem, acceptance, and self-love. Step Six says we become entirely ready to have God take our defects of character. Step Seven says we humbly ask God to remove our shortcomings. The work isn't easy, but it is worthwhile.

For now it's enough to become willing to let go of our low self-esteem and all the ways that low self-esteem manifests in our lives.

God, please replace my low self-esteem with self-acceptance.

Activity: Sometimes, we can have healthy self-esteem functioning in one area of our lives, but not in another. For instance, we may feel good about our work skills, but we may feel poorly about our personal relationships. We may have great confidence in our athletic skills, but feel bad about our finances. Decide if there are areas where you may be manifesting low self-esteem. What areas do you feel good about? Also, look at dreams you have not pursued because of your lack of self-confidence.

September 4   Look at your attachments

A friend called me one day. His shiny new car was in the garage for repairs again. "I should have gotten a truck, something practical, that would start every day and get me to work," he said. "If ever, ever I start screaming that I have to have something and can't live without it, start screaming back at me until I stop."

What's attached to your self-esteem?

Some people attach their cars to their worth. Other people can feel good about themselves only if they're involved in a romantic relationship. Some people need a home in a certain neighborhood. Some people tie their self-esteem to future events. *If I could only achieve this, then I'd be complete.*

Take a moment. Look at your life. Is your self-worth attached to certain conditions?

We say we want others to love us unconditionally, but the problem is, that's not often the way we love ourselves. We say we need money in the bank, a Mercedes, or a Gucci bag first.

Is there a certain level of success you've been striving to attain? Are you telling yourself you have to have it to be complete? Maybe it's someone's approval that you're holding out for.

There's an easy way to see what we've become overly attached to. We can ask ourselves this: What is the thing in my life that I can't let go of and release? What makes me craziest?

Don't be hard on yourself. We all want and need daily necessities, such as cars, jobs, and money. And having someone to love is a delightful part of being human.

But that's a different issue than telling ourselves we can't be happy without these persons or things. Help yourself to a healthy dose of completeness and letting go. Tell yourself that you're complete and can be happy, just as you are. Let go of your attachment to whatever you're clinging to. It may or may not come back to you. But if it does, you can more happily enjoy it knowing you don't need it to be complete.

God, help me let go of my unhealthy attachments.

Activity: What are you holding on to, telling yourself you can't live without? Is there a person who you fear will go away? Is there a job or a particular level of success you've attached yourself to? Is there a level of finances that you're waiting to have before you let yourself feel complete? Do an inventory of your life. Discern what you've convinced yourself you need to be complete. Now, transfer these people or things to a list in your journal. Make the title of that list "people and things I need to release and detach from my self-esteem." You can still have these people or things in your life, but your goal here is to get clear on your motives for wanting them in your life.

September 5   Love yourself for who you are

"I'm tired of working so hard to be skinny, wearing the latest clothes, and trying to get my makeup just right," Gina, a beautiful woman, said to me one day. "I just want to be loved for me, for what's in my heart."

It's healthy to look our best, but some of us substitute self-esteem for what we wear, how much money we make, and the things we possess.

One day, I met a woman who had long hair, bright eyes, and she played beautiful Irish folk music. She loved to sing and dance. Her eyes lit up when she talked about her music. I could see how passionate and alive she was. Her band performed for people, but usually for a nominal fee or for free, she explained.

"But we want to get better," she said. "I really want to be somebody some day."

"You are somebody now," I said.

Pursue your dreams. Drive that car. Wear nice clothes. Have your hair done up, just right. But don't forget to love yourself without those things.

You are somebody now.

God, help me see beyond all the exterior trappings I surround myself with. Help me see the real beauty in myself and the people in my life.

September 6   Stand up to your fear of abandonment

"I'm in a relationship with someone who isn't good for me," a woman said to me one day. "My boyfriend manipulates me, and he often doesn't tell me the truth. But every time I get ready to kick him to the curb, my fear of abandonment sets in."

Many of us have a fear of abandonment. Some of us let it rule our lives. We'll do anything just so that person doesn't walk out and leave us alone.

I spent many years letting fear of abandonment control me. After a while, I finally wore out that belief. I just got sick and tired of worrying about whether I was good enough for that person.

Then a new thought set me free: *If you don't want to be my friend, or my lover, or my employer, I don't want you in my life.*

No more emotional blackmail. No more stress. No more having to second-guess what that other person is feeling.

Are you spending your time worried about someone leaving you? Does your fear of being abandoned leave you feeling like an underdog in your relationships? Let it go. Stand fast. And listen to what I'm about to tell you: If that person doesn't want to be in your life, just let him or her leave. Do you want someone in your life who really doesn't want to be there? Of course not. Let him or her go.

Once you adopt this belief, it's easy to send the bad relationships packing, and the good people want to stay.

God, help me believe that I deserve only the best of relationships.

Scott was sixty-nine when he took up skydiving for the second time in his life. He had jumped in the British military in World War II. When the opportunity arose to make a demonstration jump into one of the old military bases, he came to California to learn how to skydive.

His body was old and stiff. But his heart was full of youth and fun. As he worked his way slowly through the levels, repeating many of the jumps until he got the skills dialed in, each jump took a little more out of his body. Despite his resolve, the training was more than he could handle and he had to stop short of his goal. As he left, he vowed to begin strength-training exercises and to return later to complete his training. "I'll be there; it'll just take longer than I thought," he said.

At the same time Scott started training, Tim started his skydiving training, too. Tim had never jumped before, though he had been skiing, mountain biking, and sailing. Tim was terrified. He was fearful that he would fail, afraid that he wouldn't respond well in an emergency, afraid that he would forget how to land, afraid to get out of a plane nearly two miles above the earth.

Scott talked to Tim. Scott laughed at him and laughed with him. And Tim kept getting back on the plane and passing his levels. He graduated. "I would have quit after the first jump," Tim said. "But if Scott can do it, so can I. I'm glad he was here. He gave me the faith to do something I believed was impossible."

We are each to walk our own path regardless of the fears and desires of those around us. Maybe you are like Scott, trying something new, something that may be a little beyond you. Great! Maybe you'll succeed; maybe you'll fail. Only you can decide what you'll do with the results. Scott could have taken his setbacks bitterly and dragged Tim down with him. Instead he built Tim up, enabling him to achieve something that he might not have done on his own.

Maybe you're like Tim, wanting to grow, but afraid of what you might lose in the trying. Follow your heart, and if you can find a mentor to help you on your way, thank that person for lifting you up.

Keep walking the path.

Some paths may lead to fame and recognition, others to quiet support of our fellow travelers. Walk your own path. Learn your own lessons.

God, thank you for my life.

September 8   Be a team player

You may have heard this saying: "Unless you're the lead dog, the view never changes."

Not everyone is the lead dog. Not everyone is the CEO or leading man. Better to be a working actor than an out-of-work star. At least you're in the play.

Every person who has accomplished anything of value in this world and is honest, recognizes that he or she hasn't done it alone. They're part of a team. Even Christ had a group of Apostles.

If you're in a supporting role, accept it. Not everyone is a leader every time. By being a part of the cast, you can make the entire production stronger. You can do your part to make it work. And you'll learn the humility and team spirit that will be so important if you do get that lead.

Take a look at your life. Are you living as fully as you can where you are right now? Or are you waiting until someone recognizes your true talent to really give it your all? If you're in a supporting rather than a starring role, maybe it's because the cast needs the strength and talents that you can provide. Maybe the team needs a blocker. Life is not so much about the greatness of the role we're given as it is the heart with which we play it.

It's great to strive for the lead-dog position, but give yourself permission to enjoy and contribute from the level that you're at right now.

God, help me to accept the role that I have been given and to play it with dignity and to the best of my ability.

September 9   Discover what works for you

"Enroll in this weight loss program and you'll lose thirty pounds in five days!" "Come to this free seminar and after spending one hundred dollars on books you'll be a millionaire!"

There is no quick fix, no panacea that will work for every person. Success rarely happens overnight or in five days. Even the Twelve Steps are only suggestions. Although proven to work, the details and decisions about how we apply those Steps in our lives are left to each one of us.

And few things happen overnight, except the beginning of a new day.

Listen to your mentors. Examine what's been tried and true, and has worked and helped countless others along their paths. The Twelve Steps are one of those approaches. But don't be taken in by false claims of overnight success and instant enlightenment along your path.

True change takes time and effort, especially when we're changing and tackling big issues. We can often get exactly the help we need at times from a therapist, book, or seminar—the best things in life really are free and available to each one of us. The Twelve Steps, again, qualify in this area.

Discover what works for you.

Trust that you'll be guided along your path and receive exactly the help and guidance you need. Then give it time.

There really isn't an easier, softer way.

God, give me perseverance to tackle my problems.

September 10   Be who and where you are

One day when I was new to recovery from chemical dependency, I looked around at my living situation, my job, my relationships. Nothing felt right. A chronic sense of being in the wrong place at the wrong time was overriding everything I did. My life felt like an ongoing series of errors.

I had heard talk about a brilliant therapist, one who was particularly effective in getting to core issues. Whatever was going on in my core, I wanted it to be resolved.

The problem was that this therapist lived way out in a rural area. I didn't have a car. I'd need to take the bus. He saw people only during the week. I worked nine-to-five, Monday through Friday. And his fees, although well-deserved, were high for my budget.

I saved enough money to pay for a session. Then I made an appointment. I was so excited.

The big day arrived. I started my series of bus rides (I had to transfer three times) at 5:00 P.M., when I finished work. By 7:30 that evening, I arrived at the estate where this therapist lived and worked. I was exhausted but elated when I finally sat down across from this teddy bear of a man who had helped so many people progress in their lives.

In elaborate detail, I began spilling out what was going on in my life. I explained that I was recovering, trying to do the right things, going to my support groups, making my amends to people I had hurt—but nothing felt right. A chronic sense of uneasiness plagued my life, no matter what I did.

He listened to what I said. Then he leaned back in his chair.

"Melody," he said calmly, confidently.

"Yes?"

"You're right where you need to be."

Session ended.

I gathered my things, walked the two blocks to the bus stop, and rode the several buses back to my small cubicle of an apartment in South Minneapolis. The lesson stayed with me for life. When nothing in our lives feels right, sometimes the answer isn't doing more or searching frantically for the miracle we need. The miracle comes when we accept, believe, and trust that who we are right now is who we need to be.

Save yourself the time, the money, and the trip.

Be your own guru.

God, thank you for where I am today. Help me trust that when I need to be someplace else, you'll naturally move me to that place.

September 11   Listen to yourself

In the Bible, God tells us, "Be still and know that I am God." Learn to silence the chattering of your ego, whether through prayer, meditation, or a long walk in the park. Find that place where you can detach from the pressures of the world. Find that place where your body and spirit work together in harmony.

Being aware of your true self is the best way to free yourself from the controlling, manipulative behaviors of others.

You don't need the right car, the right shoes, the right girl-friend to be complete. All you really need is to be yourself.

Your spirit is the real you. Let it guide you.

Be still. Listen to your spirit say, *I am, and I am enough.*

In the silence, you'll hear God.

God, help me be quiet so I can hear you.

September 12   Look at the roles you play

In his book *Ethics for a New Millennium,* the Dalai Lama spoke of the idea that most of us aren't a static personality. There isn't just one side to us; we play many roles in life.

I am a recovering alcoholic and a recovering codependent. I am a mother. I am a writer. I am someone's girlfriend. I am a sky diver. I am a business person, a negotiator, a woman. In each of these roles, my personality expresses itself differently. I use different talents and traits.

What are all the different roles you play in your life? Most of us are aware that we're one person at work, somewhat different at home, and sometimes a lot different when we play. Some of us tend to feel guilty about this. "Oh, if they only knew what I was like at home, they'd never respect me as a boss," one man said.

Take the time to get to know all the different parts of yourself. Honor and respect each one. Each has an important role to play in your life. When you're trying to move forward, take a moment. Make certain that all of your I am's are working together for your best.

You don't have to behave the same at home as you do at work. You get to be a mother, and a wife, too. Honor and respect all the different roles you play in life, understanding that each one has its own important place.

Then remember to practice the principles we're striving to live by in everything we do.

Our roles might change, but the ideals and values we live by don't.

God, help me honor and accept all my past and present I am's. Help me leave enough room to create new sides or parts of myself, too.

Activity: Take some time to write in your journal about all the different roles you play in your life right now. Describe each role as accurately as you can. The next time you get stuck, consult each one of these personalities. For instance, the worker in you may want to make a particular decision about moving forward in your career, but the parent self may have some objections. Understand every part of your personality and learn to make decisions that benefit the whole.

September 13   **Who do you say you are?**

I was driving out to the skydiving center one day, mulling things over in my head. Before long, I'd be on the plane and it would be my time to walk to that door and jump out. The fears started brewing and building up. *I don't know if I can do this,* I thought. *I don't even know if I want to become a sky diver or if this path is right for me.*

"You already are a sky diver," a quiet voice said.

That's right, I thought.

When I first began recovering from my chemical dependency, I preferred to identify myself as a drug addict. "My name is Melody, and I am a drug addict," I'd say quietly at the group. One member of the group started harping at me after hearing me identify myself this way. "You're an alcoholic, too," he said. "And you should label yourself as that."

I resisted what he said for a while, and then I decided to give it a try. Finally at one meeting, I said the words aloud. "My name is Melody, and I am an alcoholic."

Now, I understand why it was so important—not to him but to me—to label myself as an alcoholic. Number one, it was important because it was the truth. In order to focus on my recovery, I needed to abstain from using both alcohol and drugs. Number two, whether this friend knew it or not, he knew the power of the *Great I Am.*

He wasn't asking me to degrade or limit myself. All he was asking me to do was identify who I really was and am. And by saying and acknowledging this, I helped create a new role, a new personality. I am now, at the time of this writing, by the grace of God, a recovering alcoholic and addict.

Most of us aren't one single thing. We're a parent, a student, maybe a recovering person, and a grown child. We form many new I am's as we go through life.

Watch each time you say the words *I am* in a conversation or thought. Pay attention to the times you say *I'm not,* as well. Then spend some time reflecting not only on who you are, but who you want to become.

Discover the power in your life from saying *I am.*

Who do you say you are and you aren't?

Give yourself a chance to become someone new.

God, help me understand and use correctly, to the best possible benefit of my growth, the power of the Great I Am.

September 14   Affirm yourself

When I began flying and skydiving, I found myself fumbling inadequately with new roles or parts of myself. When I began writing, I found myself fumbling with that part of myself. *I want to be a writer,* I'd think, *but I'm not, at least not yet. I have to get this number of books published and this number of good reviews first.*

It can take years and many successes in any new area in our lives before we can confidently say to ourselves and others, *I am.* I am a sky diver. I am a pilot. I am a writer. Oh, the power of those words *I am.*

You may not have much parenting experience if your first child was just born last week, but you are a mother. I didn't have my ten-year medallion yet, but on the first day of my recovery I could honestly say, "I'm a recovering addict and alcoholic."

Who or what do you want to become? A good parent? A sober, recovering person? A good girlfriend, boyfriend, or spouse? Do you want to become happy, peaceful, tolerant? Don't wait until you're successful to tell yourself you're that. Start now by saying you are what you want to become instead of reinforcing the words *I'm not.* Yes, you have much to learn. Yes, there's a ways to go on that path. And you may not be proficient at it, or an expert, yet. But you don't have to be to say those two little words *I am.*

Help create the new part of your personality by using and affirming those powerful words *I am.* Then watch as a new part of yourself emerges.

God, help me use my creative powers to create a better, more fulfilling life. Help me use the words I am *to create who you and I want me to be.*

Activity: Create your own affirmations. We each have our own path to follow; we each have different needs at different times. Pick out one area of your life that you're working on. Then give yourself one affirmation that helps you create the new reality you're working hard to create. The first two words of the affirmation need to be *I am*. Say this affirmation out loud seven times while looking in the mirror. Do this three times a day, once in the morning, once midday, and once before retiring at night. Do this for twenty-one consecutive days, without missing one day—or until you don't need to say it aloud anymore because you believe it.

September 15   **You are a work of art**

All the arts we practice are apprenticeship. The big art is our life.

— *M. C. Richards*

What you *do* is not who you *are*.

You are more, much more, than that.

It's easy to get so caught up in what we do that we're only identifying ourselves through our daily tasks. I am a mechanic. I am a parking lot attendant. I am a doctor. I am a dishwasher. When we link ourselves too closely to our jobs, we deny ourselves the chance to ever be anything else. We limit ourselves by believing that's all we are and all we'll ever be.

Our concept of who we are is one of the hardest, but most rewarding, ideas we can change. If you have been brought up believing that you are clumsy, you will probably demonstrate this belief in your actions—until you identify that idea, let go of it, and let yourself be something else.

Don't limit yourself by saying you are just what you do. Stop seeing yourself as a static being. If I am "just" a parking lot attendant, then how can I hope to ever influence someone through my words, my art, my music, my life? But if I am a vital, living, growing soul who happens to be parking people's cars, then everything I do can become a symphony. I can have an influence for good in the lives of everyone I touch. I can learn from them, and they from me. I can learn the lessons that I am supposed to learn at this place in my life, and I can move on to other lessons.

God gave us the power to change. You're more than what you do. You're a vital vibrant soul that came here to experience, grow, and change. Make a masterpiece out of your life.

God, help me realize the glory of my soul. Thank you for my mortality and for the ability to learn and grow.

September 16   **Let your creative self flow**

To live a creative life, we must lose our fear of being wrong.
                                        — Joseph Chilton Pearce

Creativity isn't just something we do.

Being creative doesn't mean just drawing pictures, writing books, or sculpting statues out of clay. There's not a limited pot of creativity available only to the artists.

Creativity is a vital living force in the universe that is available to each of us, to assist us in living our lives. All we need to do to align ourselves with that force is let go of our fears.

Need a new idea on how to fix that room, that thesis, that relationship? Need an idea about how to fix your life? Let yourself be creative. Encourage your ideas to flow. Listen to your intuition, to your spirit.

Listen to that small idea you have, the one you have so much passion for. Let go of your rational thought process just for a moment. Let creativity help you live your life. Ask the Creator to help.

God, show me how creative I am and can be. Give me the courage to be willing to make mistakes as I create my path with heart.

September 17   Refresh yourself

There's a "refresh" button you can click on the computer when you're on-line. It makes the computer operate more efficiently.

Sometimes we get a little sluggish, too. We've been pushing too hard. Mulling the same thoughts over and over. Doing the same things over and over. Sometimes we need a change of scenery. Sometimes we need to refresh our thoughts with prayer, meditation, a few words from a friend, or spending some time with a good book.

Maybe it's our bodies that need refreshing. We need a cold beverage, a brisk walk, a nap, or a hot shower.

Maybe we need a bigger refreshment: a weekend at a spa, a vacation. Even if our budget is low, we can pitch a tent in a park and take in the refreshing beauty of the world around us.

Look around. The world abounds with refreshments. The next time you get bogged down, stop pushing so hard. Do what you need to do to become efficient and operate with ease.

Refresh yourself.

God, help me understand the power of taking the time to refresh myself. Then help me stop thinking about it and actually do it.

September 18   Rise to the occasion

"You should have seen me when I was younger. I was something else then."

"Just wait until I'm older and bigger. Then I'll show you what I can do."

If all we do is remember the strength of our past, then we're denying ourselves the wisdom and abilities we carry with us in the present. And we deny the lessons that age teaches us about slowing down, being still, and letting things be the way they are. If we're waiting for the future to be happy, we're robbing ourselves of the vitality and joy in our lives right now.

Stop reminiscing about the past and anticipating the joys of the future—that time when you become all powerful, bigger, and better than you are now.

You're as good as you need to be today. Let yourself be who you are, then enjoy being exactly that.

Rise to the occasion of today.

God, help me be the best me that I can be.

September 19   What do you expect?

The key to life and power is simple. It's knowing who we are. It's knowing what we think, what we feel, what we believe, what we know, and even what we sense. It's understanding where we've been, where we are, and where we want to go. That's often different from who we think we should be, from whom others want us to be, tell us to be, and sometimes even tell us we are.

— *Melody Beattie*, Stop Being Mean to Yourself

It's easy to get hooked into other people's expectations of us. Sometimes, it's even easier to get hooked into what we think they expect of us.

One of the biggest traps is locking ourselves into a preconceived notion of ourselves. We can keep ourselves so busy living up to an image of ourselves that we forget who we really are. It's tough enough to break free of the expectations, spoken and unspoken, that others put on us. It's more insidious when we start telling ourselves to be what we think other people are expecting us to be—whether they are or not.

Look in the mirror. If you see a person who has been confined with a limiting image that doesn't fit or feel right anymore, set yourself free.

God, help me let go of ego. Help me stop living up to self-imposed caricatures of who I think I'm supposed to be.

Activity: This week, do two things you want to do that you think other people wouldn't normally expect of you. Don't do anything that hurts yourself or maliciously causes pain to another. You might surprise yourself with how easy and fun it is to be you.

September 20   Experience your life

As soon as you say, "I want to change"—make a program—a counter-force is created that prevents you from change. Changes are taking place by themselves. If you go deeper into what you are, if you accept what is there, then a change automatically occurs by itself. This is the paradox of change.
                                                    — *Frederick S. Perls*

Dr. Frederick S. Perls, founder of Gestalt therapy, profoundly influenced my life. When I worked in therapeutic communities, to "Gestalt" a feeling meant to go fully into that feeling, to become one with that feeling, to totally and completely accept the feeling and the experience as a means of transcending, healing, or dealing with it.

How do we change? Don't force yourself. Let yourself change. Let yourself be. Go as fully into the experience of your life, your feelings, and being you that you can.

When you come out, you'll be different.

Accept who you are then, too.

Don't intellectualize your life. Experience it.

God, help me accept who and where I am, and how I feel today. Then tomorrow, help me do the same.

September 21   Revere your connections

Things derive their being and nature from mutual dependence and are nothing by themselves.

— *Nagarjuna*

We are dependent on much around us, not just for our survival, but for our joy. We need food, water, and the company of our fellow travelers on this great journey.

We can be self-sufficient in our attitude to take care of ourselves, yet we need the world around us in order to live and to be fully alive.

We are one part of a whole. We are a complete part, but nonetheless, a part. We need the other parts. The other parts need us.

Just as we're influenced and impacted by those who touch us, we influence and impact them with our thoughts, words, and behaviors. We cannot control others. Look at the difference in our relationships when we speak gently and lovingly, and when we scream.

While it is great to revel in the blessing of existence, the world becomes more interesting and alive when we recognize everyone and everything else in it, too. This body cannot be without the sustenance of food, and our soul's experience here would be greatly reduced were it not for the company of other spirits we have met.

While we do not need to live up to anyone's expectations of us, we need to remember that our actions will impact those around us. Yes, we have the liberty to think, feel, and behave however we choose. But what we do will touch the lives of others.

We are not responsible for other people. But we have responsibilities to them.

Revel in your freedom. But revere and honor your connection to the world around you. Take responsibility for how you touch and connect with everything and everyone in your life today.

Live reverently, compassionately, and respectfully toward yourself and all else in the world.

God, give me reverence and respect for all life.

September 22   Be uniquely you

We will discover the nature of our particular genius when we stop trying to conform to our own or to other peoples' models, learn to be ourselves, and allow our natural channels to open.
— Shakti Gawain

We have much in common with each other. And recovery, growth, and change are strengthened by honoring these similarities. But each of us is unique. We each have our own strengths, weaknesses, gifts, vulnerabilities—our own personalities.

The purpose of spiritual growth is not to eliminate the

personality. It is to refine and enhance it, and allow each of us to express ourselves creatively.

We are not meant to be just like anyone else. Comparison will leave us uncomfortable, either on the side of pride or of inadequacy.

You are you. The wonder of life comes in finding your own rhythm to the dance, your own way of seeing the world, your own brush stroke, phrase, or special combination.

There is an old story about a writer who goes to his teacher and says, "Teacher, all the stories have already been told. There is no need for me to write. Everything that needs to be said has already been written."

"It's true that there are no new stories," the teacher said. "The universal lessons have been taking place for a long, long time. And the same themes have influenced humanity since time began. But no one sees that story through your eyes. And no one else in the world will tell that story exactly the way you will. Now return to your desk, pick up your pen, and tell the world what you see."

The beauty of the world lies both in our differences and in our similarities. Allow the beauty that is channeled through you to be flavored with your own special perspective on the world.

There's a difference between ego and personality. Drop the ego. Let your personality, in all its glories and foibles and eccentricities, come shining through.

Respect how much you have in common with other people.

Then be uniquely you.

God, thank you for making me unique.

If you see Buddha, kill him.

— *Zen koan*

For the first several hundred years after the Buddha died, there were no images of him. Only his dharma, or teachings, were passed on from generation to generation. Eventually, however, the people wanted an image to remind them of their ideal, and that's when and how Buddha statues came to be.

The good thing about having statues of Buddha is they remind followers of the ideals they're striving for in their lives. The difficult thing about Buddha statues is that people may be tempted to idolize the statue, and forget to seek the state of consciousness the Buddha represented.

It's easy for us to idolize our mentors and teachers, the people who encourage and help us to grow. It can be easy to look around us and think others have the key to enlightenment, success, joy.

Stop idolizing other people.

Look in the mirror.

You have everything you need to learn your lessons, grow, achieve success. You have all the courage you need to fail, then try again. You have everything you need, within you, to live and follow your own path with heart.

Not only are you right where you need to be, but you can get wherever you want to go from here. And you and I have all the power we need to learn the lessons we came here to learn.

God, teach me that all I need is within me.

God must become an activity in our consciousness.
                                   — Joel S. Goldsmith

God is not separate from this beautiful world that he created. He is the creative force behind everything we do. He is the sunrise, the moonrise, the tides, and the eclipse. He created us from nothing, and we are special for no other reason than that we are.

When we let go of our separateness and welcome the fact that we are a part of the universe, an amazing thing happens: we see we are a part of the glory of the universe.

God is more than a great father standing judgmentally above looking down with a mix of love and anger at his creation. We were created in God's image. We are a part of God, and a part of God's spirit resides in each of us.

We are a part of universal consciousness.

Today, whether you are feeling down and sad or joyous and free, take a moment and get in touch with the part of God that resides within you. You're a part of something bigger than all the petty victories and losses in your life. Enjoy your uniqueness; embrace your universality, too. Find comfort and humility in all that is.

See God in your life and in the world. Pray. Meditate.

Make conscious contact with your God.

God, help me make conscious contact with you today.

September 25   **Fill in the blanks**

The magic of a story lies in the spaces between the words. When we read a novel, we often find that the writer gives us only the barest elements of a scene, and yet our imagination fills in all the blank spaces from our experiences, our hopes, our desires. We don't need the author to give us all of the details.

So it is with life. Often we are given only the barest outline of the path that we are to follow, and yet if we are silent and listen to our hearts, we can hear all of the details of our path spelled out for us, a step at a time. There is no need to have everything laid out for us beforehand. If it were, there would be no need to take the trip. We could simply read about it.

Get up.

Live your path with heart.

Fill in the blanks yourself.

God, give me the strength to find out how the story ends by living until the end of it, instead of wanting it read to me beforehand.

September 26   Connect yourself

What did the Buddhist monk say to the hot-dog vendor? Can you make me one with everything?

I was buckling my seat belt in the little Cessna one day, getting ready for flight training, when my instructor Rob turned to me.

"I just take a second when I strap myself in and tell myself I'm becoming one with the plane as I do," Rob said. "It really helped me in the beginning when I was nervous and felt so separate from the airplane."

What a great idea, I thought. That day turned into one of my most comfortable flying sessions. It reminded me of a lesson I had learned a while back.

For most of my life, I felt disconnected from things: from

myself, from other people, from life. That feeling of separateness haunted me. It explains why I tried so desperately to attach myself codependently to people, places, and things.

Over the years, I began to see that my separateness was an illusion. The same energy, the same life force, that runs through all the universe runs through you and me, too.

We're connected, whether we know it or not.

Nobody has to make you one with everything. You already are.

Let go of your illusion of separateness.

Connect yourself.

God, help me know my oneness with the world. Help me know how connected I really am so I don't have to connect in ways that don't work.

September 27   Own your life

Are you willing to take responsibility for this mat, to own it? That doesn't mean it isn't everybody else's mat, too. If you're big enough to own the mat as yours, you're big enough to let it be theirs, too.

— *George Leonard*

In his book *The Way of Aikido*, George Leonard wrote about the concept of *owning the mat*. He was talking about aikido. He was referring to an air of ownership, a certain presence he learned to demonstrate both on the mats while practicing martial arts and in his life.

Many subtle attitudes and past conditioning can affect our sense of ownership of our lives and of the world we live in—guilt, a haunting sense of victimization, laziness, living with repressive, angry, or abusive people may have tamed our sense of ownership of our lives.

One day, I was at my daughter's house. She had recently acquired a new dog, Stanley. Stanley huddled in the corner timidly instead of scampering over to greet me like her other dog did.

"We got Stanley from the pound," Nichole explained. "His previous owners abused him real badly. He's afraid to move around too much. He's afraid he'll get hit. So he sits real quietly, hoping not to make anyone mad."

I thought, *That dog reminds me of me.*

Let go of negative conditioning. No matter what happened, today is a new day. And it's your lucky day. You've just received an inheritance. You now own your world—your life, your emotions, your finances, your relationships, your decisions. Walk onto the mat of your life with an air of confidence. Welcome others graciously because it's their world, too. Whether you're walking into your cubicle at work or pushing a shopping cart down the aisle at the grocery store, stand tall, move from your center, and walk with an open heart.

Welcome to your world.

God, teach me what it means to live and let live.

Activity: Review each of these areas of your life: work, relationships, finances, leisure time, emotions, your body, and your spiritual growth. Have you forfeited or given up ownership in any of these areas? If you have, today's a good day to take it back.

September 28   You're responsible for you

We can delegate tasks, but we can't delegate responsibility, if the responsibility is really ours.

Sometimes, it's normal to delegate tasks to other people. We may hire people to do certain things for us. We may engage in contracts with a therapist or a healer to help us work through a certain issue. But the responsibility for which pieces of advice we follow, and the decisions we make in our lives, ultimately belongs to us.

It's easy to get lazy. We can let a friend, an employee, or even a skilled therapist begin making our decisions for us. We can listen to what they say and blindly take their advice. Then we don't have to take responsibility for our lives. If the decision doesn't work out, we can say, "You were wrong. Look at the mess you've gotten me into. I'm a victim, again."

Yes you are. But you're a victim of yourself.

We can listen to advice and let other people help us, but if they're helping us do something that is our responsibility, the ultimate responsibility for the decision still belongs to us.

Get help when you need it. Delegate tasks. But don't give away your power. Remember you can think, you can feel, you can take care of yourself, you can figure out your problems.

Don't get lazy. Don't give away responsibility for your life.

God, help me remember that I am responsible for me.

September 29   Remember to take care of yourself

Jenna started dating a new man. Like many women, she was a little frustrated with all the losers that had come along before. She thought she'd put this one to the test. She wanted to see how good he'd be to her.

So when he called her up and asked her what she wanted to do, she told him she thought he should take her on a little trip.

"Hawaii would be nice," she said. "You get us the tickets. And find someplace nice for us to stay when we get there. I don't want to be in a cheesy hotel."

He had enough money in the bank. The trip, she thought, would be exquisite and luxurious. She envisioned the first-class air travel, the limos, and the home he'd rent complete with maid service and a cook.

When the day of the trip arrived, they took a taxi, not a limo, to the airport. And when she boarded the airplane, he led her back to coach. When the flight attendant came around asking if people wanted to rent movies, her boyfriend shook his head and went back to reading his book. She had to dig out the four dollars to pay for the movie.

She sat scrunched up in her seat, all the way to Hawaii. When they got there, he took her to a time-share condo. Then he drove her in the rental car to the grocery store and said, "Pick out what you want to cook."

Throughout the vacation she spent a lot of time stewing in her head, but when they got home, she decided to give him one more chance.

So when he called her up and asked her what she wanted to do Friday night, she said she thought a movie would be nice. She hung up the phone, then dressed up and did her hair. She thought maybe he'd take her to a nice theater.

He picked her up, then drove to the nearest Blockbuster. "Go in and pick out whatever video you'd like to rent," he said. "Do you want to watch it at your place or mine?

The moral of this story is twofold and simple. The first lesson is if you know exactly what you want, you need to spell it out clearly. The second is that it's better not to expect people to take care of us. Even if they agree to do it, we might not like how they do the job.

While it's nice to have people love us and do things for us, it's better to plan on taking care of ourselves.

God, help me remember that it's my job to take care of myself.

September 30   Own your power

I was in an airplane on the way up. I was doing my fidgeting thing, as usual. Brady Michaels, a stunt man and sky diver I had come to know and respect, was sitting across the aisle from me.

"How are you doing, Melody," he asked in a gentle way, like he really wanted to know.

"I'm scared," I said.

"Do you believe in God?" he asked.

"Yes," I said.

"Well then walk to that door, jump, and pull your rip cord when it's time," he said. "And don't forget to have some fun, too."

Owning our power can be one of the most illusive issues we face in recovery. How much is my part? When do I do it? How much is God's part? Which parts of my life am I responsible for, and which parts are destiny?

You can spend years in therapy talking about feelings, but that isn't the same as releasing your feelings and fears and moving forward in your life. You can go to college and train to do the thing you want to do in life. You can sleep every night with your wish list underneath your pillow. But that's different from stepping up to the plate and doing it, whether that means writing a romance novel, starting your own business, learning to bake a cake, or buying an easel and painting a picture. You can read all the travel books in the library—but that's different from getting on an airplane and taking a trip to someplace you've always wanted to see.

We can go to a million Twelve Step meetings, but that's different from actually working each of the Steps.

As my favorite skydiving instructor, Andy, told me, there's three things to remember:

Gravity always works. The earth won't move out of your way. And God won't pull your rip cord.

We've surrendered our lives and will to the care of God. Now, it's time to learn what it means to align with and own our power.

God, help me own my power to take care of myself. Help me learn to do the job well.

October

Say I See

I was out at the drop zone one day soon after I'd begun skydiving, when the idea occurred to me. *I know*, I thought, *I'll get a cabin out here, on a little hill with a hot tub, fireplace, and lined inside with scented cedar wood.*

Wouldn't it be nice, I thought, *to live high up on a hill and look down at night at the twinkling lights, overlooking the city and the lake?*

I didn't think much more about it, until the cold, rainy season started. Then, despite all my efforts to repress the dream of the cabin, it just popped up and sprang right out from inside of me.

I called my friend Kyle and asked him if he was busy. He said no. So I asked him if he had some time to go driving around with me.

"I just want to check out the area," I said. "Let's see if the cabin's there. Let's just drive to where my intuition takes me."

We drove down highway fifteen when an exit approached. Taking the exit felt like the thing to do. We turned off and started driving west. I looked to my right and suddenly felt an urge to drive up the hill. So we followed the road, driving by one house after another. Finally, at the end of the road, there was a small cabin at the top of a hill. The outside was covered with rough-sawn cedar. A brick fireplace covered the front of the house. A hot tub sat in the backyard. And a for sale sign was posted in the frontyard.

There are other pieces to this story. Chip got in on the dream. At some point we stopped calling it "the cabin," and it became the Blue Sky Lodge. Pat and Andy came along and helped make the dream real. It was going to be a comfortable place for people who liked to do things in the air. We'd have extra beds available. It wouldn't be a hotel, but it was open to any guest who wanted to spread his or her wings and learn how to fly.

We camped at the Lodge during construction. Everything took longer than we thought, but eventually it turned into the place of our dreams.

There's a pool table, a dartboard, a whimsical guest room called the clown room, a comfy guest bedroom, a living room with a massive stone fireplace and a big-screen TV. Then there's the Blue Room, a master bedroom with blue plaid material on the walls. It houses the biggest, most comfortable bed in the world—the Cloud Bed—and my desk.

Red beams line the cedar wood ceiling. Chip has a desk in the foyer, and there's video cameras and regular cameras and computers on top of it. And there's books and CDs and flight bags and parachutes and helmets and climbing ropes lying around all over the house.

The Blue Sky Lodge is really about learning that your dreams can come true.

Whether your dreams for yourself come to you in bits and pieces, over a period of time, or whether you practice visualization to see and focus on your dreams yourself, dreams are just another way of God communicating with us.

She's saying, "Look at what you *can* have."

An important part of the language of letting go is learning to say, "I see what I can have, who I am, where I am, and what I have right now."

God, help me become aware.

In the skydiving world, at drop zones, there's usually a small office where the sky diver goes. This office or place is called *manifest*. The potential sky diver must submit the ticket and be assigned to a particular flight. Sometimes things happen. The winds might pick up, canceling that particular flight. The sky might cloud over. Something could happen that would change that sky diver's mind about getting on the plane. But for all purposes, once you've been to manifest, you're going to be at the door of the airplane looking down 12,500 feet with a group of sky divers yelling at you to jump.

It you don't want to be at that door, trying to let go and wondering how you got yourself there, don't make the trip to manifest.

It's easy to see how events get manifested in the skydiving world. Sometimes it's more difficult to see the manifest office in our daily lives.

"How did I get here," we say, looking around at the city we live in, the person we married, or the job we have. Of course, destiny and our Higher Power play a large part in where we are.

But so do we.

Choices we make lead us along. The big decisions we make help shape our destiny. Our thoughts, intentions, and imagination have more to do with shaping our present moment than we could ever imagine.

The problem is that usually there's a gap between our intentions or behavior and seeing them manifest in reality. By the time an event takes place, we've forgotten that B happened because we did A. It's difficult to see the progressive effect of the many choices we make in a day.

I'm not saying that we create everything that happens to

us. We don't have that much power. But God alone didn't send a lot of the stuff that comes our way. We created much of it ourselves.

Be aware of the words you use, especially those combined with powerful emotion or will. If we're going to manifest something in reality, let's make it good.

God, show me the creative powers I possess, especially my power to manifest events in my life. Teach me to use these powers to create harmony and beauty in the world.

October 3   Be aware of your intentions

Your inner self is literal and does not understand ambiguity so whenever you direct it to manifest your desires, give it absolutely literal instructions. . . . Your natural self is quite fond of accomplishing the tasks you give it. It loves to display its skills and perform for you and others, and can do nearly anything (within the realm of possibility and probability) that you can conceive.

— Enid Hoffman

Be clear on your intentions.

Intentions are more than mere wishes. An intention is will mixed with emotions and desire. For instance, I can sit here and wish the house were cleaner. When I put all else aside, take my frustration about the mess and channel it into energy and my desire for tidiness, I can say, "I will spend one hour straightening up."

Sometimes we make our intentions known to other people. For instance, we might start dating someone, and it's our intention to eventually marry. Intentions can turn into manipulation when we don't make them clear. They can also involve control, in the worst sense, when they involve changing the free will of someone else.

The best place to start is by making our intentions clear to ourselves. What do you want? In regards to your life situations, like work or finances, what are you intentions?

Sometimes our good intentions can run totally amok. For instance, we might intend to get a person sober, but they may have no desire to sober up. We can avoid a lot of painful manipulations, if we're clear about our intentions.

Watch yourself as you go through life encountering different situations. Do you have an agenda? Do you even know what it is? Sometimes our intentions are less than conscious, hidden right below the surface. For instance, we may have an intention to get married and have someone support us so we don't have to support ourselves. Are someone else's intentions influencing your own?

When you start any project, a new relationship, or just a new day, spend a moment and get quiet. Be clear with yourself and others on what your intentions are. Then surrender those intentions to God.

God, please help me align my intentions and desires with your highest good will for my life.

October 4   Value your dreams

I always wanted to be a writer. Long ago I talked to God about it, then asked God to bring it to pass if that dream was from Him. Or Her. Within twenty-four hours, I had my first writing assignment from a community newspaper. I got paid five dollars a story, and I've been writing ever since.

Sometimes, we get a vision of ourselves doing something. We might get an inkling or even have a dream where we see ourselves doing something in the future. We might get a feeling that we're about to become pregnant. Or we might have a dream in which we see ourselves moving into a new home. We might be driving by a neighborhood one day and get a special feeling that it would be right for us to live there.

We might get a hunch about a career-oriented event.

Some people think these little hunches or dreams are our soul's way of remembering what it came here to do.

We see a flash: a dream, vision, or special feeling of what's coming next. Maybe your dreams about what you want and what you'd like are more important than you think.

God, show me what you want me to do and experience in life. Then give me enough consciousness to relax and see what you're pointing out.

Activity: Have an *I see* page in your journal. As you go about the days ahead, pay special attention to the dreams that pop into your head. Nighttime dreams are important. It's good to write in your journal about those, too. Often they give us clues. But what I'm talking about here are our daytime dreams and feelings—those things we think we want or can see ourselves doing. Have you buried any dreams from childhood or adulthood, things you really wanted to pursue but forgot along the way? Tell yourself it's time to remember. Then let it go. Pay attention to what pops up into sight. Write it down, even if it's just a sentence or two. Then let the dream go again. Don't try to control the future. It will happen of its own accord.

"Go over your skydive in your mind," my jump master taught me, when I first began learning to jump out of the plane. "Sit down by yourself and see yourself going through every movement, from the time you get into the plane until you come back to earth."

Visualization has been a helpful tool to me in skydiving and in most areas of my life.

In the 1980s, Shakti Gawain wrote a best-seller, *Creative Visualization*. She talked about the powerful impact of using your mind to imagine yourself in some activity before actually doing it in reality.

Visualization has been a self-help tool that's been around even longer than that. Many people in all walks of life, from therapists to sports professionals, agree that seeing yourself doing it beforehand is the best way to do it well.

We can use the tool of visualization to help create matter out of spiritual energy, simply by spending quiet time during our meditation focusing on what we want, seeing ourselves having it, doing it, touching it, and feeling it. One woman told me she used visualization to help see herself letting go of a partner.

"I get quiet and I actually see myself living happily without the person I thought I had to have in my life," she said to me. "I get into the details of myself, too. How unencumbered I feel. How grateful I am for the lessons that person taught me. How I'm free of the burden of obsessing about this person. It really helps me let go."

Visualization is an important tool. It's a gift when we can see ourselves doing something and then having that activity manifested in reality.

Visualization only works if you use it. Make it a regular practice in your life.

Visualize yourself living with one of your dreams. Visualize yourself doing something you're nervous about doing. Take a few moments and run through the entire scenario in your head, until you can see yourself doing that thing calmly, clearly, and successfully with all obstacles cleared from your path.

God, help me use visualization as a regular tool in my life. Help me do my part in creating positive situations by taking the time first to see it, to visualize it.

Activity. Become an expert at visualization. Go to the library or bookstore and get a couple books on visualization. Then, read these books and begin applying the tool of visualization in your life.

October 6   See it simple

"It's too much," I said to my instructor. "Jumping out of a plane is too much for my mind to comprehend."

"Then keep it simple," he said. "Break it down into parts. You have the ride up, where you practice relaxing, your exit, your free-fall time; then you deploy your parachute. Then you decide if it's working or if you need to go to plan B. Next set up your landing pattern. When you get near the ground, pull your strings and flare."

I could handle the steps, but the big picture of jumping out of an airplane was too much to envision. But exiting, falling stable, pulling, and flaring were simple parts that felt manageable. My mind could comprehend these simple tasks.

You may never make a skydive. Or maybe you will. But there's a lot of things in life that seem like too much if we try to see them all as one big thing. I never thought I could stay sober and drug-free for twenty-seven years. But with God's help and the help of the program, I believed I could refrain from using drugs and alcohol for twenty-four hours. Then the next day, I got up and believed the same thing again.

There have been times I didn't think I could start my life over. But I could get up in the morning and do the things I thought best for that day.

Are you facing something now in your life that feels too overwhelming? Then simplify it. Break it down into manageable parts until you can see how simple it is.

God, if I'm complicating a task or making it too big and unmanageable in my mind, help me to simplify what I see.

October 7   Tell yourself how simple it is

Here's another example about the power of simplification.

For years, I heard about hiking. It sounded so elusive, difficult, and mysterious. I didn't do it, but I thought about hiking wistfully. One day, a friend asked me to go hiking with him. "Sure," I said. As the day of our hike approached, I began thinking things through. I was getting a little nervous. What if I couldn't do it well enough? What if I didn't know how to do it at all?

Don't be ridiculous, I scolded myself. *You're making this much more complicated than it really is. Hiking is just walking, and you've been doing that since you were ten months old.*

The next day, I arose at 6:00 A.M., and my friend and I left for our hike. I followed my friend as he began walking up the steep incline.

Just walk, I told myself after the first ten steps. *Put one foot in front of another. Walk like you've done all your life.*

I didn't make it to the top of the mountain that day, but I

made it almost halfway.

Is there something you've wanted to do but have put off because it sounds too difficult and complicated? Are you saying no to something in your life that you'd like to say yes to, but it seems elusive and out of your reach? Try reducing the task or activity to its simplest form.

I have a friend who hadn't dated for years. One day, a girl he liked asked him to go to the movies. He was anxious and nervous.

"Going to a movie is just sitting down and staring at the screen, then getting up and going home when you've finished," I said. "I think you can do that."

"You're right," he said. He went and had a great time.

Sometimes, we can scare ourselves out of doing the easiest things in life. Yes, hiking involves more than walking. And going on a date with someone involves a little more than sitting and staring at a screen. But not that much more. Simplify things. Bring them down to their most manageable level. Instead of talking yourself out of living, learn to talk yourself into it.

God, give me the courage to fully live my life. Help me deliberately talk myself into doing things, instead of scaring myself away.

October 8   Go at your own pace

This part of the path was steep. And the altitude change was severe. I was gasping for breath and trying not to grimace at the ache in my legs as my hiking partner strode up the path in front of me.

He stopped and looked back. I was definitely trailing behind. If his legs were aching the way mine were, his stride didn't show it. I knew how it felt to hold yourself back to someone else's pace. I didn't want to do that to him just because I was out of shape.

"You go on ahead," I yelled.

He looked reluctant.

"Go. Hike at your own pace. I'll hike at mine."

I convinced him to leave me behind. Just because we came together didn't mean that we had to hike, or walk as I preferred to call it, in the same stride. My friend went on ahead of me and disappeared from sight. I hiked, then rested, then hiked, then rested. Once, I stopped, took off my backpack, and took a nap.

My friend and I joined up toward the end of the day. We made the trek down the mountain together, side by side.

Even though we simplify things, most things are harder than we think. It's important to let each person go at their own pace. Whether it's working through an issue or tackling a project in your life, find the pace that works for you. Let others do the same.

Don't compare yourself to those around you. Let yourself be energized by their pace, but respect the rhythm that works for you.

God, help me know that each of us has our own rhythm for getting through life. Help me honor and enjoy the rhythms that work for me.

October 9   Lower your expectations

When you're starting a first creative project or beginning the study of an art or craft, what I want you to do is lower your standards until they disappear. That's right. You're not supposed to be any good at the beginning. So you might as well give yourself the liberating gift of joyously expecting yourself to be bad.
— Barbara Sheer and Annie Gotlieb, Wishcraft

When I first began writing newspaper and magazine articles, it took me anywhere from one to three months to complete a short article. After writing for a few years, I brought a timer into my office one day. I told myself I knew how to do what I was doing, now I was going to learn to do it more quickly. Before long, I was able to write in two hours what had previously taken me months to accomplish. The key words here are *in time.*

When I first began recovering from chemical dependency, it took me eight months of treatment to understand what other people were comprehending in six weeks. In time, I became a chemical dependency counselor. In time, I wrote books on the subject. The key words here are *in time.*

When I first began recovering from codependency, I couldn't tell a control gesture from setting a boundary. I didn't know when I was taking care of myself or what that even meant. I didn't know manipulation from an honest attempt at expressing my emotions. In time, I wrote a best-seller on the subject. Again, the key words here are *in time.*

Start where you are. Start poorly. Just begin. Let yourself fumble, be awkward and confused. If you already knew how to do it, it wouldn't be a lesson in your life. And you wouldn't get the thrill of victory two, five, or ten years from now when you look back and say, "Wow. I've gotten good at that over time."

All things are possible to him or her that believeth, the Bible says. Enjoy those awkward beginnings. Revel in them. They're the key to your success.

God, help me stop putting off living out of fear of doing it poorly. Help me lower my expectations to allow room for awkward beginnings.

Activity: What have you been putting off or avoiding out of fear of beginning badly? Make a list of each accomplishment you have, whether it's graduating from elementary school or college, learning a new skill at a job, or being a parent. Then, write in your journal about how it felt in the beginning. Now, make a list of the things you want to do. Next to your goal, write these words to yourself: I give you permission to do this poorly in the beginning. Document your performance each time you attempt that goal. Keep coming back to this section of your journal until you find yourself logging how well you did.

October 10   See how it feels to do it right

In skydiving, there's an activity called *dirt diving*. At the drop zone, you'll see people lying on their bellies on contraptions that look like skateboards. They make all the moves on the ground as if they were free-falling through the air. They're training their bodies and themselves to do it *right*. They're experiencing how it feels to do it right.

Do you have something you're trying to learn how to do? Are you struggling to let go of someone? Are you trying to do something for the first time—conquer your fear of flying or write a book? Do you have a meeting scheduled that's causing you some strain? Maybe you need to approach your boss and ask for a raise.

See yourself doing it. Quiet yourself first by deliberately relaxing each part of your body and mind. Then imagine yourself doing it, whatever it is. See how it feels to do it right. Go into each detail of how you would feel if you were doing it right.

If you encounter a block that keeps you from moving forward smoothly in your visualization time, ask your Higher

Power or yourself how to remedy or release that block. Do you have a fear that's blocking you? Is it a new or an old fear? Maybe it's concern over what somebody told you long ago about your inadequacy. Release that energy, then start all over again, seeing what it feels like to do it right. Keep at your visualization until you can go through the entire process smoothly, from beginning to end.

If you try but can't imagine yourself doing something, much less see how it feels to do it right, maybe you're trying to do something that's not right for you. Ask your Higher Power for guidance about that, too.

Visualization can give us time to safely dirt-dive and work through awkwardness, fears, and potential blocks and problems. Sometimes spending quiet time trying to visualize how it feels to do it right can give us a message that either this is or isn't the right time or thing for us.

God, help me use my mental powers to create the most positive scenes I can imagine taking place in my life.

October 11   Make use of your imaginative powers

It was a small ad in a catalog for an electric flossing machine. "I don't have the time or energy to floss," the man in the ad declared. "That's why I need this machine to do it for me."

Too busy and too tired?

Some of us complain about all the things we have to do to maintain spiritual health. Prayer. Meditation. Attending support groups. All these things take time and energy, even though we get a good return on the time we invest. Now, we're considering adding another activity to our already full self-care activities list: spending time and energy visualizing to help create positive events in our lives.

When someone first suggested I use visualization as a tool, my reaction was similar to one of the man in the ad. *I don't have the time. I'm too busy and tired.*

But we're always thinking about something and creating pictures in our minds. Usually what we see are worst case scenarios. So why not take the time, effort, and energy we're already using to see things not working out and instead visualize things working out? If we've got enough time and energy to see the negative what if's, we've got the time and energy to visualize positive events, too.

Visualizing isn't a form of control. Just because we see things working out well doesn't guarantee that they will. But if we can see it, it's more likely to happen than if we can't see it at all.

God, help me use the powers of thought and imagination in the most creative way I can.

October 12   See it and let it go

This is a reminder. While you're using your imagination, embracing your dreams, and spending your time visualizing positive performance, don't forget to let go.

Don't worry about how things will come to pass. Your part is seeing the best for yourself. Then return to the details of your daily life.

It's safe to let go and let God. Just because we have the creative powers to imagine doesn't mean we have to control the rest. Say, *I see,* then let it go.

Let God work the manifest.

God, after I've seen my dreams and visualizations, help me give them back to you.

October 13   Let go of what you can't see, too

Let life unfold, even if you can't see the good that you want coming your way. Are you worried about what's going to happen next? Has there been a shift in your job or relationship that makes you tense?

Let life unfold. Don't limit it by the past or even by what you can see and visualize. Don't deny that you feel discouraged or anxious. Let today unfold. Then tomorrow, do the same. If you've been worrying about something and you can't see how it could possibly work out and there's nothing to do now, then relax and let things unfold.

Sometimes the unexpected things that manifest are better than what we can imagine or see. Even if we can't see the good coming our way, God can.

God, help me know that what is unseen today will be made clear when the time is right.

October 14   See naturally

I was talking to a friend one day about using visualization as a tool to help create the present and the future we desire. Visualization, or using the spiritual energy of thought as a tool, can create physical reality.

"I don't really do that much," he said. "I'm not one for visualization."

Later, we were talking about a project we were working on together. He began to describe the next stage of the process. "I see us working together on it like this," he said. He described in great detail how he saw things coming to pass.

I listened. When he finished, I told him, "You said you don't use visualization as a tool. But you just used it naturally, without thinking, to describe how we are going to work on the next stage of this project."

He thought for a moment, then said he guessed I was right.

Don't talk yourself out of using visualization as a tool. Most of us often use our imagination to consider things that are taking place now or in the future. Be aware of what you say and see, so that you can use this powerful tool, your imagination, to help create whatever it is that you really want to see.

Pay attention to the ways you use your imagination in your daily life, the number of times you naturally say how you see things working out. If you find yourself using your imaginative powers to create negative events, stop! Erase that scene and create something else.

God, help me become aware of how I see naturally. Help me use and respect my imagination as the powerful creative tool it is.

October 15   Look where you're going

"I have the controls!" Rob, my flight instructor said. He grabbed the yoke and turned the little Cessna away from an approaching plane. "Did you see him or hear him on the radio?" Rob asked.

"No," I said. "I was concentrating too much on the flight panel instruments inside to scan outside for other planes."

"The airplane wants to fly," Rob said. "Learn to feel what coordinated flight feels like so you won't need to be glued to the instruments. You need to be looking outside for other aircraft."

Sometimes we get so engrossed in the world inside our heads that we forget to look outside. We can become so involved with the minor details of a project, something we're trying to do, that we don't see the big problem coming at us until it crashes into us. We can get so absorbed in our emotions that we neglect the rest of our lives. We can become so engrossed with our agenda—trying to get someone to like us, to get that job, to buy that house, or to control an outcome—that we don't see the warning signs and realize that person, thing, or place might not be good for us.

Learn to feel your life and understand intuitively when you're on the right path. Be aware. Sometimes we can spot potential problems when they're still small and far away. If you can do this, then only minor corrections to your course may be necessary to avoid conflicts down the road.

Remember, the airplane wants to fly, but you've got to keep from hitting anything if you want a safe flight. Relax and look where you're going. That's how you stay on course.

God, help me become aware of danger signals before it's too late.

October 16   You'll go where you look

There was only one tree in the landing area. Most of its leaves had been stripped away by the winter winds. I didn't want to hit it, but that's exactly what I did.

My parachute opened up right over the student landing area, a blessing for someone as new and unsure as I. I flew along the side of the field, turned onto the base leg, and then carefully turned into my final approach just as I'd been taught. There it was, the tree, its scrawny branches reaching up for me. It was all I could see from that point on. I couldn't take my eyes off of it. For a moment I thought I might clear it. "NO LOW TURNS, NO LOW TURNS," kept screaming in my ear as I drifted lower and lower, straight toward that tree.

I watched myself sink right into it.

Laughter and applause drifted out from the packing area.

Later another jumper pulled me aside to talk. "Do you know why you hit the tree?" she asked.

"Yes," I said. "It was in my way."

"There's more to it than that," she said. "You had plenty of time to turn out of the way of the tree. Instead, you watched yourself land right in it. You'll always go where you look. Look at something long enough to be aware of the potential for trouble, but don't fixate on the object. If you don't want to land on top of something, quit staring at it so hard."

Sometimes we get so focused on what we don't want and what we're afraid of, that's all we can see. We obsess about it, worry, and mull it around in our heads. It's all we can talk about, think, or feel. Then when we come crashing right into it, we wonder where we went wrong. After all, it was the very thing we had been trying to avoid.

The moral of this story is simple and sweet. Look at where you're going, but remember you'll go where you look.

Know what you don't want. Release your fears. Stay aware and alert to the dangers looming in your peripheral view. Your mind is more powerful than you might believe. If you put all your concentration and energy on something, that's exactly where you'll go.

God, help me stay aware and focus my energy on where you want me to go.

October 17   The beauty is easy to see

It is good to have an end to journey toward; but it is the journey that matters, in the end.

— *Ursula K. Le Guin*

324

One lesson road trips have taught me is that while it's good to have a destination, it's good to see what the trip has to offer rather than waiting for it to bring us what we expected.

Recently, a friend and I made a trip to Santuario de Chimayo to visit the church and bring home some of the healing dust from the sacred place. Along the way, we planned to pass through other beautiful places in the Southwest, a spiritual pilgrimage we thought. We left the house ready to be enlightened. But something happened. In the hot Arizona air, we stopped letting the trip happen and started looking for a specific experience. The Indian ruins were overrun with tourist groups and the beautiful red rock vortex center had been reduced to strip malls and time-share condos. Our spiritual quest had yielded nothing but disappointment so far. We felt antsy, irritable, and let down.

Then we saw the sign: *Meteor Crater road next right*. We turned down that road, giving in to the cheesy kitsch of the trip. A mile wide and over five hundred feet deep the crater was left over fifty thousand years ago in the middle of what is now the Arizona desert. A man bought the land and he and his family became meteor experts—marketing experts as well since they now charge ten dollars to see a big hole in the ground. Nice enough folks though, and we smiled for the first time on the trip.

I'd always wanted to see the Petrified Forest, though I feared that once again the hype would overpower the reality of what it was. It didn't. The giant logs-turned-to-stone were scarce but the place had a powerful timelessness to it. The sky was pastel blue. I lay on a giant wave of sand while Chip ran around taking pictures that would end up overexposed.

Later that evening we crossed the border into New Mexico. *Chelle's—a nice place to eat* read the sign on the side of a building in Gallup. And it was nice, just like the sign said.

We can search for joy and enlightenment so frantically that we don't see the brilliance at our own feet. Sometimes in the search for enlightenment, it helps to remember to lighten up. To paraphrase Winnie the Pooh, if you're looking for enlightenment and only find the ordinary, then try looking at the ordinary and let it be what it is. You might then find something you weren't looking for, which might be just what you were looking for when you began.

Don't let your hopes and expectations be so high that you miss the beauty in what is. Joy and enlightenment, after all, aren't that hard to see.

God, help me let go of my expectations and delight in what is.

October 18   Take another look

It's amazing the difference
A bit of sky can make.

— *Shel Silverstein*

We spend mornings at the Blue Sky Lodge drinking coffee on the back porch watching the world wake up. One morning, after grabbing my cup, I walked out back to find Frank, a skydiving friend staying at the Lodge while visiting from the United Kingdom, busily snapping pictures of the surrounding terrain.

"Frank, why are you taking pictures of this?" I asked. "If you want, we can take you to some of the more scenic areas around here."

"No way," he replied. "No one back home will believe that I got to spend my time in a place with a view like this!"

I looked around and tried to see the view through his eyes. The rolling hills of southern California were bathed in golden early morning sunlight, while a light marine layer curled over the ridgeline of the Ortega Mountains just three miles to the west. San Jacinto rose high in the eastern sky, a pale silhouette in the morning sun.

I smiled and for the first time in a while took in the sheer beauty of the view. Lately all I had been seeing were the piles of leaves and construction materials scattered around the yard or the cars driving along the road in the valley below us. I had been surrounded with beauty and yet had grown so accustomed to it that I didn't even notice it anymore.

Many times what we need isn't a change of scenery, but a renewed vision of what's already there. Take another look at your life—where you live, your friends, your work—all your gifts. Maybe the view in your life is better than you think.

God, renew my spirit. Help me look at my life with a fresh vision. If I don't like what I see, help me look again.

October 19   See for yourself

I have a friend who likes to hike and backpack. He always takes beautiful pictures of the places that he visits. After one trip he was telling me about a camp high in the California Sierras while showing me a photo of a stunning sunset. He told me about the night that he returned to camp after walking to the top of the mountain.

"When I got down, I found that everyone else had packed up and left camp. I was alone at twelve thousand feet. The silence was so thick I could almost touch it. You should have seen the sunset that night. It was even better than this picture."

"Why didn't you take a picture if the sunset was even more beautiful?" I asked.

"I figured that no one else cared to see the world from that viewpoint that night but me, so I just kept the sunset all to myself," he explained. "If you weren't there, you just missed out."

This summer I watched the sun set over a lake in a corner of New Mexico, then I spent the night under the stars in a sleeping bag. The stars were so clear, so close, so brilliant I felt like I could touch them. And no, I didn't take a picture. If you weren't there, you just missed out.

You can read a meditation book, make a list, and even talk to people who live their lives fully, but unless you make the trip yourself, you won't see all this life has to offer.

Is there a picture that you've been too busy to see lately? Break out of the ordinary. See something new or see the ordinary in a new way. Don't just glance. Really look. Then bring back the picture in your heart. Unless you're there, you're just missing out. Some things you just need to see for yourself.

God, help me live my life to the fullest. Help me see and treasure all the beauty in the world.

October 20   Be present now

Take time, but not too much, to see where you want to go. Learn the lessons from your past. Then let go of yesterday. Let tomorrow take care of itself. Even our best prediction about what may come in the future is only an educated guess, no matter how diligently we try to see ahead. If all you look at is where you're going, you'll miss all the wonder and beauty along the way. And once you get there—your future—you may not even remember where you've been. Rushing may be such a habit that you won't enjoy your future once it arrives.

Be where you are right now. See what's in front of you, not

what you wish were there. Take time to see, enjoy, and appreciate what's present. Take action if you need to. Or just enjoy the view. You've worked hard to get here. Enjoy it.

The past is important. It's where we've been. The future is important, too. But there's no time—and no time as real—as the present.

Learn to be here, now.

God, heighten my awareness and appreciation of each moment in my life.

October 21   Cultivate awareness

Often the words "consciousness" and "awareness" are used interchangeably. . . . Consciousness is the pulsing vibration that is the essence of all things. Awareness is the individuating "I AM" in each of us. Wherever I am, my awareness is also. When I move, my awareness goes with me. When I focus my awareness on something, I perceive that thing. Through my physical sensory organs I am aware of sights, sounds, tastes, smells and touch. Through higher sensory perception I am aware of much more.

— Enid Hoffman

Use all your senses, whether you are visualizing the future or sinking into a joyful awareness of where you are right now. Don't just look at the flower—touch it. Smell it. Feel it.

Don't just gaze at the people in your life. Hear them. Feel their power and presence.

Slow down. Don't move so fast. You'll miss important things. Cultivate awareness. Bring your senses, all of them, into the heart of your life.

Awareness isn't about looking. It's about seeing with more

than our eyes. Often when we look for a thing, whether it's a home or a girlfriend, all we can see is our projections—our hopes, fears, past, and desires.

Relax. Stop projecting yourself onto the world. Let go of judgments. Let things and people be what and who they are.

Cultivate awareness by using all your senses.

Learn to see what is.

God, help me slow down and become aware.

October 22   Be aware of your heroes

Heroes and mentors can inspire and teach us to do great things with our lives. They can help point us in the right direction when we're unsure. They can bring us just the right message, at just the right time. Usually we can find someone who has walked the path before us, and can lead us with his or her example. The problem comes when he or she stops being a mentor to us and becomes an idol instead. If we spend too much time revering an individual, we can easily lose sight of the message.

Take a look at the people in your life that you have chosen as mentors, heroes, sponsors, or teachers. Appreciate all the help they give you. But be aware that they don't and can't have all the answers. They're human, too. They too have blind spots, prejudices, and their own lessons to go through. And yes, they'll make mistakes. But if their hearts are true, they'll come back to the path. And if your heart is true, maybe you'll be a light helping guide them there.

Listen to your mentors. Respect them for who they are. Be grateful for the inspiration and messages that come through them to you. But don't worship your heroes.

Learn to think for yourself as well.

God, help me remember that it's the message, not the messenger, that counts. Thank you for my heroes, teachers, and mentors, but help me remember not to lift them up too high.

October 23   Find and respect your own stride

Do not seek to follow in the footsteps of the men of old; seek what they sought.

> — Basho

One of the dangers of following a hero is the temptation to emulate them too much instead of walking our own path. John quit his job and started his own company when he was twenty-four years old. Five years later he sold out for millions of dollars. We want to be like John so we try the same thing and go broke. What happened? Is the universe against us? No. We just got confused about the difference between learning from a hero and trying to walk his path. John's path may have led him to start a company; your path may also lead you on that course, just not at the same time in your life.

We can still learn much from our heroes and the people we admire. Just be aware that their path and time frame may be different from ours.

When the time comes for you to start that business, learn a new skill, enter into a relationship, or whatever you're hoping to do, the experience will be there. The experience will be ready for you when you're ready for it. Your timing may be different from everyone else's.

I know people who got married after knowing each other only two weeks and then stayed mostly happily married for more than thirty years. I know people who date each other for years and still can't decide if they're ready to commit. My friend made the transition from living in the Midwest to living in California in months. That transition took me several years.

We each have our own stride and path. And while many of our lessons are similar, each of us is unique. If we spend our time trying to emulate a person rather than an idea, we'll at best be an inferior version of our teacher and at worst will never discover our own path. Their stride will be too long or too short for us, and we won't learn the true lesson, which is to trust our inner guide.

Gautama Buddha found enlightenment while sitting under a banyan tree; Milarepa found it while living as a hermit in a Himalayan cave. Gaining enlightenment isn't an exercise in following a person; it's an exercise in following your heart.

God, help me let go of any expectations of perfection I may have of myself or others. Help me be aware of the messages you send me, then help me discern my own truth.

October 24   What you see isn't always what you get

I was walking through the mall when I saw a photo booth at one of the kiosks. A large green screen hung as a backdrop and the photographer had her subjects stand in front of it in various poses. After taking the photo, she used a computer to paste it into a scene. You might then look like an alligator wrestler, a snowboarder, a hapless adventurer getting run over by his own jeep.

What you see is not always what you get. People are not always what they seem. It's easy for others to paint an inaccurate picture either to impress or manipulate us into doing what they want us to do. Understand that while many, even most, of the people in your life will be honest, there will be those who will paint a false picture. They will claim to have experience that you don't; they will claim to know the secret of how to live your life; they will claim to be something they're not. They will try to use their self-exalted position to control and manipulate you.

Be aware of people who would manipulate you by pasting themselves into a false background or scene. Don't just take things at face value. Take your time, as much time as you need, to see what the real background is.

Most of us get misled from time to time. Sometimes people con us. Other times we trick ourselves. Let go of naïveté.

God, if I start getting conned or manipulated, please show me and help me see the truth.

October 25   Stop tricking yourself

Even the best of us get tricked from time to time. Someone comes along and impresses us with magic. Later we discover it wasn't magic, just illusions.

Sometimes the issue isn't that people were trying to trick us. We tricked ourselves. We saw what we wanted to see, regardless of what reality was. Then, when reality started to creep in, we told ourselves if we held our breath and didn't feel our feelings and hoped long and hard enough, reality would change.

We don't have to get mad at ourselves when we get tricked, even if we've fooled ourselves. We need to see and acknowledge the truth and become aware of what reality is.

Don't let your embarrassment over finding yourself in a bad situation cloud your view of yourself. Sometimes all we need to do is acknowledge the truth, including the truth about how we feel. In a few days or a few months, the solution will become clear.

When all the illusions drop away, that's when real magic begins. You'll be guided along your path.

God, help me remember that when I admit and accept the truth, I'll be given the power and guidance to change.

October 26   Be aware of how you feel

What happened today? How did you feel about it?

Just like all those stuffed feelings from childhood that we could not deal with then, any feelings that we repress or deny today don't go away. They linger in our energy field until we give them their due. Sometimes these repressed feelings block our view of the truth.

For many of us, resisting our feelings is an ancient pattern and a habitual way of life. Take your time to debrief from your day, but don't just say what you did and what you liked. Say how you felt about each thing that occurred.

You might make a discovery that surprises even you. You don't necessarily have to tell the other person how you feel, but you might. For certain, you at least need to tell yourself.

Today is just a simple reminder of something you already know. Be aware each day of what happens. And be aware of how you feel.

God, help me remember that it's okay to be who I am and feel what I feel, no matter what those feelings are. Remind me when I believe my feelings are a nuisance that they're the key to my power.

October 27   Be aware of the illusion of control

Remember how it feels when we try to control someone else.

"I was driving down the road one day behind a car that I decided was driving too slowly," a friend said to me. "I was yelling, raging, and carrying on about the driver in front of me, trying to mentally will him out of my way. I wanted him to move over and let me by.

"While I was driving I observed myself. Then I started to laugh. I wasn't angry about this driver in front of me. I was angry because I was trying to control something that I couldn't change."

Be aware of all your feelings. But also remember to be aware that sometimes it's not the other person that's making us crazy. We're doing it to ourselves.

God, help me be aware of the self-created drama in my life. Help me let go of my need to control. Give me the courage of my feelings. And help me be aware of when my self-will is running riot.

October 28   Let enlightenment come

Sometimes, the harder we try to see a lesson, the more lost and confused we become. "What does it mean?" we ask, squinting at the problem.

Relax. Let go of your expectations and your interpretations. Quit trying so hard to see.

Sometimes the lesson may be a simple reminder to see the sacred in your ordinary life or to practice compassion for yourself as well as for others. Sometimes what we're going through is part of a larger lesson, one that may take us years to complete and comprehend. It's easy to fall into the false belief that there's some lesson that we have to push and struggle to learn. There isn't.

We only have to see what we see and know what we know right now.

Experience your life.
More shall be revealed when it's time.
Practice seeing without squinting.

God, help me be present to the situations in my life without trying to read too deeply into them. Help me trust that my lessons will become clear when it's time.

October 29   Ask to see what you're being shown

I was in a small shopping center dropping off film to be developed. When I returned to my car, I realized I had locked my keys inside it. Disbelief shortly turned to acceptance. I walked down to the police station, a few doors down. I had locked my purse in the car, too. I didn't have a quarter on me to use the phone.

The police called the automobile club for me. They told me help was on the way. I went outside and sat on the curb. Then I began staring at a small kitchen furnishings store across the street. I stared and stared. Then I decided to go browse for a while, even though I didn't have my purse.

For months I'd been searching all over Southern California looking for a particular brand of pots and pans. I'd almost given up. Although this was a small store, I decided to inquire if they carried that brand.

"Oh, yes," the clerk said. "We sure do."

Sometimes an inconvenient incident is just that—inconvenient. Sometimes we just need to slow down, come back to earth, and be aware. Sometimes there's something our Higher Power would like us to see. And once in a while that unexpected problem is really a blessing in disguise.

Take interruptions and inconveniences in stride. Instead of being angry, try to be quietly present to your life. Be aware.

See if something's being pointed out to you.

God, help me open my eyes to see what you want me to see.

October 30   God's aware of you

Dear God,
Are you really invisible or is that just a trick?
                              — Children's Letters to God

Sometimes we cannot see more than a few feet in front of us along the path. The path is still there. All we have to do is keep walking it until we're out of the darkness and into the Light. Just take one small step at a time.

Surrender to the circumstances in your life. Feel your feelings. Be aware of your pain and your suffering, if that's what you're going through. But remember that even when you can't see God, God can see you.

And God cares.

God, help me feel your active presence and love in my life today.

October 31   Practice awareness of God

I can remember the moment when I was willing to be truly vulnerable with life again. I was walking around in a beach town, talking to my friend. I was talking about my safe little life back in Stillwater, Minnesota, where I thought I had everything under control. I had avoided living in big cities and thought small town living would be safe. In that small town, working for its daily newspaper, I had found all the potential held in life. I got that big break that put me, an unknown author, on the *New York Times* best-seller list. And my son had died. Small town life wasn't as limiting as I feared or as safe as I had hoped.

I told my friend about the time, many years later, I was wandering around the Middle East. I was talking to my daughter on a cell phone. She was on her cell, too, driving through the heart of Los Angeles.

"Aren't you scared over there?" she asked. "Isn't your life in danger?"

Just then a man honked at her. I heard him scream through her window, "If you don't get that car out of the way, I'm going to have you killed."

"Complete safety is an illusion," I said to my friend. "Maybe the only time we're really safe is when we're willing to acknowledge how vulnerable we really are, no matter what we're doing, and be okay with that."

"Ask God to be with me," I said to an older woman who was my mentor at the time.

"Foolish child," she said. "You don't have to ask God to be with you. He's already there, wherever you are."

God, help me feel safe, comfortable, and in your presence wherever I am today.

November

Learn to Say I Can

"This is for you," my friend said on my birthday.

I opened the tiny box with that feeling most women get when they know they're about to receive jewelry. I was right. I lifted out the necklace and held it in my hand.

"Read the brochure that comes with it," my friend encouraged.

I picked up the tiny leaflet. The necklace was more than a piece of jewelry. It was an ancient symbol that represented self-confidence—that intangible *thing* that can so easily enhance, or distract from, our ability to joyfully and peacefully live our lives.

It was exactly the reminder I needed.

The next day, I drove to the airport for my flying lesson. I wasn't exhilarated to be flying that day, but I wasn't dreading it, either. I was simply living each moment. It was time for me to get into the pilot's seat and fly the plane.

I taxied down the runway, then pushed in the throttle, wearing the self-confidence medallion around my neck. The plane lifted happily into the air. I gently took us up to five thousand five hundred feet. Following Rob's instructions, I turned left, steeply. Then I did a steep turn to the right. I did a power-on stall, something that had horrified me in the past, then a power-off stall. The airplane and my flying worked!

It was a breakthrough day in flying. Until then, I had been acting as if, going through the motions, making myself fly. Today, I genuinely enjoyed my time in the air.

The necklace didn't have any power. The power came from remembering to believe in myself.

It's easy to give up confidence in ourselves. We can give it to people from the past who encouraged us to not believe in ourselves. We can give it to mistakes we've made, building a solid case against ourselves based on some lessons we went through, past errors in judgment, and learning experiences. We can forfeit our confidence to a traumatic event—like a divorce, a death, or a loss.

Don't panic.

Breath.

Stop saying, *I can't.*

Part of the language of letting go is learning to say, *I can.*

Give the gift of confidence to yourself.

God, I believe in you. Now help me learn to believe in myself, too.

November 2   Yes, you can

Came to believe that a Power greater than ourselves could restore us to sanity.

— Step Two

Oh, no. I couldn't possibly do that.

Well, maybe I could try.

I guess I can do it, but not very well.

I'm doing it, but I'm very, very frightened.

Oh, my. I'm doing it better.

Oops! I made a mistake. Guess I can't do it, after all.

Oh well. I'll try again.

See! I'm not doing any better this time.

Okay, I'll try one more time. Maybe twice.

Hey look! I'm pretty good!

I guess I can do it, after all.

Wow! This is really fun.

There's a learning curve for anything we want to learn to do. We don't just know how to do something, and do it well.

One good reason to have a Higher Power is that He or She believes in us, even when we don't believe in ourselves. We don't just need to come to believe in God. We need to come to believe in ourselves.

Let your *I can't* turn into an *I can.* Take all the time you need. Learn to enjoy the process of coming to believe you can. Be patient. Accept where you are in your learning curve today.

God, please grant me a humble confidence that allows me to enjoy the gift of life, myself, and all the things you've given me to do.

November 3   You're learning something new

"What are we supposed to be looking for?" Stanley asked him.
"You're not looking for anything. You're digging to build character." . . .

[Stanley] glanced helplessly at his shovel. It wasn't defective. He was defective.

— Louis Sachar, Holes

Sometimes when faced with a difficult obstacle in life—a new job, new school, new anything—it's easy to feel overwhelmed and to start believing the worst about ourselves. Maybe we really don't have what it takes after all, we think. Maybe we should just stay where we are—whether we like that place or not.

One of the wonderful things about being human is our ability to adapt to new situations. Another is our ability to change and grow.

What new situation is facing you? Whether it's beginning a recovery process, starting a new job, going for your master's degree, learning to be divorced, or learning to be a happy spouse, you're up to whatever life is asking you to do.

It is important to start at the beginning of things, and often that means feeling ill prepared for the task ahead. That's good. If you were completely comfortable with everything going on around you, then chances are you wouldn't be growing and learning anything new.

Be aware of how you talk to yourself, whether you're telling yourself *I can* or *I can't*. Then let the words be filled with cheerful confidence. Recognize any feelings that prevent you from believing in yourself. Then let those feelings go. Let go of fear and feeling overwhelmed.

You can learn the new task. You can harmonize with your new boss. You can learn to take care of yourself. You can. You can. And you will. You can and will grow into this role.

You're not defective. Neither is your shovel. Grab it, and dig in.

God, give me the strength and the confidence to grow, learn, and see the wonder of this world.

November 4   Let yourself be uncomfortable

"It seems as though everything you do for fun terrifies you," my friend Andy said to me one day. "What's that about?"

I thought about his question. It was true. Flying scared me. Jumping out of that airplane for the first time was a terrifying prospect. I wasn't comfortable at all. I started hyperventilating and thought I was having a heart attack, at first.

The first day I decided to be sober and clean and not use alcohol and drugs anymore, I was faced with changing my entire life. The prospect of starting this new life scared me to death.

The day my divorce from the children's father was finalized, I was exhilarated for one moment, then I was terrified. I had an anxiety attack and called 911.

I was paralyzed with fear the first day I sat at my cubicle at the newspaper office staring at the blank screen while the deadline for the front-page story I'd been assigned was only two hours away.

"It's not that I'm an adrenaline junkie," I said to my friend. "At least the issue isn't entirely that. It's that everything new and worthwhile I've ever done on my path has required me to be uncomfortable and sometimes downright scared for a while. I've had to walk through a wall of fear."

I enjoy creating a comfortable place to live with down-filled sofas and beds that make me feel like I'm sleeping in the clouds. Learning to relax and learning to identify what makes us comfortable is an important part of learning to take good care of ourselves.

But sometimes we need to leave that nice, comfy, cozy place.

"I can't do this. I'm not comfortable," I'd say time and time again to my flight instructor Rob as he insisted that I take the controls of the plane.

"Yes, you can," he'd say, not feeding into my fear. "Just breathe. And relax."

Sometimes fear is a good thing. It warns us of real dangers and imminent threats. It tells us "don't do that" or "stay away."

Sometimes afraid and uncomfortable is just how we're feeling because we're learning something new. Relax. Breathe deeply. Do it—whatever it is—anyway. You're supposed to feel that way.

Is your fear based on an intuitive feeling of self-protection or something new and unknown? If your fear isn't based on a legitimate intuitive threat, then get comfortable feeling uncomfortable.

Walk through your wall of fear.

Do the thing that scares you. Grow. Then check your fear and do it again.

God, teach me to overcome my fears. Help me mature by becoming comfortable with the discomfort of growth.

November 5   A miracle is taking place

One evening, I was sitting with my children around the dinner table. Shane was talking about his plans for the next day. Nichole was planning a pajama party. I was working on some project at that time. I was partly thinking about it but still enjoying listening to the children talk.

It was a friendly, relaxed supper. Later, I put the children to bed and quietly went to my room, peacefully getting ready to retire for the night.

That's when it hit me. Like the proverbial bolt of lightening, it struck out of the blue.

I was so terrified when I had begun the journey of being a single parent. After ten years of being married, I was scared of little things like sleeping alone in bed at night and falling asleep without a man in the house.

Sometimes I went to bed with the phone in my hand, ready to dial 911. Everything about this new life as a single parent had overwhelmed me. I didn't feel up to the task. But somewhere along the line, I had come to believe I could. I didn't know when it had happened. It wasn't an instant transformation. It had happened slowly, bit by bit.

"Woohoo!" I said, doing a victory dance in the room.

"I didn't think I could do this. But I can and I am."

Celebrate the miracle of transformation in your life—whatever you're trying to become, do, or learn. Let it happen as quickly, or as slowly, as it needs.

Day by day, month by month, then year after year, the feeling of quiet confidence will slowly replace the overwhelming fear. That task or job that first seemed so overwhelming will begin to feel natural and right. You'll gradually become so comfortable you may not even know when that miraculous transformation took place.

Enjoy where you are today in your process of growth. You might not see it or know it yet, but an ordinary miracle is taking place.

God, thank you for where I am in my learning curve and growth process today. Help me know that whether I see it or not, a miracle is taking place.

November 6   **Become willing**

*There's nothing against you to fall down flat
But to lie there—that's disgrace.*

— *Edmund Vance Cooke*

Sometimes the problem isn't that we don't believe we can. The problem is that we don't want to do it, whatever the current task or challenge is.

When I began my writing and recovery, I wanted to do these things. The challenge was invigorating. I wanted to get back up. I wanted to push ahead. I wanted to get into the game.

When my son Shane died, I didn't want to get up.

I didn't want the challenge. It wasn't invigorating. I didn't want the loss, and I didn't want to heal from my grief.

One day in those painful, awful early years of grief, a

friend stopped by the house. I had known him for a long time. He had suffered a permanent loss, too—the use of his leg muscles from a form of polio he had suffered during his teenage years.

People hadn't known what to do with me back then. They had watched me flounder in my grief. They had tried to be compassionate, and that was good. But right now compassion wasn't exactly what I needed to hear.

"You've got to get up," my friend said in a loud voice. "You've got to get back up on your feet again. Stand up to life."

Sometimes life's problems and challenges are invigorating. Sometimes they're not. But no matter what we get hit with, we need to get up again.

Let yourself grieve. Let yourself become enraged over your losses, if you must. Then, whether you want the loss or not, get back up again. You don't have to want to; you don't even have to believe you can. Sometimes all we need to do is be open to wanting to and then believe we can.

God, help me believe in life.

November 7   **What can you do?**

Mr. Potter celebrated his hundredth birthday by doing a bungee jump from a 210 foot tower. When his physician of many years advised him against it, he simply got a new doctor.
— *Stella Resnick,* The Pleasure Zone

I almost have the local record for number of tandems jumped. A tandem is a skydive you do attached to your jump master. The harness hooks you up to the front of him; all you do is go along for the ride. I've done a lot of my training during tandems, to get body memory of how to skydive and to build my confidence.

I haven't met the woman who actually holds the tandem record for the area, but I've heard about her. I've done twenty-eight. She's done many, many more. She even participates in skydiving team events doing tandems.

When she's on the ground, she's labeled a paraplegic. In the air, she can fly.

Sure, there are things we can't do, things we can't have, and things we really want. Stop worrying about those things; there's an even longer list of things we can do and have.

What sounds good to you?

No matter what our limitations or disabilities or what we *can't* have in life, we *can* fulfill our purpose and have some fun while we're doing it.

If Mr. Potter and the tandem record holder can, so can you.

God, please show me what I can do.

November 8   Take the lid off the box

The world shrinks or expands in proportion to one's courage.
— Anaïs Nin

First you crawled; then you learned to walk, and the world grew a little bigger. You learned to ride a bike, and it grew even more. Then you learned to drive a car and bought a plane ticket. Suddenly, the horizons were limitless. But then, those doubts crept in. *I can't go to L.A. I'll never find my way around.* And the world shrinks a little bit. *I shouldn't take that trip this year; I've got too many responsibilities.* And it shrinks a little more. Enough excuses and rationalizations and you're left sitting in a little box with the lid tightly affixed.

No experiences, no lessons, no life.

Boxes can be comfortable. I've spent some time in them myself. But no matter how cozy you make it, a box is still a box. They come in all sizes and shapes. But whenever we start letting unrealistic fears hold us back and down, we can be fairly certain we're climbing inside another box, again. It may take a while, but sooner or later we'll run into the walls.

Find one small *I can't* in your life and take the lid off of the box. Look around. It's a big world out there. If it looks small, it's because you've made it that way. Try for a minor impossibility. Go apply for that dream job. The worst that will happen is that you'll learn something new about yourself. If you don't actually get the job, you may find out what it will take to get it, and then the world will grow when you stop wishing for a miracle and begin pursuing your dreams yourself. Pick up some brochures for that photo safari you've always wanted to take. Learn how to speak a foreign language. One woman I know had claustrophobia. For her birthday this year, she rode in a elevator for the first time. Then she went back and did it again.

Go ahead. Poke the top off from your box. Stick your head out. Look around. See! The world is a marvelous, amazing place.

Find a fear, then turn it into a ladder. Get out of the box of doubt and insecurity and into the freedom of courage and belief in yourself.

God, give me the courage to climb out of my box.

On the last day of my retreat, I told the guestmaster that I didn't think that I would be able to get back soon because I didn't have the time. He came right back with "The problem isn't TIME; the problem is HEAVINESS." He turned and went downstairs returning with a little carpet. "Here take this. It is a magic carpet. If you sit on it and let go of your heaviness, you can go anywhere you want. It's not a question of time." I have come to know that this is true. People laugh at me when I tell them. Will you laugh too? All right. Then stay there.

— *Theophane the Monk,* Tales of a Magic Monastery

Often, the problem in our lives isn't time; it's heaviness.

We aren't too busy. In reality, we're too worried, obsessed, doubtful, overly concerned, and afraid.

Release all that heaviness in your mind and heart. Let it sink away so you can stand free from its weight. When all that heaviness drops away, you can float through and above your ordinary life. You'll decide how you want to live rather than letting the circumstances of the day control you.

Find the heaviness in your life, the overpowering worry that ties you down, and then let it go. Are you fraid that you will be laid off from your job? You either will or you won't, but all the worry does is stifle your creative flow.

Find the heaviness; let it drop away. Then get on your magic carpet and sail through your day.

God, help me lighten my load by letting go of worry, doubt, and fear. Help me learn the power of quiet confidence. Teach me to say I can.

Slowly I began to see that many of the boxes I found myself in were of my own making. I tended to construct them, crawl in, then wonder who I could blame for putting me there. Who did this to me? I would wonder and sometimes ask aloud. That's when I'd hear the answer: You did, Melody. You put yourself in this box. Now it's up to you to get out.
— Melody Beattie, Stop Being Mean to Yourself

Each of us has our own degree of freedom. We have certain things we can do and certain things we can't. Sometimes this freedom fluctuates at different times in our lives. Sometimes we are bound by our responsibilities to other people. Sometimes we have financial limitations. Sometimes we're limited by what our body can or cannot do at any given point in time.

Alcoholics who know they cannot drink because they lose control when they do are people who are in touch with their power. They can't drink, but they get to have a manageable life instead.

Healthy, happy people know and recognize what they can do and what they truly can't—at least not without unwanted repercussions. But sometimes we put too many limitations on ourselves. We look around. Because we're so used to accepting our limitations, we automatically tell ourselves, *I can't do that, so I can't do anything else.*

I've been to the house, touched the rock collection, of the author George Sands who lived in southern France years and years ago during a time when women had few rights. It turned out that George was really a woman who took on a man's name so she could write and sell her books. Her legend and her books still live on.

Identify what you legitimately can't do or what you'd be better off and more powerful if you didn't. Learn to live within those limitations. That's how you'll own your power.

But don't stop there. Look around and see what you can do, too. Be creative. Knowing what we truly can't do is often a stepping stone to discovering what we can do.

God, help me own my power by surrendering to what I can't do. Then help me own my power some more by discovering what I can.

November 11   Create a path with heart

"I've reached my career and family goals," a successful woman in her late thirties said. "Now, it's time to start taking care of myself. I'm going to begin by resolving to spend one hour each week doing something I want to do."

One hour? What a small percentage of time to devote to doing what we want. Yet, how easy it is to fall into the trap of denying what we want to do. We may call it God's will for our lives. We may legitimately be in a situation where our responsibilities, including our commitments to other people, consume much of our time. And sometimes we have to do things we don't want to do to accomplish the things we want.

The trap is when our entire life begins to shift over to the "should be doing" category. This is what I should be doing in my career; this is what I should be doing for my family; this is where I should live; and this is probably how I should spend my spare time. This is what I should be doing in my religion, or spirituality; this is what I should be doing with my money, time, and energy.

Who said?

Take a moment. Examine whose should's are running your

life. Are the things you tell yourself you need to be doing true expressions of your legitimate goals, responsibilities, and commitments? Or have you wandered so far away from yourself that your life is no longer a genuine expression of who you are, and what you want, in your heart?

How many hours a week do you spend doing what you want to be doing or doing what you need to be doing to have what you want—whether that's sobriety, a family, or the career that's right for you? How many hours each week are spent doing what you think you *should* be doing, whether you need to or not?

Getting the things we want in life entails responsibility. We need to tend to our liberations—the career we want, the family life we want, and our avocations, as well. Tend to the things we've set free. But, don't forget to tend to the liberation of yourself, too. Maybe the things you're grumbling about doing are part of doing what you want. If that's the case, stop grumbling and thank God. Maybe you've forgotten that the things you're doing are what you really want to do. But maybe when you assess your daily life, you'll realize that some of the things you're doing aren't necessary, aren't what you want, and won't lead to where you want to go. You're telling yourself you have to, but you don't.

Start today by spending one hour doing something you want to do. In time, you may want to increase that to two hours a day. Eventually, you may get to that place where your should's intersect with your wants. That's when you've created and are walking a path with heart.

God, help me find a path with heart; help me walk the one I'm on with heart.

As I glanced through the pages of a writer's magazine one morning, I realized how important this magazine had been in my life. When I began writing back in the late seventies, I had no writer friends. I was on my own with a dream and a sketchy one at that. But by reading this monthly magazine aimed at aspiring writers, I knew I wasn't alone. Other people had done what I wanted to do; they had started where I was at. This magazine was an important part of my believing *I can.*

From time to time, we all need connections that help us believe. If we're beginning recovery from an issue like code-pendency or chemical dependency, our group meetings help us believe *I can.* If we're learning a new skill, like skydiving or flying a plane, sometimes talking to someone that can remember what it felt like to be unsure, awkward, and unskilled goes much further than talking to someone that can only remember being in mastery of the craft.

One day at the drop zone, I grabbed a man who had jumped out of an airplane over ten thousand times. "I'm so scared each time I jump," I said. "Is it normal to be that afraid?" This skydiving professional—who was so assured and respected—looked at me and smiled. "I was so frightened my first one hundred jumps that I couldn't even breathe!"

When you're trying to believe you can, whether it's believ-ing you can stay sober for the next twenty-four hours, learn-ing to take care of yourself, being a single parent, being in a good relationship, learning to write, learning to type, or learning to jump out of a plane, make good solid connections to people, places, and things that help you believe *I can.*

And if you run into someone who's walking a path that you've already walked, remember and share how it felt in the beginning so they can come to believe, too.

God, thank you for sending me the connections I need. Let me be of service whenever possible by being honest and speaking from my heart so I can be a good connection, as well.

Activity: Make a list of your connections. What are the areas in your life where you want to believe you can do it? Examples might be sobriety, taking care of yourself, being a single parent, learning to write, learning to be in a relationship, going through a divorce, surviving the loss of a loved one, getting your finances in order, or learning to speak a new language. Once you have your list of I can's, list in detail your present or potential connections for coming to believe. For instance, in recovery from chemical dependency, your connections might include your Twelve Step groups, the Big Book, a daily meditation book, a counselor, some recovering friends, and a medallion you received—whether it's for one hour or one day. If you're learning a new skill, such as writing, your connections might include a teacher, a friend, a book that's particularly helpful and encouraging, a magazine, and a piece of writing you've already done that either has been published or received good responses from friends. This list is solely to help you believe you can. Once you have your connection lists written, use them whenever you need a big dose of *I can*.

November 13 **Set the switches yourself**

One day, when I was getting ready to do a coached skydive, my coach sat me down. He gave me an exercise to do.

"When I skydive," he said, "I go into my switch room, and I set the switches where I want them to be. He explained how he set his alertness and awareness switch at about eight. If he put it any higher, all the way up to ten, he said he became too tense, hyper vigilant.

For many years, we've let a lot of people push our buttons. Why don't we try setting these switches ourselves instead?

Create a switch panel for yourself. Let the switches indicate the issues you'd like to work on. You might create one switch for fear. Don't turn it all the way off. You need some fear to help be your guide. Maybe set the fear switch at two, or a level you're comfortable with. Then go to the switch that says humble confidence. Maybe set that one at eight. Then go to the having fun and playing switch. How about cranking that one up to ten?

Create switches for any attribute in your life that you'd like to turn up or turn down. Then, from time to time, go in there and make sure the switches are still set and your circuit breaker is turned on.

God, help me own my power.

November 14　　　　There's freedom in letting go

Sometimes we gain freedom not only by letting go ourselves, but by helping someone else let go of us.

A child rounds a corner on her little purple bike, one training wheel clattering on the sidewalk, the other high in the air. Her father calls her over and tells her that today is special. Today, she has finally outgrown those training wheels and will learn to ride the bike like the big kids! Tears follow the happy news.

"But what if I fall? Or I can't balance? I'm not ready!" she complains.

Finally, after many assurances that he will be right beside

her, she lets daddy take the wheels off.

At first he holds tightly to the bike, and she sits there frozen, unable to pedal, rigidly gripping the handlebars.

"Relax," he says. "It's okay. I'm right here by your side."

She relaxes. Then she starts to pedal. Dad releases his grip slightly. He lets go and runs alongside. She looks over and laughs. "Daddy, don't let go! I'll fall!" And then, the inevitable happens; she falls.

But she gets back up. He holds on again. And again. And again. Until near suppertime, daddy runs beside, lets go of the bike, slows to a walk, and watches his little girl ride off on two wheels.

Is there something or someone in your life that you need to let go of in order to grow? Is there someone you need to help let go of you? Sometimes it's tempting to keep people dependent on us. It makes us feel needed and powerful. It makes us feel good. But it may be holding them and us back.

Go ahead. It's time. Take off the training wheels. Help them ride off into the sunset. Set both of you free.

God, help me resist the temptation to keep people dependent on me. Give me the courage to help other people let go of me.

November 15   Teach others they can, too

One good way to help ourselves believe we can is by helping others learn they can, too.

Some of us call this "being of service."

In Twelve Step programs, they call this "carrying the message." No matter how much recovery time we have, we can share our experience, strength, and hope with others. We can tell them how we were set free, how it felt it the beginning, and how it feels now, so they'll believe they can do it, too.

I've found even in skydiving that it helps me to share my experience, strength, and hope with sky divers newer to the sport than I am. When I am telling them that it's okay, that they can do it, I'm really telling myself I can do it, too.

Often in my everyday life, the things I'm telling others they need to do, or can learn, are the very things I need to be telling myself. Repetition forms belief. If we tell others, we're telling ourselves. The belief in them grows stronger. The belief in us is strengthened, too.

Some people say, "When the student is ready, the teacher will appear." That may be true. But sometimes when the student appears, it's because the teacher is ready to learn the lesson, too.

Sometimes helping others is how we help ourselves. And giving it away is often how we get to have some ourselves.

God, help me be of service. Help me remember the value of serving others—that it strengthens and uplifts them and blesses and helps me, too.

November 16   Be persistent

Earlier in this book, I talked about how little drops of rain, over the years, could wear pockets and indentations into stones. I used this as an analogy to demonstrate how negative influences could wear away our resolve.

It goes both ways.

When I first was in recovery, one of the treatment center staff gave me one good quality about myself when I couldn't see or find anything about myself to like.

"You're persistent," he said.

"Yes," I thought. "You're right. I am."

I also thought if I took one-half the energy I used doing

destructive things and channeled it into doing positive activities, there wouldn't be anything in the world I couldn't do.

Most of us are persistent. We persistently dwell. We have persistently tried to change what we cannot, usually a circumstance or someone else's behavior. Take that energy, that persistence, that determination, that almost obsessive resolve, and persevere with the things you can do.

Don't push.

Let go of concern about the seemingly impossible tasks in your life. Softly, steadily, like the rain, let your kind spirit naturally remove the obstacles in your path.

Life is better when we flow.

But sometimes it takes a persistent flow to change the things we can.

Enough water, persistently applied, can be more powerful than rock.

God, grant me the courage to persevere and the strength to persist.

November 17   Undo your mistakes

"Continued to take personal inventory and when we were wrong promptly admitted it." This is the Tenth Step of the Alcoholics Anonymous Twelve Step program. It's also a step that many wise people *not* working a program practice, too.

Sometimes the mistakes we make are teeny, tiny ones. We say something that hurts another person. Or we behave in a way we know is inappropriate, and we feel badly about it. Sometimes the mistakes are bigger. We may have taken a job or gotten ourselves into a relationship thinking it was a good idea only to discover later that it wasn't.

For whatever the reasons motivating us at the time, we made a mistake. We took a wrong turn on the path, and the direction we're going isn't where we meant to go and isn't where we want to be. Or we've arrived at a dead end.

Step Ten is part of the program, one-twelfth of the program, because someone knew we were going to need it, maybe one-twelfth of the time. The words *I'm sorry* are in our language because we've developed a need for that phrase, too.

Not making amends can damage our relationships. When pride or shame prevent us from making amends, we close our hearts to God, ourselves, and the people we love.

Admit your mistake. Take any actions necessary to correct the situation for yourself and the people involved.

Just open your heart and say these five words: I'm sorry. I was wrong.

Then let it go, and get on with your life. Have the courage to do what you need to do to get on track with your life.

God, help me admit to myself, to you, and others when I'm wrong and have made a mistake—whether it's a small one or a major wrong turn in my life. Then, help me to undo my actions and get back on track again.

November 18   Improvise

Do not fear mistakes; there are none.

— *Miles Davis*

Life is a jazz tune. Sometimes it's raucous, sometimes blue, but always full of unexpected twists and turns, and here and there a delightful new sound emerges. Viewed from a staunch classical viewpoint we might be tempted to call the new note or harmonization a mistake, but in the free flowing world of jazz, it becomes just another piece of the melodic whole.

So you took the wrong job, chose a career based on what others expected of you rather than what you expected of yourself. Was it a mistake? Only if you spent all your time there dwelling on the fact that you would rather be someplace else and missed the chance to learn something about yourself.

Admit your mistakes. Say *sorry* when you're wrong.

But don't feel trapped by the mistakes of your past and don't trap yourself now by the possibility of future mistakes. Sure, we'll continue to screw up. But, we just might invent a new note or two along the way.

God, help me learn from my mistakes and to turn my blunders into successes.

November 19   Respect the powers that be

I watched the man out the window as he dragged his kayak out to sea. Just as he'd get ready to launch, a huge frothy wave would come barreling over the top of him. The kayak would fly off in one direction. Then I'd see a paddle emerge from the sea. He'd walk back to his boat, try again, only to have himself and the boat tossed around by the wave. Finally, the last wave took the boat and threw it all the way to shore. When the man, in his thirties, stood up, he looked up at the heavens and stretched out his arms.

It was the surrender posture, the *what can I do but resign myself to the powers that be* stance that some of us know so well.

Yes, we're learning to believe in ourselves. We're learning to say I can. But an important part of self-confidence and self-esteem is learning humility and respect for the powers that be. Set your goals. Pursue your dreams. Say what you want and learn to say when. Hold your head up high, but learn to sublimate yourself, too.

Sometimes you've just got to throw your hands up in the air and surrender to the powers that be.

God, help me let go of arrogance and receive the blessings that humility brings.

November 20   Be prepared

Did you ever have a teacher in school who warned you at the beginning of the year that he would give tests without previous notice, so be prepared? We might not have liked it, but we appreciated being warned. We knew in that class that we needed to do our homework in a timely manner if we wanted a good grade. We kept our awareness up. We knew we couldn't slide by.

When that test came, we were either prepared for it or at the very least, aware. We had been warned. We knew the test was coming.

When I decided to stop using alcohol and drugs and live a life of abstinence and recovery, I was tested many times. People put drugs and alcohol in my hand. Once, in the early months, soon after my decision, I failed the test and felt awful. Then I learned that important lesson, life would challenge my decision from time to time. I had to be prepared not only to make the choice to be sober, but to stand behind that decision each day.

When I decided to become a writer, things moved along well for the first few years, then I began hitting some walls. I hit a dry spell. No words came out. The results weren't as I had planned. It was time to decide if I wanted to stand behind my decision or fold.

We will be given tests, without notice, on almost every decision we make and boundary we set. Each time we say

I can, we will be tested. And drawing from personal experience, the test is never one we would have chosen. It's often ugly, inconvenient, and hits us at our weakest spot.

Don't feel victimized or tortured when your test comes. Be prepared. Let it teach you more about yourself, what you want, and how badly you want it. Use it as resistance, the kind we can push against to become clearer about who we are and what we want. Sometimes we don't really want what we thought we did. Other times we do. We aren't in school anymore, at least not grade school. The test isn't for the teacher's benefit. It's for our benefit—to teach us how much we've learned.

Don't worry. I've been told we'll never be given a test we can't pass.

So get ready. You've been warned.

Be aware.

The test could come at any time.

God, help me let go of my resistance to the little tests life throws my way. Instead, help me use these tests as a chance to get to know myself and you better. Help me do my best.

November 21   You won't get more than you can handle

. . . God is faithful, who will not allow you to be tempted beyond that which ye are able, but with the temptation, will also make a way of escape, that you may be able to bear it.
                                                                        — The Bible

"I'm taking care of my roommate and worrying about three of my clients. People always say that you'll never get more than you can handle. But that's not true if you're trying to handle other people's stuff. That can be too much," a therapist and friend of mine said.

Most of us have heard throughout our lives that we'll never get more than we can handle or bear. The load will not be too heavy. If we're given it, we can rise to the occasion and accomplish the task.

They didn't say the load wouldn't be heavy. They didn't say the task could easily be done. And they didn't say we'd be given the grace and strength to bear the load of burdens that weren't ours.

Sometimes, it feels like too much. I know how that feels.

It's not.

You're up to the task, whatever it is, whether it feels like you are or not.

God, please give me all I need today, including enough joy.

November 22   Practice the basics

Not being codependent? That's a decision I need to make each day.

— Anonymous

Remember to practice the basics.

There's a saying floating around that people talk about a lot: *Lessons won't go away until they're learned. We can move, duck, hide, run, or escape by doing something else, but that lesson will still follow us around.*

There's another saying, too, one that's not talked about as much. But it's an important lesson to remember as we go through our daily lives: *Just because the lesson has been learned doesn't mean it will go away. Sometimes it appears in different shapes and forms.*

I used to believe that once a lesson was learned, I had it under my belt. The pain from that lesson would stop once I realized what it was. Then I could just go on with my life and put that graduation certificate in a drawer.

It took me a while to realize that that wasn't necessarily true. I was learning these lessons because I would need to use that skill, awakening, value, discipline, or practice as a tool for the rest of my life.

If you've got some important life lessons under your belt, congratulations. But don't put that certificate away quite yet. Instead, why don't you leave it out in plain sight?

When I first began skydiving, the first fifty jumps or so were dedicated to basic training. I was learning to save my life. After that, I began to add new skills to my repertoire. I was able to move my body around and have some fun in the air. I began to learn to fly. But each time I get to the door of the plane and get ready to jump, it's important to remember everything I learned in the beginning—the basics—about how to save my life.

Practice the basics every day or as often as you need. Whether you're in recovery, working at a craft, working on a relationship, or flying a plane, review your basics and remember to apply these principles each day in your life.

Spread your wings. Learn to fly. Have a ball with your life. Learn about all the mystery and magic the universe has to offer. See how good you can get. But don't forget what you learned in the beginning.

Remember to save your own life.

God, help me remember to practice the basics of self-care every day of my life.

Kevin was unhappy. He had stopped doing what he wanted to do in his life and found himself in a dull, boring routine at work. His job had turned on him. In the past, he and others had considered him brilliant, an asset. Opportunities, one after another, had just been handed to him. Now, no new opportunities were coming his way.

He wondered, "What happened? What went wrong? Why aren't things coming my way?"

"Maybe you need to do something. Maybe you need to help create the opportunity you want," his friend suggested.

Kevin's first response was, "I can't do that. I've never been a leader before. I've never had to take the initiative. I just sat back and good things came my way."

"Maybe times are different now. Maybe you need to take some action on your behalf first," his friend replied.

Kevin decided his friend was right. He began taking some steps to create the job he wanted with another company. The pay wasn't great, but at least he'd be doing more of the work he wanted to do. He began taking more of a leadership role in his life.

It took a lot of work and effort on his part. He had to travel a lot. He had to make things happen. And he had to use some of his money to make what he wanted to happen occur. He wasn't exactly where he wanted to be, but he was closer than he was before.

About three months after Kevin decided to take the initiative, he came home from work one night. There was a message on his machine. Some people that owned a business had an opening. They had heard about Kevin and wondered if he would be interested in interviewing with them, maybe becoming part of their organization?

The position was a leadership role, doing exactly what Kevin had hoped he could do. The pay and benefits were great. It took him only took a moment to realize that this was that golden opportunity.

Sometimes it's not just enough to say *I can.* You need to show yourself and the universe that you mean what you say. If good things aren't coming your way, maybe you need to walk toward them. Once you take those first steps, the universe can guide you along the path.

Whether it's writing that book, meeting a friend, moving, getting a sponsor, making a career switch, or acquiring a new skill, it may be time for you to show the universe that you mean what you say. Take those first steps, awkward and clumsy as they may be. Work with the raw materials of your life that you have on hand today—even if those materials aren't ideal. Do your best. Make an actual step toward fulfilling your dream. Then let the universe and your Higher Power help guide you, once you've taken those first steps. Just because something isn't being handed to you out of the blue doesn't mean it can't be yours.

Is there a dream, a vision, or a goal that you've been waiting to magically manifest in your life? Could it be that you need to take some first steps toward it, instead of waiting for it to come to you? Your first efforts may be just that, first efforts. But from those first steps, you'll be guided into what you want to do.

Sometimes letting go means more than sitting back and passively waiting. Sometimes taking the initiative is an important part of the work you need to do. Showing the universe and yourself that you mean business is part of how you learn to manifest your power.

God, show me the steps I can take today, and help me start walking so you can guide me along my path.

Activity: Take out your goal list today. Is there a dream, a vision, or a goal that you've been waiting to magically manifest in your life? Could it be that you need to take some first steps? Today, take the initiative. Start to use the power of *I can* in your life.

November 24   Move from your center

Whatsoever thy hand findeth to do, do it with all thy might.
— *Ecclesiastes 9:10*

Move from your center.

It's a lesson I learned in aikido. But it's more than a lesson about martial arts; it's an ancient lesson about how we're to live.

Try this exercise. Walk across the room wishing you were someplace else—in your chair, in your car, or with your friend. Then do an activity for five minutes, like washing dishes, concentrating the entire time on something else you'd rather be doing, or something you're worrying about. Then, walk back to where you started.

Now, walk across the room conscious of each step, fully present for each move. Pay attention to where you're at and how each step feels. And be willing and intending to be right where you are. Wash the dishes, present for the feel of the hot water, the smell of the soap, and for how the floor feels under your feet. Be conscious and aware. Be intending to wash those dishes. Be right there, in that moment in time. Be aware of washing until the dishes are clean and rinsing until they're clear. Be happy and grateful for the task. Give that task your all.

That's moving from your center. It means we're right there, completely present, focused, and aware. We're not wishing we were someplace else. And we place great value on what we're doing, no matter what the size of the task. How much richer our lives become when we put our all into all that we do. The colors are brighter, the success sweeter, the loss sharper, and the lessons more true.

Move from your center in all that you do, even the ordinary tasks and moments of life. Pour all of your heart into your relationships. Give your best ideas at work. Don't worry; the universe has more where those came from. Stop the car on the side of the road and watch the sunset.

Whatsoever you find to do, do it with all your might.

God, remind me to live my life fully every day.

November 25   Express your power gently

Express your power naturally and as gently as you can.

When I started learning what it meant to take care of myself and to own my power, I talked loudly, spoke up, and yelled in order to set boundaries, limits, and to express myself. That was the way to get my point across. That's how I'd showed people I meant what I said.

I had to say it *loudly*.

About five years after I started this process of learning what it meant to own my power, I met a bear called Winnie the Pooh. The book that introduced me was *The Tao of Pooh*. Lights started coming on. The seeds of new lessons began to sprout.

To own my power, I could quietly say what I meant. The clearer I was about what I had to say and who I was, the less I had to shout. Owning my power wasn't something I had to plan out, premeditate, and obsess about.

The more I took care of myself and connected to myself

369

and the clearer I became, the more natural and easier it became to own my power. My power—including setting limits, saying no, refusing to be manipulated, and saying I'd changed my mind—often became a natural, graceful, timely expression of me.

There are still times in our lives when we have to be firm, sometimes forceful, and repeat what we've said, sometimes loudly. The quieter and more relaxed we can be when we say what we mean is usually in direct proportion to how much we believe in ourselves.

Let your power, boundaries, and expressions of who you are arise naturally.

Learn and respect the value of responding as gently, but as firmly, as you can.

God, help your power flow through me. Teach me to take care of myself gently, in a way that reflects harmony with myself and as much as possible, the people in my life.

November 26   Open the door

I was having lunch with a friend at a restaurant one day when he realized he had either misplaced his keys or locked them in his car. We had taken my car to the restaurant. His car was at my house.

He went through all the denial and fussing most of us do when we realize we've locked ourselves out.

"Maybe I brought them into your house and left them on the table," he said wistfully. "It's okay, though. I have an extra set in my . . ." He dug through his pockets. "Other pants."

Game over.

He didn't enjoy the rest of his lunch.

When we got back to the house, we looked for the keys

inside for a few moments then walked out to his car. Sure enough, there they were—right on the dashboard. We walked around the car a few times.

"Maybe I should just call AAA," he said. I offered to go get a coat hanger from the house. We walked around the car a few more times, peering longingly through the windows. You could almost touch the keys; they were that close.

I turned to go inside and get the hanger. That's when I heard it. *Popclicksqueek.* I turned, and there was my friend standing triumphantly next to his car, keys in hand, a dorky smile plastered on his face.

"The door was unlocked," he said.

So often we allow ourselves to feel like outsiders. We want to break into a new field or group but feel we don't know enough yet, that we may not be liked, that we may fail, or that we may succeed. So we stand outside wistfully looking at others and wishing we could unlock that door and join the group.

The door isn't locked.

You belong here.

Open it and walk in.

God, help me remember that the only one keeping me an outsider is me. Help me open the door and join the group. Help me live my life.

November 27   Flex your wings

Walking in the hills of Southern California, I came across a high meadow bursting with the movement of hundreds of moths. I stood for a few moments and drank in the scene, watching them dance lightly around me. There were so many of them I could actually hear their wings beating in the still air.

I walked further along and saw a caterpillar crawling along the ground. I looked more closely and saw that the tiny creature had two small but useless wings protruding from its back. At first I thought that it must have been a deformity, that this poor worm would be forced to spend its days crawling, never able to fly, but all the while having wings. Then as I walked further along, I saw another winged caterpillar—this one with slightly larger wings. It was slowly flexing its new appendages, looking anxiously at the sky. These moths grew their wings gradually, without the aid of a cocoon to protect them throughout the transformation. They just sprouted their wings right out there for the whole world to see.

We each have different levels of freedom. What I think of as a box might be unthinkable freedom for you today. In the future, when you look back at your life, you may be amazed at the levels of freedom into which you have naturally grown. Perhaps you are looking around today at the freedom of others in awe and envy. "I could never do that," you might say.

Yes, you can.

And you might.

Feel those wings on your back? They're there. And they're growing every day—whether you're flying yet or not.

Robert Thurman wrote, "The great thing about the horizon of infinity is that there is no limit to how amazing you can become."

God, help me flex my wings. Teach me how amazing I can become.

In order to develop a strong sense of the preciousness of human life, it must connect to one's belief system. The belief system doesn't need to be the Buddhist karmic system, but it has to be one that is critically aware of the uniqueness and special nature of this life form.
        — *Robert Thurman,* Circling the Sacred Mountain

Do you see it? Do you see what a special, precious opportunity each day of your life is?

Look more closely. See all the lessons you can learn. See how you can participate in your growth. See how carefully God holds your hand, guides you down the right path, offers just the right words and opportunities at the right moments, sends just the right people your way.

You can feel. You can touch. You can agonize in despair and giggle with glee. You can make jokes. You can cry at movies. You can weep in bed at night. Then get up the next day, refreshed.

You can taste an orange, a lemon, a mango—and describe in detail the difference in each of those tastes. You can smell a forest of pine trees. You can hold your friend's hand and feel how he trembles because he's afraid.

You can stumble and fall and feel abandoned, then get up and suddenly, in one moment, understand that lesson you've been trying to learn. You can jump out of airplanes, feel the smoothness of your lover's back, and hold your child to your breast.

You can wait and thank God later.

But you might as well thank God now.

Maybe the best way to thank God is by living your life fully today.

God, help me to use this opportunity, this life that I have been given to the best of my ability every day.

November 29   There's magic for you, too

I was looking at a photo of my friend Chip. In it, he's sitting beside his battered, old Volkswagen looking nearly as tired and battered as the car. But he's smiling.

He was smiling the first time I met him, too. He told me the story of this photo prominently displayed on his desk.

"That picture was taken at the trailhead to White Mountain. Elevation twelve thousand feet. The last sixteen miles of the road are two dirt-tire tracks, but I really wanted to go on that hike. You should have seen the expressions on the faces of the research group in their four-wheel drive vans when I pulled up in Carmen. [That's his name for his car.] It was so high that the carburetor could hardly breathe. I don't think I got over ten miles an hour for the last sixteen miles. When I got there, the car was on empty, and it was forty-seven miles to the closest gas station.

"After my hike, I put her in neutral and coasted all the way down the mountain. It was insane, my brakes were shot by the time I made it down, and I rolled into the gas station just as the engine died. What a trip!"

You can do things if you think that you can. You can put a backpack into your old car and take that trip with just a few dollars. You can see new things, visit new places, and amaze others and yourself. You can get the career you want, have the relationship you want, reach the dreams in your heart. You can get wherever you want to go from where you are now.

All it takes is faith, desire, and a little belief in the magic of the universe.

"Oh, but that magic only works for other people, not me," I've heard others protest in disbelief.

One of the things I like about Chip is something he always says and means, whether he has $5 in his pocket or $3,000 in the bank. He says this in both the good times and the times most of us would label as bad.

"I can't believe what a lucky individual I am. I can't believe how amazing the world is. And I can't believe and don't understand why I've been this blessed."

The magic of the universe is there waiting for each of us.

Look around. See how lucky and blessed you are. Then take another look at the limitations in your life and start letting go of those limitations, one by one. Find your dirt track with the great experience at the end. Find and follow your path with heart.

Oh, but do check the gas tank first.

God, once again, teach me the magic of I can.

November 30   Believe in the magic of life

Listen to the Never haves
Then listen close to me—
Anything can happen, child,
Anything can be.

— *Shel Silverstein*

All around us every day are those who would have us believe we can't. They haven't grown in their lives, so they tell us we can't grow and change in ours. Belief systems are strong, but ideas are stronger. In 1899, the then chief of the U.S. patent office proposed closing it down. He said, "Everything that can be invented already has been."

We look back on a statement like that today and laugh, but how often do we believe it in our own lives? I can't go back to school because I'm nearly fifty. I shouldn't change careers now; I'll lose my retirement. Sure, a boat like that is nice, but I'll never have one; I'm just not rich enough. Maybe he can stay sober, but I can't change my life.

As children we're filled with wonder at the world around us. Anything is possible, anything at all. But all too soon the weight of the shouldn'ts, impossible's, and won'ts comes sneaking in around our shoulders tying us down to lowered expectations and limited beliefs.

The world is flat. If you sail to the edge, you will fall off. Everything that can be invented already has been. Man will never walk on the moon.

Believe in yourself. Believe in a wonderful God. Believe in the programs and support structures that help you every day. Say what it is you want, the lessons you want to learn, the goals you want to achieve, the relationships that you want to have, and then go out and allow the universe to manifest them in your life.

The never have's sit on the sidelines and tell you about all that can't be. Will you join them or will you quietly go about doing the impossible on your own?

Believe in the magic of *I can*. Tell the naysayers and never have's: I can, *too. And so* can *you.*

Today, why not go to a park, sit on a bench, and think back to when you were a child. What were your dreams, your hopes? Are they really that far out of reach? Remember, anything can happen and quite often, it does.

Thank you, God, for the glory of my journey so far. Be with me as I learn more about what I can accomplish through you.

December

How Sweet It Is

Many of us have been seeking diligently for the meaning of life, at least for the meaning of *our* lives. I thought I had found it when I began recovering from chemical dependency. *Aha*, I thought. *The meaning of life is to stay sober.* Then along came codependency and my need to recover from those issues. Surely, the search for enlightenment would culminate there.

No, not yet.

It was as if there was a big locked metal door. On one side of it was supreme knowledge of why we're here, that elusive "thing" called enlightenment. I was on the other side of the door, locked out, searching for the key.

Over the years, I've been to therapists, doctors, and healers. I've used homeopathy, kinesiology, acupuncture, and acupressure. In my youth, I tried alcohol and drugs, thinking they were the answer. I looked for the answer to the meaning of life in relationships. Then I searched for enlightenment by avoiding commitment and romantic love at any cost. I've tried Gestalt therapy, transactional analysis, hypnotherapy, prayer, and meditation, too. Over the past twenty-seven years, I've actively participated in more than one Twelve Step program in this quest for truth.

I've dutifully plodded through the grinding work so many people have come to know as family of origin work. Hooray, I finally found and healed my inner child. I even have a fuzzy teddy bear on the floor next to my bed. After my son died, I stayed with every moment of my grief until I worked through it by finally accepting the lifetime handicap that I would live in spite of the loss of Shane.

I've perused *A Course in Miracles*, learning with Marianne Williamson's help about the magic of love in all its myriad shapes and forms. At last, I opened my heart. But the search for enlightenment eluded me. I wasn't depressed, but my spirit ached.

I started traveling, first around the United States and then around the world. I visited the vortexes of Sedona, the ancient Anasazi village in Chaco Canyon, and the Santuarior de Chimayo, the blessed New Mexican church. I should have been glowing in the dark. Occasionally, I glimpsed the Light. But I still didn't understand what life was all about. *Maybe tomorrow I'll find that key,* I'd think. It seemed as if enlightenment was always one day, one step, one therapist, one book, one healer away. Over twenty years ago, when I was already well immersed in this quest, a trusted friend told me that the secret to life was simple: there wasn't one. Maybe my friend was right. Maybe I was looking for something that didn't exist.

One day, I stopped looking. It wasn't that I gave up. I gave in. I stopped waiting to win the spiritual lottery. Stopped trying to become enlightened. Stopped looking for that perfect soul mate. And started surrendering to and enjoying each moment of my life—just as it is.

That's when I found joy. Or maybe joy found me.

The key to enlightenment might be simpler than we think. We're here to experience joy. Look at each moment in your life and learn to say, *How sweet it is.*

God, help me learn joy.

December 2   The lesson is joy

I was visiting a counselor in Minnesota one cold January day in 1991. We were talking about the present and speculating about the lessons to come. She grabbed my hand and looked at me, looked right into my eyes. "This I know for sure," she said. "You've been through enough pain. Now you're going to learn about joy."

One week later, my son Shane died.

Mixed in with my grief was rage. I was so angry with her for saying that. It was another instance of getting my hopes up that I could finally be happy. Now, I felt tricked and let down.

The years passed slowly. I lost almost everything, including my desire to write. Nichole graduated from high school. Then she moved out of the house, and to New York. Life kept changing and moving along, in spite of how I felt.

One year I noticed that the anniversary of Shane's death had passed, and I hadn't become depressed. Then I began to notice something else. I was beginning to feel alive, vibrant, awestruck with life. It wasn't a naïve assumption that whatever I wanted, I'd get. It was a newfound ability to surrender to each moment and enjoy what life brought my way. I made new friends. My relationships with old friends changed. What inspired me was my new relationship with life. I stopped looking for outward circumstances to provide me with happiness. I began to see that I held that key myself.

If you're going through something in your life that isn't what you planned, a transformation is at hand. While we might prefer to be transformed in the twinkling of an eye, it usually doesn't happen that fast. It takes all the moments added together, and sometimes those moments go on and on. But one day when you least expect it—a phoenix rises from the ashes. That phoenix is you.

Some of us encounter a lot of pain. Some of us have less. If I could sit across from you right now, I'd look into your eyes and say these words to you: "I know you've been through a lot. But there's a new cycle coming. You're going to learn about joy."

Life is going to take you on your own journey of personal transformation. You may have to let go of some things. But don't worry, you'll get some of those things back. And sometimes when we think something is lost, it's not. It's just moved to a different place. No pain, no gain, is what many people say. And usually they say that because when the lesson is learned, the pain stops. But then something happens. It just clicks in. The moments start getting better and better. And it's not because of what we get. It happens because we've surrendered. And although it looks like what we've surrendered to is pain and heartache, we've really surrendered to God's will.

There's a world out there—right outside your door. And the key that opens that door is in your hand. The ultimate lesson is learning joy. Put your fears aside. Live your life, whatever that means to you today. It may happen today, tomorrow, next week, or in ten years. But you won't be able to help yourself. You'll throw your hat up in the air, look around, and shout, "Oh my God, how sweet life is."

God, help me get through my lessons, one by one. Then bring me to that place where I learn about joy.

December 3   Enjoy the void

We begin to walk down a path—recovery, a new job, a new relationship. We're busy, even overwhelmed, with everything that lies before us. We work and work and walk our path and grow. Then one day the relationship changes. The job changes. Or we're far enough along to look past the next minute of sobriety and when we look, we can't see anything.

We get scared. Nothingness can be frightening. There's no way to plan for the future. We can't make the right move.

We're surrounded with decisions, and none of them feel like the right ones.

Relax. Savor this moment, too. Stop trying to fill it up. You're in the void, that magical place from which all creation arises. Breathe the air, look at the flowers, feel the sun. Or build a fire to keep you warm. There's no need to be frightened of this place; there's nothing you need to do. Keep walking your path, and the creative way will become clear to you soon.

God, help me to let go of worry when I'm in the in-between places in my life. Help me to walk in peace and let the universe show me the path that I am to follow. Help me relax in this space and garner energy for the journey ahead.

December 4   The miracle of rebirth

Birth is an exhilarating experience. Walking into a hospital room seconds after a child has been born, you can almost touch the emotion and power of the moment.

Rebirth is like that, too. Sitting in a powerful religious ceremony, standing alone atop a high hill, or walking in the footsteps of an ancient civilization, we can feel our hearts being changed as our spirit is given new birth. "What have I done to deserve this?" we whisper. And the universe whispers, "It's to move you along your path. It's to teach you to live." And we emerge from our experience reborn.

Sometimes, it goes the other way, too. In a single moment, all that we know can be stripped away—the death of a loved one, a divorce, the loss of a job—and suddenly we're left standing at the mercy of the universe. "Why did this happen? What did I do to deserve this?" we cry. And the universe answers, "It's to move you along your path. It's to teach you to live." And once again, we rise from the ashes, reborn.

Surrender to the exhilarating moments of creation in your life, both the uplifting and the heartrending ones. Touch the emotion and power.

Trust that you're being moved along your path. You're learning how to live.

Let yourself be reborn.

God, please help me to accept all the life changing experiences that I may have. Help me to see the wonder in rebirth and to learn your lessons.

December 5   Be happy now

"Time is what keeps everything from happening at once," the bumper sticker ahead of me read.

Maybe, I thought. I was racing back home from the computer store, busily doing my errands, trying to get things done. I noticed a restaurant and shopping center to my right, on the freeway. I'd been curious about this place for almost a year. Today, instead of driving by, I turned off the highway and pulled into the parking lot. I spent the next three hours browsing through the stores filled with antiques, trinkets, and gourmet foods. Then I enjoyed a leisurely dinner—a juicy hamburger and a chocolate malt—at the restaurant before returning home. The stores had always been there; I'd always driven past. Today I stopped, satisfied my curiosity, and enjoyed myself.

It's easy to spend our lives working toward a goal, convinced that if we could only get there, we'd be truly happy then. Today is the only moment we have. If we wait until tomorrow to be happy, we'll miss out on the beauty of today.

Have your plans. Set goals.
Let yourself be happy now.

God, help me be aware of the joy that's in front of me now instead of waiting for tomorrow to bring me happiness.

December 6   Celebrate

Look at your life. Look back at the path that you've walked this far and celebrate!

One of the joys of walking to the top of a mountain is looking back at how far you've come. It's wonderful to stand on a high ridge and see the tiny footpath stretching off into the distance.

Celebrate with awe how far you've come in those first few steps of sobriety and in your faith and willingness to let go of your fears. Celebrate those first faltering moments of learning what it meant to take care of yourself. Even now, with each step you take, you are being transformed. Celebrate!

Turn around. Look. See how far you've come. Celebrate the journey that you've taken so far.

And look forward to the adventure that lies ahead.

God, help me celebrate all our triumphs. Thank you for walking with me, even when I felt like I was walking alone.

December 7   Enjoy your successes

Eventually, if you put enough effort into something, it gets finished. The house is built, the picture is painted, the report is completed. Let yourself rest and relax in those moments. Take a moment to enjoy the feeling of completeness. That moment will be a fleeting one. There are many more ideas and tasks waiting around the bend.

Gaining experience and learning lessons from failed efforts is an important part of our path. But success feels good, too, and it's meant to be enjoyed.

If you've had a recent accomplishment in your life, take some time off. Celebrate it. Celebrate those smaller moments of victory, too. Sit back, look at what you've done, and say, "It is good." Take yourself out to dinner, take a vacation, or even a short trip to the beach.

Reflect on your past successes. Forget about your failures and the things that went wrong. Think about all that you've done right in your life, the things that have worked out, the answered prayers. Don't just stare at your problems and everything that's gone wrong. Look at what's right about your life, too.

Sit back and rest for a moment Then say, *How sweet it is.*

God, thank you for all my victories, for all the challenges you've helped me meet. Thanks for all those times you answered my prayers and met my needs. Help me rest and celebrate the good in my life.

December 8   Enjoy the ordinary

Days before, there had been a tremendous storm out in the Pacific Ocean. Now the swells from the storm were smashing against the shore in California. The tide rose and rose. The house shook with each wave as the breaking water slammed into the pilings under the house.

I went to bed but couldn't sleep. I got up and walked outside to check on the kayak. It was still there, but the water was far up under the house, threatening to grab the boat. I went back to bed and eventually drifted off to sleep in spite of the noisy, angry sea.

The next day, the sea returned to normal. That night when I went to bed, the gentle rolling of the sea lulled me to sleep. Soon, I forgot about the storm, how loud and angry the waves had been. I once again began to take the gentle soothing sound of the surf for granted.

It's easy to take many things in our life for granted: health, the presence of a loved one in our life, friends, food, even sobriety and recovery. When life proceeds smoothly, it's easy to take the ordinary for granted.

Look at the ordinary in your life. How would you feel if it was taken away? Don't just be grateful for successes. Be grateful for and celebrate the ordinary in your world.

God, help me to not take anything for granted. Teach me to recognize, appreciate, and celebrate the ordinary in this world. Help me see how beautiful and meaningful the ordinary really is.

December 9   Discover a sense of wonder and awe

After lunch at Paradise Cove, one of our favorite places to eat, my friend and I went for a walk along the beach. Suddenly he bent down and picked up a little purple ball with spines all over it. "Look," he said, "a sea urchin!" It was just an empty shell, but the purple was glowing, almost the color of amethyst. Neither of us had ever seen an urchin lying on the beach before. We touched it and debated whether we should take it home and put it on a shelf.

"Why don't we leave it here," he said. "Some kids will find it, and they can take it home. We've got enough stuff lying around."

As soon as he put the treasure back on the sand, two children and their mother rounded the point in front of us. The oldest child, a girl about twelve, was curious and delighted when we called her over and handed her the little purple ball. Soon her brother and her mom crowded around. The boy couldn't wait to touch the urchin's tiny spines. My friend and I were both smiling as we walked back to the car.

Two of the sweetest experiences in life are discovering new things and sharing those things with someone else. Be aware of the new and exciting things that come into your life. They don't have to be that big to give you a sense of delight. Enjoy them, learn from them, play with them. And then, for an even greater experience, share them with a friend.

God, help me rediscover a sense of wonder and awe about life. Then help me pass that feeling on to someone else.

December 10   Become amazed at what you see

We were on a trip through the Southwest when we turned around a bend in New Mexico. Lake Albiquiu, the sign said. The campground was seated on a bluff overlooking a large man-made lake. We decided it was so beautiful we'd camp there for the night. We selected just the right spot to give us the best view of the sun rising in the morning. We wanted to see the light hit the red rock cliffs in the distance.

Hiking around the edge of the bluff, we found a tiny cactus bursting with bright red flowers sitting in the shade of a windblown tree. We sat for a while then scrambled down to the water and sat on a big rock that jutted out into the lake. We swam. The water was cold, but refreshing, and the early summer sun felt good on our skin.

Later we cooked supper on the little gas stove. "Should we set up the tent?" I asked, eager to see the new tent set up in the wilderness.

"The weather is nice," my friend said. "Let's just throw our bags on the ground and sleep out."

That was an idea! I had never slept under the stars before. We lay there in the gathering darkness and watched as one by one the stars softly glowed into view. I closed my eyes and dozed.

Moments later, a bird sang a goodnight song from a nearby tree, and I opened my eyes to see a blanket of stars overhead. The Milky Way cut a path through the night sky, and there were so many unfamiliar stars that I could hardly distinguish the constellations I knew. I didn't want to close my eyes; I didn't want to miss a moment of this incredible sight.

Camping in a state park may not count to some of the hard-core wilderness folks. But we each have different levels of freedom in our lives. Freedom means tasting new things, having new experiences, and pursuing our dreams no matter how small they might be. Recapture the magic of a time in your life when everything was new and amazing. Discover what's possible for you. Then be amazed at what you see.

God, give me a sense of the possible in my life. Then help me be amazed at just how beautiful life can be.

December 11   Touch and taste your life

Tonight, the sun set like a red ball over the hill to the west of the house. There's an eclipse coming in just a few days, and the ocean knows it. She can feel the moon. She rises high on her haunches, ready to pounce, then slowly rolls forward. The waves build and stretch until finally the lip crumbles and the back of the wave chases the front of the wave culminating in a massive waterfall. She smashes against the pilings, shaking the entire house. The sky is rose, lavender, and black. The house smells richly of the pasta and meat sauce in the pots on the stove. A cedar log burning in the fireplace warms the room.

This is my experience now. It's an enchanted moment when the world rests but is still alive.

Experience is the privilege of being human. I can taste the spaghetti. I can smell the salt of the ocean. I can feel the burning cedar taking the chill out of the air. I can love. I can hurt. What a sweet experience this is. And I thank God for every moment and feeling of each experience I've been given.

Do you taste your life? Or do you float through it unaware of the beauty that surrounds you each day? We weren't meant to sleep all the time. Sometimes when we first become sober or begin recovering from codependency, we wonder what we'll ever do with all this time and all the feelings that we're left with now that the alcohol and drama have been taken away.

Revel in the experience you're going through. Feel, touch, and taste each moment of your life. Then be aware of how exquisitely beautiful it is.

What's your experience right now?

God, help me be aware of the beauty and power that flows through this universe. Help me remember how connected I am to that beauty and power through each experience I've been given.

December 12 — Create an extraordinary life

I ran into my friend one day on the street. I asked him how he was. He said not very good. But if he won the lottery— and he showed me a few tickets—he'd be happy then. I asked him if business was slow. He said, yes, income was down and bills were up. He needed a big hit to balance the ledger sheet.

We talked for a while. I asked him what he made an hour. He said $100, but he was mostly getting appointments for half-hour sessions. He was a therapist, and business wasn't very promising right now.

"Gee," I said, counting up the hours in a week, "if you worked four half hours a day, that's $1,000 dollars a week and $4,000 a month. Sounds like pretty good income, at least to me."

"I never thought of it that way," he said.

"Instead of trying to win the lottery or get that big break, why don't you try to happily do just four half hours of work a day? Then you don't have to win the lottery to break the bank. You'll be pretty well off right now."

It's easy to want to win the big one or think of a windfall as the only solution to the problems we face. And the lottery we want to win might not be just in money. We can easily take that kind of thinking into our relationships or our work. Buy a chance to win the lottery, if that's what you want to do. But maybe you could look at things a different way. What if you stopped going for the big one and tried to do a lot of little things well? You could work on being the best friend that you could be. Or maybe you could get closer to that person you are dating. Instead of waiting for the perfect soul mate to come along, just be the best boyfriend or girlfriend in the relationship you already have. Instead of waiting to win the lottery, make the most out of all the ordinary moments in your life today.

You're richer than you think.

God, help me remember that many ordinary moments, when well-lived, add up to an extraordinary life.

December 13   Let go of afflicted emotional streams

Step out of afflicted streams.

I was walking through a national park one day when I came upon a stream. I wasn't looking closely; I decided to step into the water and walk through it to get to the other side. When I looked more closely, I gasped and stood back. The stream was all murky and gross. I didn't want to wade in it.

Most teachers of our times and from times long past—from the Dalai Lama to Emmet Fox—agree on one thing: stay away from murky, afflicted emotional streams. Avoid them at all costs.

There's a lot of afflicted streams out there: greed, envy, negativity, regret, revenge, resentment, arrogance, victimization, hard-heartedness, bitterness, control, hatred, resentment, and paralyzing fear are just a few. When we step into an afflicted emotional stream, that emotion colors everything we do.

An afflicted stream is more than an isolated emotion. It's a position, a posture, an attitude, a pattern that will poison us and our lives. Look around. Be aware. Don't be careless and step into an afflicted stream. If you've inadvertently slipped into one, then quickly step out.

Feeling restless, irritable, and discontented is definitely an afflicted stream. If you find yourself in that one, step right out into gratitude.

God, help me let go of my emotions before that feeling becomes a way of life. Guide my thinking and outlook on life. Keep me out of afflicted streams.

Many years ago, I asked a fellow therapist what the one thing was that hallmarked the unhappy state of being many of us have come to label as *codependency*.

"It's the Karpman Drama Triangle," he said. "People rescue someone by doing something they don't want to do, or it's not their business to do. Then they get angry and persecute the person. Then they walk away, feeling like a victim. Again."

A light went on in that moment. Like a gerbil on a wheel, I could see myself spinning around this triangle. I was regularly rescuing somebody, then getting angry, and ultimately feeling victimized by it all.

I was creating the pain and the drama in my life.

Over the years, I stopped rescuing alcoholics. Many of us have gotten off that painful wheel. We know we can't control another person's chemical dependency, depression, problems, or life. But we may have stepped off that wheel and gotten ourselves into another more subtle drama spin.

A friend recently cleaned out his entire house—closets, garage, drawers. He had to hire a truck to come and take everything away.

"I can't believe everything I collected and hung onto," he said. "Most of it was junk that I didn't want in the first place. I guess that came from being poor and going without for so long. I convinced myself that if it was free or cheap, I'd better grab it and take it home."

Many of us were survivors at one time. We either genuinely didn't have a choice or convinced ourselves we didn't. So we clung to whoever and whatever came along our path.

You may have survived what you went through, but you're not a survivor anymore. There is no need to desperately cling to whatever comes along. You're living now. You're living fully and freely.

Choose what you want.

God, help me give myself permission to walk a path with heart.

December 15   Fall in love with life

I was sitting in the chair at the beauty shop getting my hair cut one day and listening to my beautician chatter away. She showed me a picture of one of her friends, a woman who had gotten married and recently had a baby girl.

"She's been so in love since that child was born," she said, showing me a picture of the new mother's smiling face.

"In love with her husband?" I asked.

"No," she said. "Well, that, too. I mean in love with life."

Have you ever been in love, had your heart beat fast when you anticipated the call of your lover, felt the way the sun felt warmer on your face, the sky appeared bluer, the clouds more fluffy, and the sunset more grand?

What if you could fall in love with your life and feel that way each day? I'm not saying romantic relationships are bad. They're not. They're part of being human and getting our needs met. But what if we could take all that passion and focus it into falling in love with life?

Maybe that is what is meant by universal love. Maybe that's the part we give back.

Fall in love with your life today.

God, help me feel passionate about my life and all the possibilities that stretch out before me.

"The entire skydive is great," a friend said to me. "But one of my favorite moments is when we open the door, and I can see the whole sky spread out in front of me."

I remember that feeling the day I was given the choice to recover from chemical dependency or go to jail, the day I got my first writing job, the day my daughter gave birth to her first child. It's that split second when now freezes and stretches out into infinity. For just a moment all that has been and all that might be crown into a single arc in time and the power of the universe rushes through us.

Get a little of that feeling every day just to remind yourself of the power and potential of now.

Sure, we can envision our rosy future after the big project pays off, or when we've got fifteen years of sobriety, or after we reach retirement. But what about that moment when the minister pronounces you husband and wife, or the moment after you tell your parents you're gay, or the day you walk out on someone, or the day someone walks out on you?

The power isn't out there somewhere in the distant horizon. Feel the rush of the moment. It really is your life. You have all of the power you need, right now.

God, help me tap into the rush of power available to me right here and right now.

Oh, the glory of the ordinary!

I wake up, roll over, and look out the sliding glass door at the sun rising over the distant layers of hills.

Today will be a day of errands. We're out of milk, so we'll

make a run to the grocery store, probably returning home with too much chocolate and no milk. The pictures from the last trip need to be dropped off. We have a flying lesson at 2:00. Then it will be supper at the Lodge with our friend Andy. It'll probably be something simple, like burgers on the grill.

An ordinary day.

I remember a time when the ordinary meant searching for another high, searching for money to get drugs. I'm grateful for the ordinary life that I lead.

"When we have a toothache, we know that not having a toothache is happiness. But later, when we don't have a toothache, we don't treasure our non-toothache," Thich Nhat Hanh gently reminds us in his book *The Heart of the Buddha's Teaching*.

Take another look at your ordinary world.

See how glorious it is.

God, help me cherish each moment of my life.

December 18   Savor each moment

Enjoy each moment as it comes.

It's so easy to relish that final moment, when the project is finished and the work is turned in. It's easy to trick ourselves into thinking that peak moments in life are the only ones that count.

In Benjamin Hoff's *The Tao of Pooh*, Pooh talks about the anticipation of eating his honey. The moment when the honey touches your lips is good, Pooh says. But there's the moment right before, that moment of anticipation, that might be just as good if not better.

Go for your dreams. Go for those peak moments of performance and pleasure, too. The day you get your ten-year medallion for sobriety is a good day. Achieving that success in your career—that special award—is a wonderful moment, indeed. And those peak moments in love are indescribably delicious to experience and reminisce about.

While many people talk about being in that peak zone of pleasure all the time, most of us know that peak moments are only a very small fraction of our lives. If we only enjoy those peak moments, or those moments just before, we'll forget to notice the importance of a lot of our lives.

Go for peak moments. But open up your heart and let the sheer raw beauty of all the moments in. When you stop looking and waiting for those peak experiences, you might find out how sweet and delicious each single moment really is.

Savor each moment of your life.

God, help me let go of anything that's sabotaging my joy. Help me release the belief that I can only find happiness, pleasure, and joy when I'm on top of a peak.

December 19   Have the time of your life

Make every moment count.

The first time I heard the words, I was sitting in the movie theater with Shane. He was eleven at the time. There were only a few other people in the theater; we had snuck out to see a show together. It was one of our favorite mother-son things to do, especially on Sunday nights.

Until about a year before, I had been very goal oriented. I was always looking toward the future, moving toward the next level in my life. First there was getting through the poverty, then struggling to get beyond being an impoverished single parent. Then I began working toward the next level of success in my career. I was always trying to make my world and my children's lives better.

As I sat in the theater staring at the screen, I had a flash of my own mortality—at least I thought it was mine. *I won't be here forever*, I thought. *Someday, this time in my life will have passed. It'll just be a memory.*

Shane put his feet up on the back of the seat in front of us. I started to nag him about this, then I changed my mind. There was nobody sitting there. It wasn't that big of a deal; I didn't need to fuss about something that unimportant.

Make every moment count, were the words I heard in my heart.

It's so easy to get hooked into the busyness of life. It's easy to focus on the destination and tell ourselves we'll be happy when we get there and forget to be happy and cherish the beauty of each moment of the trip. So often, we don't even know that we're living the best, most beautiful part of our lives right now.

I worried a lot as a struggling single parent, trying to write articles for the *Gazette* for $25 an article. How will I make ends meet? Am I writing well enough? Geez, I don't have time to date. Am I being a good enough mother? God, there's a lot to do raising these kids. In retrospect, it was one of the best times in my life.

No matter what emotions you're feeling, no matter the nature of your problems, this moment is the best time in your life.

Stop waiting to win the lottery. Or maybe, don't stop waiting. Buy your ticket. Then put it away and forget about it. Be happy now. Don't wait until later when you look back at this time in your life.

Say *how sweet it is* right now. Make every moment count.

God, teach me to be happy now.

It was an odd friendship right from the start. I was in a local store, trying to buy some new rocks—a crystal, maybe some lapis—something beautiful to change the energy in my house. "Kyle can help you out," the salesclerk said. "He knows all about our stones."

Kyle talked to me for a while about what stones I might like. Then I left the store. A few days later, I wandered back in, and we talked a little more.

By the time the first year passed, we had become pretty good friends. At that time, neither of us had a romantic relationship in our lives. We just hung out, went to restaurants, saw movies together, and talked on the phone.

One year passed, then two, then three, then five. We started a bookstore together, and together we closed it down.

Now Kyle's seeing someone romantically. I am, too. We're still best friends, but the wheel of life has turned again. We were talking on the phone just the other day.

"For all our complaining and grumbling and carrying on, we sure had some good times," I said. "Yes," he agreed. "This is one of the best times in my life."

The ordinary moments that we each live through, in retrospect, look so rich and full. Why don't we take all that wisdom and all that poignant reminiscing and realize that we're having the best time in our life right now?

God, this is the day you have made. I will rejoice and be glad in it.

So you meet someone, become infatuated, date, and allow your mind to create an exaggerated image of that person.

Soon you find that he's your *soul mate*. You don't want to live without him; he means everything to you. And then he stumbles, somewhere around three months, maybe six months. He fails to meet your expectations.

He loses soul mate status.

"You just aren't the person I thought you were," you say, walking out the door.

Of course he isn't. He's a person, not a figment of your imagination. Lighten up. Let each person be themselves.

When we're with someone, either as a friend or as a lover, a good deal of the success or failure of the relationship can be traced to our expectations. We get angry when we expect someone to behave in a certain way and he or she doesn't. We feel cheated, lied to, and disappointed. Here we stacked all of our chips on a certain number coming up, and when it doesn't, we get mad.

Lose those expectations. If you enjoy another person's company, then enjoy it cleanly and without any expectations. People are people. They will stumble; they will get back up again—or not. You cannot control them. All you can do is learn from them, love them, and enjoy their company when they're around.

Drop the expectations. Allow people to just be themselves. Appreciate them for who they are. Let the love that you have for them grow out of that appreciation, instead of out of what you expect in what writer Natalie Goldberg calls "your monkey mind."

God, help me remember that when I lose my expectations I just might find real love.

There's so much talk about finding that extraordinary love of our life. Maybe everything we need to know about romantic love can be learned from our friends.

We don't expect our friends to change our life and make everything that's wrong, right. We just expect them to be who they are, and then we let them be that. It's part of being a friend.

We don't expect to like everything about our friends. We know they have defects of character. They do things occasionally that irritate us.

We don't expect our friends to entertain and amuse us, keeping us laughing and smiling all the time. We let them go through their ups and downs. Sometimes we just sit in silence with our friends, and we each keep our thoughts to ourselves.

We don't pick fights and create drama with our friends, just to keep passion alive. Usually we do everything we can to avoid fighting with our friends. We want our friendship to be a quiet, safe, peaceful place, a haven in our lives.

We don't expect our friends to turn our lives upside down, distracting us from our path. Usually if a friend attempts to wreak havoc in our lives, we run the other way.

We wouldn't let a friend hit us. And friends don't talk mean. If an issue comes up, we usually carefully weigh the best way to talk about this issue with her or him.

We don't expect friends to be in perfect health all the time. We know that they will have issues to deal with as they walk along their own paths. We encourage them. We pray for them. But we don't take their issues as our own, and we don't take it personally when they need some time to focus on their own personal growth.

In friendships, one person does not hold all the power. So despite the differences in our lives, we try to relate as equals.

We're tolerant of cycles in our friendships, knowing that at different times, each person has different needs, different experiences to go through. Sometimes there's more time and energy to devote to the friendships. Other times, there's less.

We don't expect our friends to be at our side twenty-four hours a day. We have our time together and value that, but then we each go our own way. We don't try to force bonding with friends, or even force the relationship to be a friendship too fast. We let ourselves go through experiences together naturally, knowing that that's how bonding takes place.

I'm not an expert on marital love, but we might have a better chance at finding love if we treated our lover like a friend.

God, help me find the middle ground between unrealistic expectations and no expectations at all. Help me cherish my relationships and not confuse heavy drama with romantic love.

Activity: Honestly look at the expectations you place on romantic relationships. Are you expecting a lover or spouse to change your life, or are you looking for a friend with whom you can share the additional elements of romantic and sexual love?

December 23   How sweet and precious the moments

It had seemed like such an ordinary time. He was staying at the house, helping me out. I had funeral arrangements to make and to attend. My mother was coming into town. I had a lot to do.

Then the busy days and nights settled into the quiet rhythm of California winters—short days, fires in the fireplace at night, a pot of spaghetti sauce on the stove. January at the beach was a time to stay in the house and be quiet and cozy.

Sometimes he cooked a wonderful dinner—Philly steak sandwiches with real melted cream cheese. Other times, we ordered pizza and just ate in. Sometimes I read. Other times I talked on the phone or puttered around the house.

At night, right before sleep came, bringing a gentle end to another day, he put a Sarah McLaughlin CD in the stereo. She sang about being in the arms of angels as she gently sang me to sleep.

Then the time came. He was ready to leave. Our time together was done. So be it, I thought. What comes around doesn't come to stay. It always comes to pass.

As he walked out the door, I waved good-bye. Then a wave of emotions rushed through me, flooding my heart. It had seemed like such an ordinary time. And it was. But until it was over, until he walked out that door, I didn't know how rich and beautiful the ordinary was.

"Hmm," I thought, watching him leave. Maybe the time hasn't passed yet.

How sweet and precious are the moments of our lives, especially the ordinary ones. Don't let them pass unnoticed or unexperienced. Those ordinary moments can easily become the richest part of our lives.

God, help me remember that the way to live a life filled with wonder and awe is to surrender to and live each moment fully, expecting and allowing each one to simply be what it is.

Timothy attended one of those seminars, the kind that talks about personal growth and encourages people to open their hearts. After the seminar, he was so moved by what he'd heard that he called his father on the phone. He hadn't talked to his father for many years. They had a squabble years earlier when Timothy left home. Neither one wanted to make the first move or to forgive the other person for the harsh words that had transpired. Timothy made the first move. He and his father have been close ever since.

Jessica had her share of troubled times with her mother, too. Over the years there had been times when they'd been close, times when they didn't talk, and times when Jessica just did the minimum in the relationship, mostly out of a sense of obligation and guilt. As Jessica got older, she began feeling bad about her troubled relationship with her mother. She'd done her family of origin work. She knew her mother had been troubled; but after all, her mother was just a person. Why not forgive and forget? Jessica planned a big trip for the two of them to take, a mother-daughter vacation that would melt away the irritation and conflict from all the years. Jessica had so many hopes the day she met her mother at the airport. But when they got together in the same room for their two weeks of joy, Jessica realized she felt the same way she always had when she was around her mother: irritable, ashamed, and not good enough.

Clarence liked his dad when he was a boy. But the older he got, the more he wanted to leave home. His father had issues; Clarence did, too. After Clarence left home, he only spent a few minutes each year talking to his father. One day, when Clarence reached his thirties, he decided it was time for him and his father to be friends. He planned a trip to his father's house. He couldn't wait for the heart-to-heart talk they'd have. Clarence would talk about the struggles of being a man and growing up, and surely his father would identify with him. But when they got together, alone in the house, after Clarence poured out his heart, all his father had to say was, "Can you come outside and help me change the tire on the car?"

Families and parents come in all different kinds. Do your family of origin work. Be grateful for the good passed on to you from your ancestors and your heritage. Reach out, if that's what your heart leads you to do. Be the best son or daughter you can, whatever that means to you. But don't torture yourself if your relationship with your parents is not what you dreamed. Let each member of your family be who he or she is. Love them as much as you can. But if you never got along all that well before, you might not get along now, even after you open your heart.

Laugh. Smile. You don't have to react. You know how to take care of yourself.

God, heal my heart toward all my family members. Help me accept each person for who he or she is. Then help me genuinely accept myself, too.

December 25   Point to the good

Identify three things you like.

I was talking to my daughter on the phone one day after I had visited her at her house. I took a moment during the conversation, and I listed the three things I most enjoyed and liked best about our visit that day.

She caught her breath. She knew I was being honest. "Really?" she asked.

"I mean it," I said. "I meant every word I just said."

Do you want to spark that relationship with your friend, your child, your lover, employee, co-worker, or boss? Instead of criticizing everything you don't like, say what you like best. Most people have their share of insecurities about themselves, their relationships, and how they do at performing a task. Instead of thinking you're the only one who feels insecure, tell people something that will help them feel good about themselves and their relationship with you.

Three is a good number, don't you think?

Look in your heart and find three things you genuinely like about someone. Then tell them clearly what those things are.

God, help me start looking at the good in the people I love.

December 26   The magic is in you

Sometimes, we play a little trick on ourselves.

We may get so close to someone, we think, *I don't have to let go.* Or we may become so successful at manifesting events in our lives, we think, *I don't have to let go.* When I want something, it just appears.

Anytime we forget to let go, life will jog us back into remembering. There is nothing that we can cling to in this world. Ultimately, all that we hold dear will require us to let go, in some shape or form. That child will grow up and leave home. That love relationship that's going so wonderfully? A new cycle will come, in its time. That friendship will change. That job you thought you'd always have? Oops, the company merged. Your position is changed.

Although long-term relationships and secure employment and living in that house feels good, remember, that's not where your security lies.

Let yourself bond. Get close to that woman, or man. Let

405

yourself enjoy being friends with the best friend you've ever had. Be a loving parent, 100 percent. Throw yourself into that job with all your heart and soul.

But your security and joy are not in that other person or job. The magic is in you.

Don't get angry when the time comes in your life to let go. Open your heart to that person, place, or thing, and say, "Thanks for teaching me to love and helping me to grow."

Then let him or her go, without resentment in your heart. Because even though that time has come to an end, love can't be lost. Even if it means an end to the best time you've had yet in your life, look around at where you are now. Don't forget to enjoy it, too.

This will be the next best time you'll have.

Remember, love is a gift from God.

God, help me keep my head up, my heart open, and know I'll always be guided along the path.

December 27   Cherish the glimmers of light

I know people who have been enmeshed in extremely hard times. One woman lost her husband and both children in a fire. Another found her teenage child hung to death—suicide—on her back porch one Sunday in the spring. I've known people struggling with chronic depression. I've known people who lost their fortunes in one swoop. I've known people who were active, healthy people one day, and the next day an accident paralyzed them for life.

I had my years of grief, too, after the death of my son. Year after year the pain pounded incessantly, threatening never to abate.

Listen carefully. I pray you will never have such a time. But even if you're going through something like that, make every moment count. And pay special attention to the moments when the pain and the suffering subside, even if it's only for a few seconds or hours. Count those moments as a gift, a glimmer of light. Hold them in your heart.

Write in your journal about how much it hurts. Feel all your pain. But take the time to document those brief moments each week when just a glimmer of pleasure sets in.

Remember, two plus two equals four. Four plus four equals eight.

Those moments will add up.

You might not be going through a time in your life that you relish, but try to find a few moments where you can catch your breath, look around, and say *how sweet it is.*

God, help me find at least one thing in my life that makes me feel good and gives me pleasure, even if it's for only one moment of my day.

December 28   Risk being alive

"I know nothing is going to last forever," Charlie said. "But the key to life and being happy is acting as though it is."

Many of us have had our illusions about security and permanency shattered. The longer we're alive, the more it gets beat into us: nothing is forever. We can plan on many things, but the only thing we can plan on with any certainty is change.

At some time in our lives, we may have convinced ourselves otherwise. We surrendered ourselves to that job, that project, or that relationship with all our hearts, only to have it crash to an end.

Some of us may have decided, after enough cycles of

beginnings, middles, and endings, that the way to deal with this was never to fully give our hearts to any person or circumstance, never to let ourselves fully be present and enjoy the moment.

If I don't get in completely, I won't get hurt when it ends, we think. Maybe. But you won't experience the pleasure and joy, the rich, sweet, full taste of those moments, either.

Okay, so you're wiser now. You know nothing lasts forever. You know the moment something begins, the ending has already been written, too. People are born. They die. A job or project begins. Then it ends. But there's an entire luscious middle waiting, inviting you to jump in fully and see how sweet life can be. Besides, when the ending does come, you'll also have been given enough wisdom, courage, and grace to deal with that, too.

What are you waiting for?

Go ahead. Stop holding back. Jump in.

Live your life.

God, give me enough faith and a well of letting go so I can live each moment fully.

December 29   Let the adventure consume you

The spirit of adventure settles over us slowly sometimes. In the beginning, when those old winds of change blow, we turn our backs, fight, and resist. We just want things to stay the same. Gradually we let go of the need to control. We allow things to change and us to change with them.

We accept the change.

Then we round a corner and find a wonderful lesson there, and then another, and another. Soon we find ourselves looking forward to taking the next step, anxious to see what lies in front of us today. Where will my path lead? Who will I meet? What will I learn? What wonderful lesson is taking place right now?

And the adventure begins to consume us.

The steps that you have been taking have been slowly leading you down a path with more wonder and goodness at every turn of the road. You learned to tolerate change. Now learn to embrace it.

Adventure isn't something you do. The adventure is your life. Recognize *how sweet it is*. Let those winds of change blow.

God, help me cultivate a spirit of adventure in my life.

December 30   Slow down and let go

On a road trip up the California coast a while back, I tried to call home only to find that the batteries in my cell phone had died. I worried. What if someone needed to get in touch with me? What if there was a problem with the house? What if my family couldn't find me and got worried?

I passed the exit to the beach that I had always wanted to see.

I obsessed some more.

I stopped for breakfast at a restaurant overlooking the Pacific Ocean. I asked if they had a pay phone. They didn't. I barely noticed the stunning view, the smell or the sound of the surf, and I can't remembering eating my eggs and toast.

I put off seeing things until another trip; I took the freeway and got home early.

When I got home, there were no messages. No one had needed me; no one had even been aware that I was gone. But I had missed out on the treasures of the trip. I had spent so much time obsessing, I could barely remember where I'd been.

Are you missing out on the wonder of your trip because you're in too big of a hurry? Let go. Breathe deeply. As long as you're taking the journey, you might as well relax and enjoy the ride.

God, help me enjoy where I am right now.

December 31   **The adventure is in the trip**

We were on our way to the drop zone when Chip turned to me.

"Let's go to San Francisco and see a widgeon."

"Widgeon?" I said. "Okay. Let's go."

These are the rules," he said, pulling off the highway and getting back on the exit ramp heading north. "We'll stop at the house for a minute. But we can't pack. We can only take with us what we have on us now. We'll have to trust ourselves to get whatever else we need on the way."

"Okay," I said. "You're on."

I didn't know what a widgeon was.

Four hours later, we were walking barefoot on Morro Beach, just south of Big Sur. A big rock, one that looked like the fossil remains of a dinosaur hunched over in the water, beckoned. So did the impending sunset. I still didn't know what a widgeon was, but I was glad we were searching for one.

"You'd better call Andy," I said, watching the waves crash against the dinosaur rock. "You guys were supposed to go climbing tomorrow."

Chip took the cell phone I was handing him.

"I've got an idea," I said. "Tell Andy to get on a plane, fly to San Francisco, wait for us to pick him up, then come with us to find the widgeon."

Chip called Andy. Thirty-five minutes later, Andy called back. "I'll be at the United gate at the San Francisco airport at 9:34. See you!" he said.

Chip and I looked at each other. It was 6:34. We were two hundred miles south of San Francisco and had already started traveling the One through Big Sur—a winding two-lane highway that climbed high banks, offered a breathtaking view, and needed to be traveled slowly and cautiously.

Half an hour later, we looked at the odometer. We had gone twelve miles.

Chip turned east on a road that suddenly appeared. It was slightly bigger than a one-lane road, winding its way through the mountains that separated us from the interstate and a sixty-five mile per hour limit. He drove like a Daytona master. Forty-five minutes later, we had traveled another twelve miles.

Focus, focus, focus. Focus on the destination, not the journey. Just get there.

At 10:35, one hour past Andy's arrival time, we pulled up in front of the baggage claim. A six-foot, two-inch Texas blond guy sat on a bench, reading a book. We honked. He looked up, waved, then lumbered over to the car and slid into the backseat.

"What's a widgeon?" he said.

The next morning, we set out for Ace Aviation, the home of the widgeon. We didn't know where it was, but we headed in what we thought was the right direction. Suddenly, Chip pointed to a sign. "Seaplanes!" We pulled off the road, and went in.

"Have you heard of Ace Aviation?" we asked.

"Yup," she said.

"Is there a widgeon there?" we asked.

"Yup," she said.

"Will you tell us where it is?" we asked.

She did.

One hour later, we pulled into the parking lot for Ace Aviation. For the next hour, we fawned over widgeons—amphibious planes with a peculiar yet immediate and undeniable charm. The name painted on one widgeon read, "Da Plane." It was the seaplane from *Fantasy Island*.

We found a hot springs motel on the last evening of the trip. Sitting in the outdoor hot tub, I found many things remarkable: the almost full moon in the sky, the calming effect of the water, and the toothpaste provided by the hotel. All along the trip, our wishes seemed to magically appear—from a restaurant on a desolate strip of beach, to a restroom in the middle of a forest, to a widgeon in a widgeon hospital.

I've said it before; I'll say it again. It's good to have a destination, but the adventure is in the trip.

Take a moment. Review where you've been this past year. Be grateful for all you've experienced and the people who have come into your life. Search your heart. Let go of any resentments. Take a moment and reflect on your successes. Be grateful for them; be grateful for all the ordinary moments, too. Take a look at your goal list. Some things have taken place. Other things may not have materialized yet. Don't give up yet. Let go. Tomorrow, you can make a new list.

God, thank you for this year. Clear my heart so I can start tomorrow with a clean slate.

About Hazelden Publishing

As part of the Hazelden Betty Ford Foundation, Hazelden Publishing offers both cutting-edge educational resources and inspirational books. Our print and digital works help guide individuals in treatment and recovery, and their loved ones. Professionals who work to prevent and treat addiction also turn to Hazelden Publishing for evidence-based curricula, digital content solutions, and videos for use in schools, treatment programs, correctional programs, and electronic health records systems. We also offer training for implementation of our curricula.

Through published and digital works, Hazelden Publishing extends the reach of healing and hope to individuals, families, and communities affected by addiction and related issues.

For more information about Hazelden publications,
please call **800-328-9000**
or visit us online at **hazelden.org/bookstore.**